POTHOLE OF THE GODS
On Holy War, Fake News &
Other Ill-Advised Ideas

Also by Richard Murff

Yellowcake
One Last Hour
Haint Punch

As editor

Memphians

POTHOLE OF THE GODS
On Holy War, Fake News &
Other Ill-Advised Ideas

BY

Richard Murff

Burnaby

Copyright © 2021 by Richard Murff

Library of Congress Control Number: Pending

ISBN: 978-0-9796988-4-2

This book was printed in the United States of America

For Marie and Bernie:

Big Sister and Little Brother,

Both great teachers, hilarious storytellers and smart enough to know how one lifts the other.

It just isn't as much fun without the two of you around.

It may help to understand human affairs to be clear that most of the great triumphs and tragedies of history are not caused by people being fundamentally good or fundamentally bad, but by people being fundamentally, people.

Good Omens
Terry Prachett & Neil Gaiman

Contents

PART TREE: BAD HAIR AND THE CREEPING APOCALYPSE

"Run and find out."
Motto of all the Mongoose family
Rudyard Kipling
Rikki-tikki-tavi

PROLOGUE:
I'VE NEVER BEEN TO KATMANDU
November 2012

I was starting to sweat. It was a cold morning, and Istanbul's Atatürk International Airport is not a cozy place. At 5:30 am, though, it is a stifling madhouse. The din of the travelers moving in the wide, high corridors drifted upward along the curving walls and hung about my head like a muffled cloud. Around me in grey and black permanent press was a quartet of Turkish airport security. They were professional but jittery. The Arab Spring that was spreading like a grease fire across North Africa and the Middle East had engulfed Syria. Just over the Turkish border one more ancient state was coming apart at the seams.

Once again, Western powers were coming in to spread the good cheer: An arms pipeline from Libya to the Free Syrian Army, organized by the US, facilitated by the Saudi and delivered by Qatar, had gone pear-shaped. Military grade weapons were everywhere - not just assault rifles, but the heavy, high tech ordinance as well. Crates of man-powered air defense weapons known as MANPADS in the charming language of the military, but by the catch-all "stingers" by the press had gone missing. This was no mere inventory control issue, those shoulder fired missiles capable of downing a commercial airliner. The CIA was frantically trying to mop up the mess and the Turks were furious over the whole thing – largely because by arming Kurdish rebels in Syria the US was, in effect, arming Kurdish rebels in Turkey – our NATO ally. All of which raised the terrifying question of why, exactly, was the US arming the same jihadists we were trying to defeat?

For my part, I was attached to an entirely different sort of mission that morning and my concerns were of a much more personal nature: That airport security was more than a little curious about an American flying into Benghazi with a black canvas duffle the size of a body bag. A bead of perspiration had formed high on the temple and was making a mad dash for my open face. I've been me long enough to know that it wouldn't be the last one.

Two months after the 11 September attacks on the US Special Mission compound in Benghazi that killed Ambassador Christopher Stevens, both the FBI and the CIA had cleared out of the city citing security concerns. Officially, at any rate. The FBI was conducting its investigation from Tripoli, as for the CIA, well, you never can tell with that crew. Here I was flying into the place with a high-tech kit I couldn't explain even if I did speak Turkish.

The three men in the security detail were engaged in a routine search - more curious than suspicious and probably wouldn't have given me any trouble if I remained generally likable. The lone female, however, stood with her feet wide apart glaring at me. She wasn't ugly, just willfully non-feminine. The lip service Turkey pays to women's rights has never really soaked through to the cultural bones, and had been receding the longer President Erdogan stayed in power. She had something to prove. Thinking about the daughter I'd left in Memphis, on any other day would have applauded Officer Smiley's determination in the face of sexism, but this morning she was problematic.

Having anticipated something like this, I was wearing a blue blazer, khakis and loafers because in these high-alert days it never hurts to look like you just stumbled out of the yacht club.* I unzipped the duffle to reveal an almost ordered jumble of sterile, sealed surgical supplies. The damn bag had been giving me hell since I'd left Memphis two days earlier and now it was about to get me arrested. Should you find yourself in a similar situation, the trick is to maintain a vague air of polite impatience without being insulting to security. They've got a job to do and rousing indignation just makes you look guilty. With an insufferable air, I handed her my paperwork: the packing list, cover letter and my Libyan visa – all in Arabic that neither one of us could read. She handled the documents badly, crushing them and giving me a good frowning as she handed them back to me in a wad. I gave her my best *aw shucks* smile and handed the official crumple over to another guard with a shrug. He didn't know what to make of them either, but did smooth the papers out apologetically before handing them back. Then, out of the corner of my eye, I saw her

_____

*My sister referred to this as "douchebag camouflage."

3

bend down and snatch a clear container of surgical cannula out of the duffle and begin to pick at the protective packaging.

If I'd thought about it things would certainly have gone differently, as it was, I didn't. Some nescient motor function took over. I rolled up my paperwork, swatted her hand – like a puppy – and snatched the container away. She stared at her empty palms for just a split second, but it felt like ten. Long enough for me to realize what I'd just done. When she did look up I can't imagine the dumb American expression that greeted her on my dumb American face helped matters. She looked stunned, but it would only buy me a few moments before the fury took hold and she did something brutal and, in Turkey, perfectly legal.

TEN DAYS EARLIER, I'd called the charming Mrs. M. at work to tell her where I was headed. "Oh fun!" she said. I thought she was taking the whole thing surprisingly well considering that the footage of that wall of black smoke rolling out of the US Special Mission compound in Benghazi had been running nonstop on the news for nearly six weeks. That easy going air of hers didn't quite make it to dinner.

While we watching the evening news, some escaped detail quietly returned to her. She turned to me and said, "Wait… did you say that you were going to *Benghazi?*" She was pointing to the infamous wall of inky, toxic smoke and heaps of excitable Arabs.

I remember exactly what was on television because it had occurred to me that too much eye-contact just then was ill-advised, so my eyes were fixed to the screen. "Yeah," I said casually, "we talked about it this morning." That, I thought would settle the matter. As it turned out, in some spasm of selective spousal hearing, she'd thought I'd told her I was heading to Katmandu.

"Why would I go to Katmandu?" I asked, trying to deflect the subject with a polite tangent into Nepal.

"WHY would you go to Benghazi?!?" she asked, sensibly.

"Well, why NOT go to Benghazi?" I most certainly did not say. What I did was heroically open a bottle of wine. The truth is, she had me there.

Why was I chasing a group of pediatric cardiac surgeons into a war zone crime scene? I'm not a doctor, that would be my twin brother – affectionately known in my family as "The Smart One." The most I could offer was that I'd been to a lot of med school parties. It was perfectly reasonable to ask why I was putting my neck on the line for a bunch of people who, if the news was to be believed, hated Americans and the core concept of America itself. Fortunately, being a writer keeps me from believing everything I read.

To get to the unguarded heart of humanity you need to quit listening to the politicos and activists in their folderol and go talk to people who actually work for a living. So with the Arab Spring trying desperately to hang-on in that dim twilight between revolution and civil war, I just felt compelled to go. I wanted some strategic assessment of the world seen from the eyes of the people not currently trying to blow it up.

And that includes us. U.S. Foreign Policy has been nothing if not inconsistent. Prior to World War II, our policy largely involved pestering the Latin Americans and politely closing the door when the Europeans or the Asians got riled up about it.

Then Hitler and Hirohito happened* and suddenly we were pulled out of our bumpkin, isolationist closet and recast as a global colossus. Almost overnight we became the New Rome, and like the old one, had a political system not at all designed for empire.

As a nation, our first instincts were reflected in a 1947 article in *Foreign Affairs* written by an American diplomat under the pseudonym "X" – his name was George Kennen and he urged US post-war policy of containment of the USSR, but not a lot else. Don't fight them, he urged, just keep them penned in.

As far as the Middle east went, we didn't have much of a policy, which suited the Arabs just fine. Then, in 1948 an explosion of immigrants and refugees in a place mostly known as Palestine declared themselves the independent nation of Israel. Muslim fury was pointed mainly at Britain for allowing it to happen in the first place *by leaving*. And then at the European Jews for showing up in unstoppable numbers in the aftermath of the Holocaust. While it's hard to believe now, most Arabs at the time considered the genocide a tragedy, just not one of their doing. Would it not be more reasonable, they argued, to carve a Jewish State out of Germany instead? The Arab view of America, never having been a traditional colonial power, was relatively positive.

By 1953, however, the Cold War was in full swing and everyone was choosing sides. The war in Korea was spinning in limbo and the USSR had gone atomic. President Eisenhower thought a more preemptive policy was in order. In the name of

---

*Mussolini happened too, but the Axis powers would have been better off without him.

freedom and self-determination, Ike agreed to help the British monkey around in Iranian politics by disposing their only freely elected leader since the dawn of civilization. The Iranians have never really forgiven us for it. Twenty six years later, President Carter claimed* he didn't want to meddle in Iranian affairs and abandoned the Shah – a royal shit to be sure – to his fate in the face a popular revolution. As it was, the revolution was hijacked by a radical cleric with the stated aim of global jihad that would trigger the apocalypse. Most Iranians haven't forgiven us for sitting that one out either.

Since then, US Presidents have tried various methods for dealing with the can of worms that Ike cracked open in the streets of Tehran. There has been meddling, which makes matters worse, and a hands-off approach that also makes matters worse. What are we missing? What are they missing?

Then, in December of 2010, an unlicensed fruit-vender in Tunisia had had enough with government corruption and harassment and, in protest, lit himself on fire and unleashed a revolution. By January, Tunisia's president Zine al-Abidine Ben Ali had fled to Saudi Arabia in exile. The protests, fueled by social media, spread quickly to Egypt, Bahrain, Libya, Syria and Yemen. The Arab Spring had started and began to spread in the name of democracy. In the chaos, foreign forces melted into the melee, eager to exploit its momentum and harness the wave to their own means.

FOR AN AMERICAN traveling on a somewhat off-the-books errand in 2012, all of this made the world very interesting.

---

*We'll get back to *that* matter.

In an age of proxy wars, it's very hard to understand just who is fighting who, but in a hospital you get to the cost of whatever it is you're fighting for with nauseating speed and clarity. Iran's revolutionary regime had been monkeying around in the Lebanese civil war since *before* they took power in Tehran. Everyone knew that the Islamic Republic had crept into Syria, but then, so has everyone else it seems. How do you negotiate a settlement with half a dozen or so belligerents when only about three will admit to actually being in the fight?

With the hysterics swirling around the attack on the US Special Mission, I was obviously very interested in the truth behind the attack. I also know that foreign, oppressive governments aren't the only ones able to exert pressure on the press. That the attack was triggered by a disrespectful video with a middle school AV club production value seemed silly and far-fetched. And weirdly convenient.

You'd do well to consider why all sweeping geopolitical events all seem to have a convenient and easily explained cause and effect, despite no one having but about 20% of the information. Contrast this with your personal and professional life. While having nearly all the information at hand, you walk around baffled, wondering what the hell just happened. Hint: You don't have a press office, they do.

Politics are muddled, and modern politics even more so. Today's wars serve the abstract: Economics, self-determination, nationalism and host of other swell-sounding ideals. When the United States got out of puberty, President Woodrow Wilson famously said he wanted to make the world 'safe for democracy.' Which is fine, but democracy is a slippery concept and it doesn't always work right out of the box. Everyone has to agree to the rules, even if they loose. Freedom is even more slippery. These are hard issues – and to look at the bill, expensive ones.

Traveling around with a group of doctors seemed like a good way to get in front of a lot of smart, educated people whose livelihood depended on realistic analysis rather than on whipping the greatest number of local knuckleheads into a deranged lather. Since most of the world's healthcare is government-run that put me in front of local government officials who weren't so far up the political food-chain that they were completely divorced from reality.

By the time I was packing for Libya, I'd been all over Hell's half acre trying to find answers and generally confusing myself. I was getting a general idea as to how politicians, technocrats and other foreign policy experts were "losing" states left and right. And there, on the side of the Mediterranean that the Italians never managed to make fashionable, a state was being lost in real time. The noble aspirations of a people to overthrow a psychotic tyrant was being hijacked - not from the Judeo-Christian West, but by a deranged version of their own religion.

YOU'D BE FORGIVEN for thinking that this grim history was pointing to a grim destiny. I certainly never said as much to Mrs. M., she's an optimist. And admittedly, this is a weird place in which to see humor, but why not? Being theatrically serious about a problem may signal its gravity, but it has never helped bring about a solution.

So, I got my shots and had a check-up: my heart rate was fine and my BMI came in at 'nicely marbled.' I was set. I attached myself to a humanitarian aid mission to gain access to government officials as well as get a worm's eye view of the situation on the ground. Politician lie wherever you go, but hospitals are where you find the rawest types of grief and joy. You can't fake that. If there was a Why to be found, it would be here. Earnest ideology be damned, what works for the people we are trying to help? Let's not be Boy Scouts about it either, what stops for the people we're trying to defeat?

Which is how I found myself in Istanbul that strange morning with a bag of supplies unidentifiable if you don't have some sort of medical degree. I knew *why* the Turks were jittery about that bag of donated surgical supplies, I just didn't care. I may have been a mule, but I was a mule with my papers in order. Once in country there was no way to re-supply the mission, so those sealed tubes and gizmos and whatsits all meant life or death to some little kid with a wrecked heart. And that's what made me so angry.

Years ago, I sat through a long, uncertain night in the hospital with my own daughter, and since then have seen it around the world. The politics and the religion of desperate parents has got nothing to do with socialism or capitalism, or whether you pray on Friday, Saturday or Sunday. It is very simple: *Please God, let her make it through the night. Take me if you have to, I won't fight you, but let her make it. See her through to the sunrise.* So, I was in no mood to have the sterile material in that bag ruined by the fussy security at the Atatürk airport.

In retrospect, taking a swat at airport security was an idiotic thing to do but my conscious mind hadn't thought about it. I'd just done it. Or my subconscious had done it while my conscious-self watched in mute horror as my arm reached out and snatched that clear box out of her hand. My conscious brain was caught between visions of *Midnight Express* style Turkish prison and the truism that a bold move – even a near suicidal one – is wasted on a weak follow up. There was nothing to do in the situation but to push through it and push hard. I doubled down. Like a real first-rate ass, I wagged my finger at her and said in the slow, halting words that Americans assume all foreigners understand, "Must. Not. Open."

The other guards looked amused. "*Docktor?*" one asked. Turkish is a harsh language. It sounds like one of those Slavic tongues that was taken round back and roughed up by Arabic. As it was the only word we had in common, I lied. Hell, I looked like a doctor. The four guards conferred as I checked the seal (it was still good) and started to put the bag back in order without anyone's permission. I zipped up and started off in an arrogant huff as they waved me through. Once out of sight I bolted upstairs to my flight check-in as fast as a husky middle-aged man hauling 57 pounds of badly balanced surgical supplies can. It lacked grace.

After a little more bad noise at the gate, I got both myself and the damn bag on the flight to Benghazi. Where I was promptly arrested again at customs.

PART ONE:

JUST ADD FLIES

NASIRIYA, IRAQ

Wars begin when you will, but they do not end when you please.

> Niccolò Machiavelli
> History of Florence (1524)

CHAPTER ONE:
JUST ADD FLIES

About five months before that bout of selective spousal hearing with Mrs. M, I was on a similar errand in Iraq's sunny Shi'a south. This was also with a global medical aid charity called the International Children's Heart Foundation (ICHF). What had attracted me to the organization was that its model did not entail rich world doctors performing a week of surgeries and then flying home to brag about it at the golf club. The foundation ran dedicated training programs of several two-week missions per year for about five years to establish home-grown pediatric cardiac programs. It was based in Memphis, but its international cadre of volunteers came from all over the world. Many of the volunteers had once been ICHF trainees.

That flight too had taken me to Istanbul for a long layover. The volunteers had gathered from points around the world the night before in Istanbul. We sat around the bar outside swapping tales – but not of war-zone derring-do. "Don't eat the shawarma." Said an anesthesiologist from Belarus.

"Ever?"I asked.

"No. Just off the street." The rest of the crew, veterans of various missions, echoed this. "Find a restaurant." He advised with Slavic stoicism. As medical professionals, all agreed that the *Istanbulii* street shawarma was a low-percentage affair. The jet lag had played hell with our systems, and so instead of grabbing some sleep, the team wandered off for all-hours tours of the city. And, as it turned out, to go get some street shawarma.

By late-morning the next day, our Turkish Airline plane was taxiing into the Basra International Airport – a big, brutal concrete building colored in dueling shades of brown. The facility isn't without its style points though: tall, Arab style windows line the front of the building and between each is a flourish that looked almost exactly like … "Why are there Star of David motifs between the windows?" I asked Tim, the team's perfusionist.

He'd been quiet most of the flight. Upset stomach. "Have you ever been to Iraq before?" he asked.

"No."

"It's so hot it's confusing."

Which, I suppose is as good an explanation as any. "What the hell is a perfusionist?"

"The guy who runs the heart/lung bypass machine. Can't do heart surgery without out it." He paused, and rubbed an unsettled belly. "Well, you can, but you don't want to."

"Like street shawarma?" I asked. "How do you spell perfusionist?"

Tim laughed, "No one really knows."

At that time and place in the universe, there was a lot that no one really knew though. It was July of 2012, six months after the withdrawal of the "last" of the American troops along with some 10,000 State Department employees. Theoretically, both the war and the American occupation was over but it didn't feel that way. The place had that strange, strained peace you find in an exhausted society trying to get back on its feet. The Western aid sorts were hopeful that the country was in the foothills of some glorious peaceful future without the typical Arab Big Man coming in a wrecking everything. Old habits die hard.

As it was, US troops would be back in less than two years. The displaced ruling Ba'athists, ousted along with Saddam Hussein, were regrouping under the banner of al-Qaeda and then as ISIS in the northern regions. In the south, Iran had crept in with money and arms to form up the Shi'a militias.

That July the local officials weren't exactly sure what to do with us. So, we got herded into a small, cramped room to wait around in a humid cluelessness. There was no signage that I could read, no big screen to tell you when flights were coming or going; just a windowless, off-white walled room filled completely with white people dressed like millennial hippies and one writer dressed like the J. Press clearance bin. At first, I didn't notice the small, elegant blonde woman when she appeared. I think it was the hair that threw me.

Nadwa Qaragholi was born in Iraq, got her degree in Beirut and has lived for most of her adult life near Washington D.C. Her children have landed in successful careers in the U.S. and Europe. As founder and executive of a pan-Arab charity called Living Light International, she jumps back and forth between the United States and the Middle East. She's so good at moving in-between worlds that it disarms people. Which I'd learn later was part of her genius. She breezed into the cramped room – not quite like she owned the place, but as if whomever *did* own the place would be just thrilled to see her. She said something to someone and suddenly all the ICHF volunteers (and myself) were moving into an even smaller room with even less fresh air that was being used as customs office. In it there were some cheap folding chairs and a sign, handwritten in English: Visas = 80US + 1,200IQD (Iraqi dinars). Why a single transaction was being conducted in two currencies I don't know, nor did I know the exchange rate* so I coughed up $82 and was handed back 1,000IQD. Which was a little like getting a ball of hair as change. The QED was that my passport was inked with a stamp that looked official enough and I got waved through.

With the withdrawal of US troops and the installation of the Shi'a Nouri al Maliki as president, the locals were trying to clean up the place, which was a little heartbreaking. I never got the impression that anyone in that airport was glad to see me, though. I got my bags searched and my nail clippers confiscated. I'm not sure what mayhem could my clippers would cause in a barely functioning state that was also currently the world's largest buyer's market in rocket propelled grenades. War has a way of making people very practical. His nails really did look awful.

Just beyond, at the baggage claim was one of those annoying testaments to the ultimate oneness of humanity: The bags of the head field surgeon for the mission, Dr. Ed Gascon, were lost. Gascon is directly out of central casting for a big ole Southern

---

*Like the proper spelling of perfusionist – this was just one of those mysteries.

guy. He's also a dead ringer for that creature called the M.Diety: arrogant and brilliant. And he is brilliant, just not as smart as he thinks he is, or as he demands to be treated. It's not personal, no one is that smart. At the Turkish Airlines desk in the Basra airport, smarts won't really help you anyway. The airline blamed the airport and vice versa. Gascon loudly opined that both were at fault and that his bags had fallen through some gaping mental defect snaking through the entirety of the Muslim world.

And into this breezed once again the figure of Nadwa Qaragholi. She'd been held back in customs because one of the nurses had left the UK without the proper papers. Nadwa kept insisting on speaking to the boss of the whomever she happened to be talking to until she got to the departmental Big Man, who (of course) remembered her through some of her charity work. It wasn't even an act, it turned out that guy running the place actually *was* thrilled to see her. Once she'd established that, she'd been able to massage the nurse through a bureaucratic and paranoid customs process – sans paperwork – through sheer force of her will.

This was also the woman who'd taken care of the in-country details. I finally put it together that I had been on a teleconference with her, I'd just never laid eyes of the lady. She carried herself like an aristocrat, but thought like a "fixer." Having been surrounded by that creature known as the Southern Belle my entire life, I am familiar with breed of lady who can handle nearly every obstacle without appearing to do much of anything. As I watched as uniformed airport officials pretending to dismiss her while doing exactly as they were told, I don't think that I'd ever seen it played with such aplomb.

She took Dr. Gascon's rage over the lost baggage with a detached smile, which is more than could be said about the frightened man in the Turkish Airlines office. She wielded the names of various big-wigs attached to the Iraqi side of the mission and how much they wanted everything to go smoothly. The TA man cowered and groveled, took down the doctor's information and photocopied it to show his good faith and promised to get our bags on the next flight from Istanbul. Then he promptly went on vacation for a week without reporting the loss to anyone.

So it was that I finally I stepped outside and onto the fabled soil of Mesopotamia. The heat smacked me in the face like a kiln with something to prove. Maybe it had been the shawarma talking, but Tim was right, the heat *was* utterly confusing.

The summer in Basra is really something. The arrivals board said that it was 55^0 outside which didn't seem all that bad until one of the British nurses gasped and I realized that the rest of the planet uses Celsius. I did the math in my head and that 55^0 degrees looked a lot like 131^0 Fahrenheit. Maybe it *is* the heat. Basra is consistently the world's hottest city, and also reckoned by many to be the site of the Garden of Eden. Both can't be true. The whole of Christian tradition unravels in the first chapter if Adam and Eve don't commit some wicked original sin, but just wander off looking for shade.

The Muslim end of the faithful have their own drollery about the environment: It is that God, having cast Lucifer out of Heaven, needed a place to send the fallen angels as punishment and thus created a place of searing heat and unbearable torment. This Hell was so awful that amid the fallen's wailing protests for mercy, even the ever loyal Angel Gabriel was moved by pity to step in and suggest that God had over-egged the pudding. "You can't make it *that* bad," Gabriel intervened, "These angles were once your own children, your favorites. Yes, punish them, Lord, but this is *too* much." Moved to pity, the Lord relented and created another, gentler Hell for the fallen scofflaws.

"Verily," the Almighty said to Gabriel, looking at his beta version of Hades, "What do we do with this?"

"Put it over there," said Gabriel, "Just add flies, and call it Mesopotamia."

It says something about the cultural temperament of the Arabs that they seem to have so many jokes involving Moses, Muhammed, Abraham, Ishmael, Gabriel and even Jesus haggling with the Almighty. What it says, however, is God's own private mystery.

What is unquestionably true is that Basra is Iraq's second city with a population of three and a half million. It is a low, flat and desert colored so that from the airport, it's easy to miss despite its size. It's a port city on the Shatt al-Arab waterway that connects the city to the Persian Gulf – once a highway for traders and merchants, then a conduit for the oil fields around the city that make up for some 90% of Iraqi oil production. After generations of war with nearly everyone in the neighborhood, the Shatt al-Arab is now chocked with trash and sunken vessels. As oil production is 95% of the Iraqi government's income, the place should glitter like Dubai instead, apart from the odd old 19th century mansion, the city is a flat expanse of low-rise apartments.

Not that I saw much of it. We were loaded into a big white van and flanked by our Iraqi Security Force escorts, before and behind us in two white pick-up trucks, smiling and armed to the teeth. Beyond the airport's concrete blast walls, there was about twenty feet of anemic shrubbery "accented" with razor wire. I searched for a withered tree of knowledge, but all I saw was more horizon.

The drive to Nasiriya is a spine rattling two-hour dash across a desert that looks less like majestic Arabian dunes than God's infinite and badly pressed khakis. I'd never seen anything quite like it. For Americans, places like Great Britain and France are more interesting than they are foreign. Gallivanting through Latin America things are a little more exotic, but in the end it's just another colonial experiment spun off from a faded European power. Arriving in a place like Iraq for the first time felt like landing on the moon.

The sand isn't like the stuff you frolic around in at the beach: This is a fine-ground grit. When it gets kicked up in the air it hangs so that in the distance horizon where the earth meets a washed-out pale blue of sky, the sand affects light refraction into a blur, like a finger ran through a line of chalk. For two hours, it was Mother Nature in her nihilist phase. The depravation of senses would have been absolute save the confusing heat and your kidneys rattling against your spine on the potholed roads.

Out in the desert, there was the odd sign of mankind here and there. A few burned out cars or military vehicles had been sitting idle on the roadside. Dotted around the security checkpoints were little hovels selling food and drink to what travelers there were. These were simple block buildings that didn't appear to be mortared at all, but held together with gravity and the will of Allah. The roofs were flat reed mats secured from blowing away with more blocks.

Some infrastructure work was going on. When the on-ramp to the convoy's single turn was blocked due to construction, the caravan hopped the median into the opposing traffic without slowing down. This threw the security fellows in the bed of the truck to their feet and they waved their assault rifles as a sort of all-purpose VIP pass. Oncoming traffic could make way as we careened the wrong way up the exit ramp. It wasn't as reckless as it seemed, information leaks out of Iraqi security forces like a sieve. Once theses fellas were asked to escort a brigade of foreign aid medics the smart money was that every dueling crackpot militia in the country knew it as well. The convoy was under strict orders to not stop for any reason. I'll say this, we made good time.

As quickly as sign of human settlement had gone blank just beyond Basra, it picked back up again at the Euphrates River. I was thrilled, this was the Cradle of Civilization, and that sort of thing really brings out the history dweeb in a guy. Although, if you grew up in Memphis on the banks of the Mississippi River with family from its Delta, there is a dim schoolboy let-down when you first cross over the Euphrates. For all its history, it really isn't much of a river.

Yet such was the wealth and arrogance of the ancient Babylonians that when Cyrus the Great led his invasion west towards what was then considered the greatest city on Earth, the eastern approach to Mesopotamia was marked by a huge phallus. Theoretically, the great wang was a fertility symbol of the alluvial plain. Sure. Cultures before and since normally used a hugely pregnant woman for that kind of symbolism, and even to the wildly chauvinist ancient man that had to make a hell of a lot more sense. Ancient man wasn't stupid, after all, but he was a man. A real archeologist might argue the point, but it seems to me that Sargon the Great placing a gigantic boner on his imperial doorstep was less a fertility symbol and more what investment bankers would dub a few millennia later, a big swingin' dick.

THE CRADLE OF CIVILIZATION seems to have turned on its mother. Over 6,000 years of human development and I watched us pass a neighborhood of people living in hovels made of grass. Iraq is poor, but it's not *that* poor. This couldn't even be entirely blamed on the war – it was just empty. Closer to Nasiriya, the landscape got greener, sort of. It was really just bare scrub that I understand gets more scrubby in the winter with more water. There were some reed and canvas homes that I also understand look a lot less desperate in the off-season as well.

The building codes definitely improved. Nasiriya is a real city. It is the place where the US-led "March Across Kuwait" stopped and rolled back in 1991. I might have even found myself in that fight, had the operation taken longer that my Econ mid-terms. The only reason most American have heard of the place today, however, is due to a couple of wrong turns by an army convoy during the 2003 invasion that led to its ambush and the capture of Pvt. Jessica Lynch and her made-for-tv rescue by the Marines was turned into a real made-for-tv movie.

The retreating Iraqi army was so unprepared for prisoners that they took her to the Ali Hussein hospital where, coincidently, we were heading. The local staff remember the whole ordeal well. One of the Iraqi doctors working with the ICHF team, Dr. Alem Ghazi, is a charming man who'd studied in Germany and spoke excellent English. Later we had a nice long chat while he drove me around the city. According to both Pvt. Lynch and Alem, the hospital staff took pains to protect the American from the disintegrating Iraqi military. A nurse held vigil at her bedside, singing gently to calm her fears. Alem told me that the doctors tried to return the poor girl to the Americans, rigging up a white flag to an ambulance, but were fired upon.

"American troops fired on an ambulance?"

"It was a warning shot, I don't think that they intended to hit us." He said, pretty graciously. "They called through a loudspeaker not to come any closer. So, we turned around with the woman and took her back to the hospital. They came and got her that night."

That daring rescue from the hospital would have been a lot more daring had the Iraqi military not all fled the day before. They left behind the doctors and nurses who'd been trying all day to get the US Army's supply clerk back to them. The Arabs are nothing if not polite.

"So why did the marines shoot up the stairwell?" I asked, "It's still riddled with bullet holes."

He rolled his eyes. "The army has its ways." Then he seemed embarrassed that a close to a decade later the hospital still hadn't gotten around to patching up the pock-marked stairwell. I felt bad for mentioning it.

As Alem was driving me through the chaotic roundabout where Pvt. Lynch's convoy had its fateful wrong turn, it was hard not to talk about the war. He pointed out the old water tower with its pan still punctured with the dinner-plate sized holes. These weren't the pin-pricks of happy fire from rifles, but the work of larger ordinance.

Nasiriya itself is only about 170 years old and most of it built in the Arab nationalist heyday of the late 1950s. In 1988, with the Iran/Iraq war over, the city finally got traffic lights. Three years later, in 1991, US tanks rolled through and pulled them all down. We also managed to knock over some of the buildings which were repaired, somewhat. Saddam was pretty chapped by the Shi'a south for its attempted uprising in the wake of the first US withdrawal, so it wasn't until 2002 when the Iraqi government finally got around to stringing up the traffic lights for the city's roughly 900,000 citizens. These, of course, were pulled down the next year in the 2003 invasion. "The army has its ways." Alem repeated again.

The polite euphemisms were stacking up, and not just from Alem, either. For whatever reason, humans hate to believe that wealth and power is largely acquired through luck. Surely the American colossus that had emerged after World War II was an exercise in superior skill and planning. No people can be *that* successful by accident, can they? What was dawning on the people of Iraq – after an invasion that pulled out in time for Saddam to crush popular uprising, followed a decade later by a second, inexplicable invasion and a nearly endless occupation – was the horrifying likelihood that the United States did not have an endgame to all this chaos; that we'd never thought it through. They were angry, sure, but they were also baffled on an almost cosmic level.

Outside the city, the scars are easily erased in the fine gritty sand. Alem and I were headed for much more ancient history in the nearby biblical city of Ur. Tradition holds that Ur is the birthplace of Abraham – although tradition is less clear on what the Ur Department of Child Services thought about that stunt he pulled on his son, Isaac, at the father/son picnic.

We were headed to the one of the oldest existing structures on the planet. You might think that the Great Ziggurat of Ur would be a kitschy tourist attraction like the pyramids of Egypt. It isn't. The whole of what is left of the ancient complex, and the city of Ur, is located on the Imam Ali Air Base. You have to hand it to Saddam there, the man knew how to work the system. Building a military base around a world heritage site like the Great Ziggurat not only keeps the tourist traffic to a minimum it also ensures that your air base never gets bombed by a liberal country with a free press.

Entrance to the site isn't exactly forbidden, but it isn't welcome either. Like everything else in this part of the world, it's all a negotiation. Or more bluntly, a tedious cerebral massage. Since no was entirely sure that the war was actually over, the soldiers guarding the entrance – well they weren't exactly on edge, we'd caught them napping – needed some convincing. My four phrases in Arabic weren't going to cut it so Alem picked out the fella with the biggest beret and chatted with him for a moment, then went into the guard house and they chatted some more. Calls were made, more chatting with the next fellow who wandered in. Eventually he came out, got behind the wheel and said. "It is all arranged. No problem. We must leave before sunset."

"How long is that?"

"Oh, I shouldn't think that it matters. There is a sandstorm coming."

Giving money and power to government is like giving whiskey and car keys to teenage boys.

P.J. O'Rourke
Parliament of Whores

CHAPTER TWO:
WE'RE ALL SOMEONE'S BITCH

THAT THE ROYAL TOMBS of Ur were filled with riches originating in such faraway places* like modern Iran and India is testament to the fact that even in those early days, someone had talked himself into being a royal. While Ur was a bit rough by today's standards, but it wasn't a bad place to rule in its heyday: The largest city on the planet with a peak population of some 65,000 and the center of the known world in the bargain. Its wealth largely came from being a major port – which is hard to visualize these days, being smack in the middle of the desert. All that land that had rattled my spine on the drive from Basra to Nasiriya looked like a dried-out sea-bed because that's exactly what it was. Beyond the coast, it was a marshy place, with beautiful farmland made fertile by flooding from the Tigris and

---

*On foot at any rate.

Euphrates rivers. People have been there for about 6,000 some odd years, which is getting us close to the dawn of anything we'd call civilization.

By the Third Dynasty of Ur, some 4,100 years ago, King Ur-Nammu had written down and enacted the Code of Ur-Nammu (which you probably haven't heard of) because to keep a population of that size in line you need a little more than threats to pull the car over. The code predates the Code of Hammurabi (which you really should have heard of) by some 300 years. These weren't just criminal codes, the government got into weights and measures and even price controls despite not having a hard currency to control. It was a barter economy with standardized pricing: According to contemporary legal documents, a beer was a certain measure of barley, and a shag with the prostitute hanging around outside the tavern was a piglet. So the people of Ur knew what the score was when they saw the fellas out on the town with their pockets bulging with barley and a piglet under the arm.

Once *that* was organized, Ur-Nammu decided that what the place needed was a great whacking Ziggurat in honor of the city's patron deity, the moon god Nanna (or Sīn depending who you asked). If there was ever a litmus test for the prosperity of civilization throughout the mists of time, it's that if a government can enact a public works project of such staggering uselessness, they must be doing alright.

The Great Ziggurat is a great stepped pyramid, the original height of which is a mystery. It was a crumbling ruin by the 6th century BC, and today only the base survives. "Originally," Alem told me, "It was like a step stool for Nanna, so he could step down from the heavens to the earth." While Ur-Nammu was on the subject of the gods, he had himself declared one to spare himself the indignity of going up to the heavens in the service elevator.

So, there I stood atop Ur-Nammu's Bronze Age boondoggle waiting for the expected storm to sand-blast my face and thinking that, noxious though it is, we need government to provide some stability if we are going to be something other than mere scavengers. While the rule of law is the single most important factor in civilization, it does not make civilization permanent.

By the Third Dynasty, Ur had started its decline. Upriver the port town of Babylon began to hit its stride. Its famous king enacted the Code of Hammurabi, which states that the gods have "called by name me, Hammurabi, the exalted prince, who feared God, to bring about the rule of righteousness in the land, to destroy the wicked and the evil doers; so that the strong should not harm the weak." Pretty self-serving, but it did create the circumstances needed for real civilization to take root.

Before we get too high and mighty, Frans de Waal, a primatologist,* observed a little less grandly: "Without agreement on rank and certain respect for authority there can be no great sensitivity to social rules, as anyone who has tried to teach simple house rules to a cat can well agree."

True enough, but it doesn't change the fact that humans are greasy little stinkers and will abuse both law and authority to their advantage if given half a chance. Consider that the same politician who is exempt from the social security that gets wrung out of *your* paycheck is also exempt from the Affordable Care Act, Freedom of Information and a raft of other laws they

---

* Studies monkeys and apes.

benignly hang around your neck so that "the strong shouldn't harm the weak." We have ditched kings and a titled aristocracy and farmed out all that foolishness to a new breed prince, princess, and pasha: Those vaguely likable but oily kids who stayed awake in social studies class and joined the Young Democrats or Republicans. You know the ones, the sort who'd show up at Kevin's "My Parents are in Aspen" kegger even though no one could figure out just who in the hell had invited them. None of whom will ever be so dedicated to public service that they'll give up *their* perks and salary – just yours.

We've always had government in one form or another, and we've never quite trusted it. History tells us we really shouldn't. For most of human history said authority meant some thug who was mean and strong enough to take from others. He grew rich enough to feed a private army of thugs to go out and rob a lot more suckers in the middle of next spring. For most of human history, in short, life really sucked for the common man. The fact remains, however, that civilizations need governments to maintain themselves. And civilization is better that the lack thereof.

Still, that one man should be king and another not, is grating to men. I suspect that it is a lot more grating to women, as throughout most of history they weren't really in the running. It's no surprise that kings have used "God wills it" to establish the legitimacy of their rule almost from the beginning. What is surprising is how long we used the same ridiculous argument given the number of kings who've been deposed by their own people. Surely it serves some purpose, or it wouldn't have worked so well for so long. The why likely rests in that "God wills it" is so much easier for the hoi polloi to swallow than the more honest, but off-putting: "I'm going to kill you."

To which the masses will have to entertain the disconcerting thought, "Yeah, he probably will,"

That's no way to build team spirit.

While the Great Ziggurat of Ur may have been a vanity project, it did serve a real political purpose, namely to make the priests look really good and feel important. They were the ones, it was believed, who could divine the will of the gods and the celestial omens in a random and dangerous world. More practically, it was they who murmured that monarchy itself was a gift from the gods who'd taken pity on the wild and disordered humans, tormented by demons in the wilderness. It was kings, they said, who would bring peace and order to the earth. Left unsaid was that it was the kings who maintained the priest's privilege.

The divine notwithstanding, on the ground you need to address more practical matters. To build a nation, or even a tribe, you need a well-defined in-group of people willing to put the tribe before their own strict self-interest. If you don't, you'll have a revolt every time you sit down for breakfast. In-groups like to tell each other that they are primarily held together by internal bonds and tradition. This isn't exactly wrong, but the primary cohesion is more likely external in nature. The best way to build that tribal in-group spirit is to have a hated out-group. As Eric Hoffer points out in his book, *The True Believer,* "Hatred is the most accessible and comprehensive of all the unifying agents. Mass movements can rise and spread without belief in a god, but never without a belief in a devil." Basically, we all need someone to hate. And if we're good at hating the bastards, the gods will smote them.

You don't have to be human for very long to see that this makes life brutish, fragile and short. Or that your fellow human is full of shit. It won't do to just walk up to your neighbors and tell them you just had a conversation with the gods, and they promoted you to Big Man and here's what we're all going to do. They'll never believe that the gods picked an ass like you out of the crowd. Better then, to tell everyone that the gods told your grandfather what the score was and, assuming that he survived to a ripe old age, killed an impressive batch of outsiders and made a pot of whatever is passing for money, people will believe that you might be onto something. Which is why so many of these fantastic origin myths seem to be written down a generation or three after the fact.* Humans love rank and rank loves a pedigree.

IN IT'S DAY, Ur may have been the world's great city, but that's all it was – a great city. Further up the Euphrates, Babylon grew rich, but it too was just one more spot of order in a seemingly endless expanse of wilderness. It sat on a great alluvial plain between the Tigris and the Euphrates that flooded and kept the soil there dark and abundant. Mesopotamia in fact, means "the land between the rivers." And because the land could support a great population, it did. Up to a point.

The fellow who would go down in the scrolls as Sargon the Great of Akkad was almost certainly not the first man to dream not only of being king of his own city but to rule over many

---

* Maybe it the journalist in me, but if I was there for some Sword of the Almighty derring-do, I'd have filed a story that same day.

lesser kings. Sometime around 2,200 BC, though, he became the first one we know of to actually pull it off. He established the Akkadian Empire and planted that enormous boner on the eastern approaches to show the neighbors who was boss. And the boss was smart enough to see that the population of his realm was outpacing its ability to feed itself. Radicals will tell you that revolution starts in the heart or the mind, but back then Sargon knew better. Revolutions start in the stomach, an empty stomach.

Sargon reasoned that if he could subjugate surrounding city-states and demand a tribute in grain and slaves then the power center would stay well-fed and tended. He was right, but it also caused the population to grow faster, so the empire needed even more to fuel feeding into the center. As innovations go, it wasn't bad, just a little lopsided. The imperial seat remained well-fed with tribute and the client kings received protection from various second tier thugs by swearing loyalty to a real first-tier thug. And both the ruler and ruled got access to wider, open markets.

The model worked well-enough that Sargon had long passed into folk legend by the time the Assyrian Empire was starting to really fire on all cylinders. It went through several dynasties of varying success but they all agreed that Babylon was the center of the world. At the time, the "world" was defined as everyone who knew that Babylon was the center of it. The problem with all empires, though, is that to keep working they need to keep expanding

In 722 BC, the ever-expanding imperial gyre was hitting the limits of existing technology and logistics. Babylon had expanded some 500 miles to the west when it hit the beach. It was there that a semi-nomadic tribe over at the edge of the world started to make a name for itself. According to tradition, a tribe calling themselves the Israelites decided that *their* god promised to deed over some real estate in their name. All they had to do was throw the current tenants, the Canaanites, out. The hitch in the divine property transfer was that no one had bothered to tell the Canaanites that their lease was up.*

While most historians regard the biblical Books of Genesis and Joshua as of little to no *historical* value, it doesn't mean that it doesn't have any *social* value or a wider meaning. And the tale Joshua tells about the City of Jericho is a doozy: That the Hebrews marched around the fortified walls of the city once a day for six days and seven times on the seventh day, and the whole thing just fell down with the blast of a ram's horn trumpet. With walls down, the Israelites came in and killed every man, woman and child, save one family. Even with complete faith in the Hand of God business, there is still a curious hole in the plot. Sitting in the middle of said hole is a prostitute named Rehad. In some accounts she's cleaned up as an innkeeper, but there is no reason she couldn't have been both. However she bought her bread, she also kept two Hebrew spies in her house while they performed a recon on the city. If God was going to knock to walls down with a righteous horn melody, why the spies? What were they going to find out from wandering around the city and sleeping on the roof of a brothel that the Almighty didn't already know from such an exalted an omnipotent vantage point?

More likely, the spies were looking for a point in which to sneak in or break the gates, which they did with Rehad's help

---

* Virgil claimed the same for Rome in the *Aeneid*. Caesar Augustus loved it.

and then killed everyone except her family. Afterwards, they slapped the "God wills it" seal of approval for future generations.

Even if actual events have been scrambled into fiction, the story is interesting because it shows that this business of a divinely inspired land grab is woven into the ethnic story almost from the beginning. And we're still dealing with it today.

To the south of Jericho is the city of Jerusalem. There is archeological evidence that people have been there since 4th millennia BC but the first real civilization, the Canaanites, dates only from about 1,400 BC. The Canaanites called it *Urusalin* which likely means City of Shalem – their god of the dusk. As it happens, this word comes from the same root as the ancient Hebrew word for peace, so when the Israelites showed up 500 years later, they thought it meant City of Peace.*

Another theory is that the Israelites never went to war with the Canaanites, but were simply a splinter group that broke off and needed a livelier origin story. And still another tradition holds that there was a United Kingdom of Israel founded in 1,053 BC which broke into the two kingdoms of Israel and Judah in 930. It's possible, archeology is a fragmentary science at best. For the most part, historians agree that the region was simply too sparsely populated to support a united kingdom of that size. You will also note the curious absence of Ziggurat style boondoggles dating from the era in question. However two cities called Israel and Judah did exist around this time and buzzed along over there on the Mediterranean until the Assyrians showed up and sacked Israel in 722 BC, carrying away heaps of Hebrews into captivity

---

* Don't tell me that God doesn't have a sense of humor. Either way, mood lighting is swell and the sunsets delightful.

in Babylon to feed the imperial machine. More practically and less heroically, Judah avoided the same fate by becoming a vassal of the Assyrian Empire. The arrangement lasted better than a century until Judah stopped paying the imperial tribute. King Nebuchadnezzar II, unable to let the snub slide, laid siege to Jerusalem in 594/93 BC and hauled off a bunch more Hebrews to captivity with their northern neighbors.

AS KING OF BABYLON, Nebuchadnezzar II ruled over an unquestioned superpower. It is the curse of the successful, true of families as it is nations, that success often breeds an entitled softness. And once an empire hits its outer limits, they don't stagnate, but contract. It was a mere 25 years after the death of Nebuchadnezzar that his royal dynasty was overthrown by a force coming from far beyond the plains of Mesopotamia, where the land rises into plateau in the east. There lived tribes called Aryans that the Assyrian's had never been able to subjugate – tough, hard people famous as breeders of the best horses and who seemed to have been born into the saddle. You know, bumpkins.

A tribe called the Meads – against all expectations, including their own – had risen as a force with which to be reckoned. To the south were other Aryans tribes, people that even the rough Meads thought were uncouth. As horsemen, they were semi-nomadic but then again most humans were in those days. They came from a place they gave their name to: Persis. The family of the dominant tribe of these bumpkins were the Achaemenids, and its chieftain was a wildly gifted man named Cyrus. A man who would, in the course of about six short, bloody years, reshuffle the great power competition of the ancient world. A millennia and change later be called a hero by a wide-spattering of people like Thomas Jefferson, the last Shah of Iran and David Ben-Gurion, the founder of modern Israel.

Cyrus was the child of a Persian chieftain Cambyses, and a Median princess, Mandane. According to lore, even that pairing was weird. The Median King Astyages had had a dream where he saw his daughter popping a squat and urinating enough to create a river that flooded his empire. A little creeped out, the king consulted his magi, who told him this was a bad omen: It meant the Persians were coming for him. So, the king married the girl off to some Persian chieftain to keep the peace. That settled, Astyages then had another dream: A vine grew out from between the Mandane's legs and just kept coming and growing until it shaded the entire world.* Astyages ordered his grandson killed, as you do. As happened with Moses and in half a dozen other of these child sacrifice stories, the kid was saved by maternal subterfuge and raised somewhere else only to extract an ironic and theatrical revenge on the infanticidal king trying to avoid a fate laid out in his dreams. Drowning the world in a river of wiz, though, is a nice touch.

As it was, the Mead's *did* fall to the Persians, but they weren't enslaved. Part of Cyrus' considerable genius lay not only in his mastery of arms, but diplomacy and his ability to refine the imperial model of the past. Once he conquered an army and a tribe's nobility, he didn't indulge in the common practice of beheading the soldiers and enslaving the rest. His innovation was to fold the conquered nobility into his court with titles and privileges and let the people just get on with it. He needed the

---

* Perhaps Astyages should have passed on that last cup of wine.

conquered to buy into his vision of an ordered world, and so tolerated local customs and religions, and even rebuilt shines to local deities the Persians found ridiculous.

When the armies of Persia arrived at Babylon and deposed its last king, one of the first things Cyrus did was to free the captives, including the Israelites. He even built them a new temple in Jerusalem.* They were still vassals of Persia, you understand, but they were back home and had a new temple. He gets a really rave review in the Bible.

By the time of his death, the Achaemenid Empire that Cyrus had established stretched nearly from India to the Levant. Impressive, yes, but Cyrus was standing on the shoulders of empires past, and he didn't have to take over every city in the Assyrian empire, just the capital. After that you just announce new management and kill all the second-tier kings who don't respond with a big sack of grain and a hearty, "Let me be the first to say how glad we are to have you at the helm."

In the Levant, the imperial eye naturally wandered up the coast to Asia Minor until it fell on Ionia – a Greek settled stretch of coastline and islands in what is modern Turkey. Cyrus didn't have anything against the Ionians *per say*, but he was in an expansive mood.

Over in the Greek mainland, news of this Persian expansion reached the proud Spartans, the scourge of the Peloponnesian peninsula. They sent a delegation to Cyrus, who duly received the long haired, scarlet cloaked ambassadors. Being congenitally devoid of diplomatic tact, the Spartan delegation warned the

---

* I trust there is no need to point out the irony of Iran's first Shah freeing Israelites and rebuilding their temple for them.

most powerful man on earth to leave the Ionian cities alone or face the wrath of mighty Sparta. It was a bold move, you've got to give the Spartans that. It would have certainly made more of an impact had Cyrus ever heard of them. As it was, he had to call over an Ionian servant and ask, "Who are these Spartans?"

Unlike the towering civilizations of the East, the Greek city-states were a fractious collection – nothing you'd call an Empire, or even a federation. Just some people who lived in a place and agreed on the basic fact that they were Greek, and very little else. They were like cousins who, forced to contest granddad's generous but finite will, admitted they were family but hated each other nonetheless. Everyone in Greece agreed that the Spartans were just the worst, but no one outside the family had ever heard of them. They certainly didn't move the needle with Cyrus, who ignored the threat, ate up Ionia anyway and installed some client kings with standing order to just get on with it.

At this point, the Persians didn't have anything we'd call a state religion, and that was part of their strength. The Egyptians could carry on worshiping cows and cats, the Greeks could continue trying to get signals from that board meeting being held on Mount Olympus, and the Persians themselves were still pretty sure that a good, white horse was divine.

Relaxed though he was on the matter, Cyrus was canny enough to know good symbolism and meaning when he saw it. Out of the eastern approaches of his growing empire – among people even the Persians thought of as bumpkins – came a religion that was radically simple and straightforward. Given the strange rites and bizarre headwear that had evolved to show the common man just how special and technically proficient someone had to be to speak to the gods, this really was novel.

The whole point of the priestly class was to keep people in awe of the semi-divine monarchy.

And here was a prophet called Zoroaster carrying on about one god above all the rest, the uncreated, called Ahura Mazda – which means Chief Wisdom. Zoroaster preached that the earth was a great battlefield between good and evil, the light and the darkness, between the truth (*Asa*) and the lie (*Druj*). Ahura Mazda had created the truth, but it needed to be tended, like fire. And like fire's pure flames, there was attendant black smoke and smudge, the lie. And what's more, the world would not just spin along forever, it would all end one day in a climactic battle between good and evil where Ahura Mazda wins.*

The beauty of what Zoroaster preached was that it was so simple: There was the truth and there was the lie, and all you had to do was pick a side. This radically changed the marketplace for ideology where seekers wandered around looking for some sympathetic magic to buy with a candle or a goat. Pick the truth and its potent symbol of fire was on your side: Warming your house, cooking your dinner, and lighting your way in the darkness. If you got on the wrong side of it, it would just as quickly burn your house down. Heady stuff.

Cyrus began building shrines to Ahura Mazda and connected his reign to the symbol of fire. He proclaimed that he wanted to bring order to the world, to reveal the truth. It's not that the man was a hippie. He died fighting in the saddle like a good Persian would, at the age of 70 in about 530 BC while on campaign against a warlike tribe beyond his eastern frontiers.

---

* … all this sounds weirdly familiar…

Although it must be pointed out that while Cyrus was very good and drawing peoples to his vision, not everyone was impressed with his vision of an enlightened and well-ordered world. The queen of that eastern tribe reportedly had Cyrus's head lopped off and stuffed into a wine-skin filled with blood so as too finally slake his thirst for the stuff.

One man's freedom fighter...

Nils desperandum
"Never Despair"

Horace 65-8 BC

CHAPTER THREE:
THE BEST LAID PLANS

THE ICHF MISSION was housed in a Ministry of Health guesthouse somewhere inside a dusty labyrinth of biscuit colored offices, a small hospital and a few other nondescript buildings that took up an entire block. All of it walled in like a fortress. The security checkpoints were manned by soldiers in discontinued US Navy surplus "blueberry" camouflage fatigues – a design useless for sailors and fatally conspicuous for desert soldiers. Worse than that, they looked hot. I was never exactly clear what criteria the guards were using to admit people, because inside the compound lots of women in black *abayahs* billowing in the wind seemed to be wandering everywhere with little children in tow.

The entire region seemed to be in the swing of the first building boom since the King Faisal II had been deposed in 1958. Given the south's relationship with Baghdad, it probably was. Unlike new American build-outs of the Danish Modern & Desperate school, Iraqi commercial construction is inspired by

41

that Ziggurat: Ur Contemporary if you will. Not that I could see many architectural details. This part of the world seems incapable of building something as quaint as a picket fence. Nearly every building of any size in Nasiriya is walled compound. The color scheme, for both wall and exterior, is the mud and water concept that has been popular here since men around here brought a piglet on a date. It isn't that the locals don't appreciate the odd splash of color here, but those sandstorms really play hell with paint job.

Inside the office of the Director of Healthcare for the Thi-Qar region, I found that splash of color. It was more like a tidal wave. Indoors, the sun-bleached palette was replaced by an orgy of garnet, purple and swirling marble as if the décor was trying to make up where a monochrome nature had short-sheeted them. The trim on the floors hadn't been laid so we stepped over a gap of about a foot over concrete rubble to the gleaming marble and headed to the elevators.

You can't fault Arab manners, but all official business was thrown completely off when Dr. Gascon casually mentioned, by way of explaining his grogginess, that he hadn't slept well and what sleeping he had done had been in the same clothes he'd been wearing since leaving Istanbul. Minions were called in and there was an impromptu council held in indignant Arabic with lots of hand waving. From the way the director was carrying on, he was contemplating a land invasion of Turkey over their national carrier's loss of the good doctor's luggage. He pointed at Gascon: This man has come to help us and just look at him. He looks like Hell! Then, in English, elaborate assurances were made that all would soon be well. This took 25 minutes.

The creation of the Nasiriya Heart Center, intended to be the regional cardiac center in southern Iraq, was the pet project Iraqi President Nouri al-Maliki, so the director was happy to have the Americans heading up the year-long training program for both the current staff of surgeons. He was less happy that Gascon and Nadwa had, more or less, strong armed him into enrolling thirteen surgical residents, with no seniority, in to the program.

It was all very pleasant, but it wasn't a social reception – only the Big Men spoke. The director behind his enormous desk and Gascon in the seat of honor. The rest of us occupied seating arranged Arab style around the walls of the cavernous room and kept our mouths shut. I'd heard of this, and used the expression myself, but I'd never actually seen someone literally hold court.

The results of previous two-week long ICHF missions in Iraq – running on and off since 2010 - had been nil. The standard modus operandi of the ICHF was pretty straightforward: Flying in teams of medical volunteers for two week missions a couple of times per year, the foundation teams perform surgeries while the local teams watch, then assist, then the foundation teams move back to assist and finally to consult. Ideally a program should last about five years and result in having two fully competent local pediatric cardiac teams with established protocols in place to train more. It's a model that has produced brilliant successes, as well as failures.

Exactly why the Iraqi mission had failed was another question, because if the Arabs have anything, its long memories. In 1989 so many Iraqi doctors had trained in the US and UK that nearly as quarter of them were Board certified. And 1989 is a good year to cite because it's the first full year after the

1980-1988 war with Iran and the last before the invasion of Kuwait. Since then the country has been invaded twice and subject to crippling sanctions. With the US troops withdrawing (again) the vibrations in the resulting vacuum were getting nasty, and Iraqi government contracts are mercurial in the best of circumstances. In short, the director needed to launch the program as fast as possible as a *fait accompli*. There however a small issue, one of those things dyed so deep in the fabric of society that the host doesn't think to mention it and the guest doesn't know to ask. When the dates of the program were established no one in Iraq pointed out to the arriving Westerners that the entire Muslim world was heading into Ramadan.

It's a time of fasting, but unlike Catholic lent you aren't given any wiggle room on making up your own rules. For an observant Muslim, this means no food, water or smoking between sun up and sun down for a month – followed by an *Iftar** feast after nightfall. The issue was a delicate one because fasting plays hell with what we'd call a "professional attitude." After twelve years of Catholic schooling with nuns, priests and Christian Brothers, I'd know. It's one thing if low blood sugar and a hankering for some nicotine causes you to snap at a kid who hasn't turned in his homework, but no one needs to be doing cardiac surgery in that state of mind. No less than a source than *The Economist* estimates that Ramadan knocks off some 8-13% off the GDP of the Arab economies every year. So, having flown from places all over the planet, the team was told that the first order of business, before starting the ambitious year-long training program

---

* I was told by a doctor who'd spent time in the US that it was like "having your Thanksgiving every night for a month."

intended to change the face of modern Iraq, was to take a break from it. For a month.

To his credit, Gascon didn't meet the religious objections head on, he just more or less ignored them and told the assembled company that we could all pack up and go home if the Iraqi's didn't want to work. They wanted to work.

Here was the foreignness that I'd felt when first landing in this country played out in the theater of professional politics of the East. It shows up mostly in things that, when taken alone, seem innocuous to the Westerner. When stacked atop each other, however, the proceedings lead to an entirely different endgame. If the director didn't know something, he signaled one of his underlings who would clarify the point *to him*. Then the director would tell Gascon the answer he'd just been provided. It's very important for the Big Man to have and dispense all the answers. Underlings do not take the floor. At the time this seemed trivial, but it reflects a reflexive hoarding of information – compounded at nearly every link up the chain of command – that creates a near fatal paralysis within the operational system. Not just in healthcare, but the entire state itself. I'd have considered this point further at the time but was distracted by the next, fairly unbelievable, item on the agenda.

The issue had nothing to do with surgery, but pediatric intensive care unit (PICU) nursing protocol. Gascon reckoned he was a surgeon so asked Karen Thames, the formidable British head field nurse attached to the mission, to take the floor. And she most certainly did not whisper her remarks to the chief. Karen dragged a chair into the center of the room and plopped herself down to join the conversation. The air on the Iraqi side to this was akin to your very proper grandmother learning at the rehearsal dinner that the bride and groom have been living together for a year and a half and she's three months pregnant. Granny will be too polite to say anything just then, but she is visibly horrified.

Karen left surgery to the surgeons - her concern was the pediatric patients in recovery afterwards, most of whom were still in diapers. As Karen understood it, for reasons of hygiene, in Iraq parents are not allowed into the PICU to see their children after surgery. While this would be unheard of in the United States, it's fairly common in places where the citizenry does as its told. Alone, that wasn't a huge problem. Now that the government was spending more on healthcare and less on an outsized army, it had started conscripting the young men who used to be cannon fodder into the nursing profession. Again, that only works on a citizenry trained to obey, and again, this wasn't a problem in and of itself. The stink, Karen explained, was that the male nurses considered changing diapers to be women's work. And there were very few female nurses. And a loaded nappy was a much larger hygiene issue than say, a parent in the PICU.

The director dismissed her concerns with a noncommittal wave of the hands and returned his attention to Gascon, who said groggily that Karen ran the PICU, and even the most elegant surgery is wasted if the patient isn't allowed to recover. The director then tried to dismiss Karen directly to her face by asking what I'm sure he meant to be a rhetorical question: "How are parents, with no medical training, crucial to the patient's recovery?"

By this time, Karen was squirming in her chair, gripping its arms with fingers that were on the edge of going white. She was physically struggling against a hydra-headed absurdity. For Gascon's part, he figured our hosts had been duly warned and let nature take its frustrating course. What followed was a shock and awe tirade that boiled down to the fact those nappies* weren't gonna change themselves, gents! So just tell the boys to do their jobs or send them out for a smoke break and issue the parents a disposable surgical gown and tell them to wash their hands. Got it fellas?

The Iraqi's threw their hands up in surrender. "Okay, okay! We'll issue the mother a surgical gown."

"Or the father!" Karen pressed.

"...yes...sure...or the father." From the far side of the room I was pretty sure I actually could hear their eyes rolling back in their head. They were making light of it, but they were also ducking for cover.

The issue with the next item on the agenda was that it was not, in fact, on the agenda. It wasn't the sort of thing that you tend to commit to paper. In earlier missions in Iraq, some 50 heart surgeries had been performed on the children of first cousins - huge causal red flag for heart defects. Permission was needed to take DNA swabs to send to the UK for genome sequencing, but finding someone willing to sign the release was difficult. The strict privacy laws made sharing patient information hard, if not impossible.

Now the subject of inbreeding is a touchy subject for any culture, but it seems to me that the problem would largely fix

---

* It is very hard to repeatedly say "nappies" and maintain the required indignation in your voice. She managed it impressively.

itself if there were a place other than your Uncle's house to go meet girls. No one asked me, though.

The argument required delicacy and ultimately it was an appeal to vanity, rather than science, that won out. President al-Maliki wanted a regional medical center and a training hospital that would host conferences so doctors could come from abroad and drop money in hotels and restaurants and all the rest of it. Since the founding modern Iraq, Baghdad's treatment of the Shi'a south had ranged from the merely negligent to actively abusive. The future was unclear and these guys needed to seize the opportunity while it was in their hands. They needed to produce a success and needed it fast. And to do that they needed to share information. The men running the program had a lot more on their minds than persuading some kid to change dirty nappies when he thought a machine gun had so much more swagger. They wanted to please the boss. If you are looking for an indicator of future success for the mission, there is was – not in the satisfaction of a baby with patched heart and a clean bum but in making a smallish river town in the south into a prestigious medical center.

Could they pull it off? Later, in the fly infested conference room the mission was using as a war room, I posed this question to Dr. Gascon, who may well be the most cynical optimist currently living. "Let me ask you a question," Gascon snorted. "What do you think we're here for?"

"To save lives?" I ventured.

"No." he didn't wait for me to finish and I had the feeling the question had been a set up. "We are NOT here to save lives!"

"Ok." I said. Honestly, he had me there. "I'll bite… so why are we here?"

He was quick with the answer and leaned into my voice recorder. "The goal of our being here is not to perform surgery on children. It is to establish a regional pediatric heart center for southern Iraq at the Nasiriya Heart Center, to establish a system that works. The goal is to work with local teams to bring the level of competence in simple to medium complexity to acceptable levels by the end of the year."

"And how, exactly, do you plan to do this?"

"I could talk all day and you wouldn't understand."

Evidently being the smartest person in the room requires the desperate belief that everyone around you is an idiot. "Okay," I said, "then don't talk all day."

He lit a cigar (yes, we were still in the hospital) and thought for a minute. "When you first learned to ride a tricycle, your father walked beside you so you wouldn't fall off, right? Then you didn't need him alongside. Then you moved to a bike with training wheels and there was dad, trotting beside you until he was confident you'd keep your balance. Then the training wheels came off and there was dad again, running alongside until you mastered the next phase." Then he pointed at me with the cigar to give gravity to an illustration that was about to fly off into the absurd. "Now extend that metaphor through a motorcycle, then a car, a Cessna and an Air 380 Jumbo Jet. ... And yeah, your dad is running beside you on the runway, just go with it. Our goal is to run alongside local surgeons as they gain experiences and move on to more complex surgeries when they no longer need us."

I'm pretty sure he was getting sick of me, and I almost hated to tell the guy that the visual might have been absurd, but the metaphor made perfect sense. This was teaching someone to fish rather than just giving them one. For all the misfires and unintended consequences of humanitarian aid, here was a model that was sustainable – if only just – that would leave a functioning system behind. "Can you do it in a year?"

This seemed to require more thought. He puffed on the cigar. "Yeah...It'll take every bit of it though."

The surgeries performed that week were, by heart surgery standards, fairly simple – a bike with training wheels, if you will. "This isn't a one size fits all operation. Nothing that we do here will work unless it fits into the existing cultural groundwork." He said, looking at a gigantic fly that had been circling the conference room all morning.

He, of course, was talking about a mission to create a pediatric heart surgery program. The man was nothing if not focused. For my part, the ICHF mission wasn't the only brief I had for being in-country. The truth is that he could have been talking about installing a new government, democracy, liberalizing trade restrictions. Pretty much anything needed in what we call nation building except teaching house rules to a cat.

The problem with so many noble sounding humanitarian ideas is that they recall, so well, Oscar Wilde's quip about second marriage being "...the triumph of hope over experience." And given the way we keep lavishing financial aid on third world dictators, hope springs eternal.

NOTHING SERVES the writer's purpose like a handy, almost unbelievable metaphor. The fates were kind enough to supply me with one on the outskirts of the ancient city where one of the earliest surviving cracks at literature, "The Epic of Gilgamesh" was penned.

We were piled into the white van, returning from the Ali Hussein hospital with the usual phalanx of blueberry clad security in white Toyota pickups as we headed through Nasiriya to the guesthouse. And it was there where I saw a kid, maybe ten or twelve, in a dirty white *dishadash*, clomping up a highway on-ramp on a tired donkey, his checked *kheffah* was secured to his head with a New York Yankee's baseball cap. He didn't notice us, he was too busy fiddling with his cellphone.

Cultural appropriation gets a bad reputation these days, but the simple exchange of ideas and adapting different ways of addressing a problem is the only way human society progresses and moves forward. Without some cross-pollination of ideas, materials and technologies created by cultural appropriation, human behavior tends toward a loop made up of self-repeating and self-enforcing fractals. And these patterns are very, very hard to break. Just ask an alcoholic, a chubby guy, a pathological liar or for that matter, the painfully honest. There doesn't have to be a right or a wrong to it, and that's what makes it so aggravating.

"Nothing that we do here will work unless it fits into the existing cultural groundwork." Gascon had said. That is as true for a surgical program as it is for democracy-in-a-box foreign policy solutions. To get anything of note done anywhere, no matter how obviously noble or beneficial, takes some massaging of the existing cultural groundwork and the one doing the cultural massaging for the ICHF was Nadwa Qaragholi. She is single-minded and determined, but a lot of people are. She is well-off and connected but you can say the same about a lot of celebrity causes. Her charity organization, the Takreem* award

---

* An Arab Humanitarian Award.

winning Living Light International (LLI) has created local programs that have more or less turned cleaning up the neighborhood garbage and gardening into a sport. These acts of civic pride are basically the price of admission into the local football league or sewing club. In addition, LLI is responsible for a cross-cultural program of sister classrooms linked via video-conferencing the Muslim world and America. She is adamant about getting children from the Arab world and the West to talk to each other the way that adolescences do, so that they get to know each other. If they do, (I'm paraphrasing here) they won't believe everything the politicians say. The remarkable aspect is that she managed to not only get the Islamist leaning government to ignore the co-ed nature of American classroom, but (for the purposes of this program) allow Iraqi classrooms to go co-ed for the program as well.* It isn't enough to stop the current war, she admits, but it just might be enough to stop the next one.

Her secret, and this really is brilliant, is that her organization accepts no cash donations, only services. She doesn't draw a salary – her "day job" is real estate development with concerns in London and the D.C. area – and LLI doesn't even have a bank account. "I know my country," she told me, "everyone wants a kick back to help out." This isn't so much a problem with the country's anemic private sector, but in socialist states it's hard to get anything done without some pay-out to a government official. What Nadwa realized was simply that you can't get bogged down in kick-backs if there is no money to kick back. How do you skim off donated services? The Big Man in the department

---

* Classrooms were integrated under Saddam Hussein, if you are looking for the man's "made the trains run on time achievement."

responsible for garbage collection will either donate trucks to help the kiddo's clean the place up or he won't.

"So, how do you get them to donate services?" I asked. Nadwa admits that it helps to be a woman here. The local Big Man goes to great lengths to ensure that he doesn't have to deal with women largely because it doesn't know how to: He rolls his eyes, he shuts down, he panics. The truth is that hyper-aggression works as well for women as it does for men, but for the Big Man – the self-proclaimed protector of a helpless sex's virtue – the optics get very tricky. And if the woman is very lady-like in the bargain, the optics get even worse. He could ignore her request for services (plenty do) but there is also that paranoid reflex to hoard information plays into her purposes: The awful fear among Big Men that there will be a loop formed with this camera-ready charity work and they won't be a part of it.

She didn't put it quite so bluntly as that. Speaking in vague pleasantries, Nadwa told me about the glue that makes the whole thing work: It was a very high-flown answer that amounted to, more or less, she pestered them until the shame became unbearable.

NASIRIYA AT NIGHT is something else altogether. It's still hot, but just a little less oppressive. Still dusty, but it isn't so apparent as the harsh glare of the sun is replaced by softer man-made lights. It being Ramadan, the streets were strung with little green lights – exactly like American Christmas lights, just all one color. After nightfall they became brighter, and so did the neighborhood. After the Ramadan fast was broken with the *Iftar* feast, the cafés were full. Thi-Qar Provence, Iraq, like Cullman County, Alabama is dry. But the tea shops were full, mostly with middle-aged men smoking ornate water pipes and sipping tea and fruit juice.

Despite what your nephew in Colorado may tell you, that's not hashish they are smoking. Not in public at any rate. It's a mild tobacco, lightly flavored, and lacks that vaguely toxic sensation of a cigarette. Over here, firing up a lung-dart is for administering nicotine into the system, but smoking a pipe is a relaxed, social act. You have to have a seat because you'd look like an ox carrying one of those pipes around. And because you have a seat, you chat. I was with some journalists around my age, although after the last deranged decade some of them looked like they had a hard 16 years on me. One my hosts feared that a nice smoke and the conversation that went with it was dying out with the new generation. "The young, they don't come to places like these," one man, Yasin, told me, "When we were young, this is what the grown men did, and we wanted to be like them. Now, they all want to play on their phones."

This is basically true. Earlier, at the guest house, we'd all had great fun typing profane and lewd things about Saddam into the iTranslate app on our phones for our in-house handlers. They were in their early twenties. They roared with laughter. So, in summary, Iraqi youths like their new-fangled gadgets and don't really like hanging out with square, middle-aged people, who think this is a shame because life was so much simpler back then.

Despite the professed equality of Saddam's secular regime, culturally, cafés are the preserve of men. To meet his family, Alem brought his three children; Ana, Ali and Mustafa for a visit to the guest house. The two younger boys – ten or eleven - were polite and friendly, with hair that refused to stay combed. The fact that they were sitting at a table didn't stop the wrestling match that had been going on all day, but it did tone it down. Ana was about thirteen and was dressed more or less like my daughter plus a head scarf. She was learning English and wanted to practice with Nurse Karen, who wanted to improve her Arabic.

Mustafa looked me over and smiled. "How do you do?"

"Just fine. How are you?" Said I.

He smiled wider, "How do you do?" Ali punched Mustafa in the arm.

Alem said, "That's as far as he's gotten." Then he said something to the boys in Arabic and they burst out laughing. Ana continued to ignore her brothers and made enthusiastic and very trendy corrections to Karen's formal Arabic.

They joked about Ramadan. It's traditional for Muslims to blame every inconvenience and mishap on the fasting. Which the kids don't do until about 14 because who wants to deal with a little kid who hasn't eaten all day? It is the same ruling as Lent. Which, I explained, is also blamed for every mood swing and parking ticket by observant Catholics.

"For Lent you fast for forty days?" The Muslim calendar is a Lunar one, so they go for 28 days.

"It's a different sort of fast. For one thing, it isn't absolute, you just eat *less*."

"What is less?"

"Honestly, you make up your own rules on the outset. It's a personal thing."

"That *is* convenient." I'm going to stop short of claiming a convert, but he looked awfully intrigued. Anyone who can joke about their religion is not a fanatic. And everyone I met was joking about Ramadan.

The women and the children who weren't out at the cafés could be found at the aptly named 'Nasiriya Fun City', an amusement park, which comes alive after dark with the kiddies riding ferris wheels and roller coasters and eating cotton candy and swilling soft drinks. If you swap out the pork hot dogs for the goat kebabs, you've pretty much got Anytown, USA. If I'd thought that Iraq was as foreign as the moon on my first ramble across the desert, suddenly it now seemed as familiar as a backyard cook-out.

Just as familiar is that the chatter of journalists. No matter where you are in the world there are recognizable patterns. You have to hone your skills at small talk and pleasantries (the side door is often left open when the front door is securely barred), but the truth is none of us really like it, it's just a means to an end. I spoke with a man I'll call Abdel regarding Iran's creeping influence in the Shi'a south. "Saddam was very hard on the Shi'a down here, and had always been fairly certain that the south was in the pocket of Iran. So did Khomeini." He laughed. "He thought that we'd rise up when Iran invaded, but we fought as Iraqi's. We *are* Iraqi's. After the first US invasion, when there was a popular uprising against Saddam, after that, it was harder. He starved the region."

Then, in the nineties Iranian money did start to come into the region. Not as foreign aid, precisely. Understand that the Ayatollah Khomeini of Iran saw Saddam Hussein as only a junior devil to the Great Satan of America – but as devil's go, he was a hell of a lot closer. The aid began to come through the Shi'a religious schools and mosques that Khomeini had cultivated while living in exile in Najif, in southern Iraq. There he cultivated the network of adherents who would help him take control of the revolution in Iran. Not surprisingly, the charity came with strings. To the locals it was, Abdel explained, less a matter of Shi'a devotion rather than public services "So, to a degree, his [Saddam's] suspicions became real."

The Shi'a make the majority in Iraqi, despite being effectively shut out of the country's power structure since the modern country came into being. So when the US deposed Saddam in order to create a working democracy, the Shi'a – and by extension the meddling Iranians – did have the advantage. Of course, we couldn't just run a completely free popular election, we had to vet someone who wouldn't let things get too out of hand. That we needed a popular Shi'a figure to be elected prime-minister makes complete sense if we're going to go around claiming the people we install in power were actually elected. To gain the broadest possible support we selected a popular Shi'a politician called Nouri al-Maliki. He'd fled into exile in 1979 and while operating abroad became a leader of the Islamic Dawa party, working with the Ba'athist Syrian regime of Hafan al-Basar,* and Tehran to overthrow Saddam's government. Maliki met with the approval of the CIA as a Shi'a who would stay independent of Iranian aims in the country.

Al-Maliki, though, had lived a large part of his exile in Tehran. He was also the candidate of choice of Qassem Sulimani, leader of Iran's Qud's force, a sort of CIA/special ops combo pack. Sulimani was the terrifying embodiment of Iran's aims abroad. He was equally convinced that Maliki would do as he was told. In 2006, some 27 years after the Ayatollah

---

* The father of the current president, Bashar al-Assad. It's counter-intuitive, but the Ba'athists Party of Syria and the Ba'athist Party of Iraq are mortal enemies.

Khomeini had first called for the overthrow of Saddam Hussein's regime in favor of a Shi'a dominated government, the United States finally obliged Iran.

Iraq, however, didn't just need a president, it needed a government. So high offices like the vice-president and parliamentary seats were doled out in a patchwork of identity politics that only an American poly-sci professor would find reasonable.

The Shi'a had been stepped on and abused simply for being themselves for a generation and they were legitimately pissed. If I'm going to be honest, no one in the little tea shop seemed too put off by Maliki's sneering at the Sunni minority. Some were downright pleased.

The US officials managed to talk Maliki into resigning in 2014, but that only led to the continuing interference by Iran shift into overdrive. Five years later, many of these same people I'd had tea and a mild smoke with - and definitely the young who had been staring at social media at the time - were shouting "Iran out!" and "Death to Khameni."* Iraqis, even in the south, were sick of the interference of Shi'a militias funded through Iran and even more brazenly, Sulimani's Quds force who were now opening agitating for a theocracy.

---

* Ali Khameni, Iran's Supreme Leader. Not to be confused with his mentor, founder of the Islamic Republic of Iran, as well as it's first Supreme Leader, Ruhollah Khomeini. This is the Persian equivalent of Thomson and Thomas.

Sometimes I wonder whether the world is being run by smart people who are putting us on, or by imbeciles who really mean it.

Mark Twain

CHAPTER FOUR:
THE FIRE AND FAKE NEWS

WHILE CYRUS THE GREAT likely did not envision his own lopped off head in a wine-skin, the man was certainly self-aware enough to wager that someone was going to kill him. As such, he had meticulously planned out his succession with profane efficiency because he knew that any shift in power, however legitimate, is tricky. Twenty-five centuries later and it is still a delicate maneuver that can easily go pear-shaped.

The American media makes an insane amount of hay about any incoming president's first hundred days in office. It gives the chattering classes something to talk about, but it also ensures that every incoming administration attempts to shove a few useless show-ponies into law before anyone has time to think it through. It's all a bunch of silly theatrics, so was the Ziggurat, but that doesn't mean that the exercise in entirely without purpose.

You could make a good argument that the single most important election in US history wasn't George Washington's:

We'd already decided to elect a president and he was a tall, rich war hero – the shock would have been if he hadn't gotten the job. John Adams' election wasn't particularly remarkable, either. Washington didn't want to run again, he had a plantation to milk in Virginia and was going to make a ton of money by not paying his taxes on shady land speculation in Pennsylvania. Adams was of the same party, the handpicked successor, if you will. It was Thomas Jefferson, winning an election running opposition that made all the difference. The voluntary and smooth transfer of power in March of 1801, and the precedent it set, created the conditions of stability that set the United States on its path and has kept the strange American experiment working*. In the course of human history, however, smooth power transfers are something of an anomaly.

Cyrus knew this and he was nothing if not thorough. He had an heir, Cambyses II, and a spare, Baraiya, along with three daughters, Attosa, Artysonna and Roxanna. Cyrus appointed Cambyses crown prince and Baraiya the governor of a rich eastern province so he'd have his brother's back from the weirdos who would eventually stick dad's head in a wine-skin. To keep any upstart noble families in their place, Cyrus had one daughter, Attosa, married off to Cambyses, and another Artysonna was hitched to Baraiya. Records are unclear at this distance, Cambyses did have a younger wife named Roxanna – and the

---

* Donald Trump's election caterwauling notwithstanding.

Egyptians sure as hell thought she was his sister. If nothing else it kept family holidays tidy.*

The Persian Empire was a polyglot affair, so there were lots of client kingdoms ready to make trouble before the untested King of Kings could secure his power base. Neither an inherited crown or elected title is actually where power lies, but where the next rung down, where the powerbroker say it is. Unfortunately for Cambyses, he was haughty and arrogant so the Persian nobility didn't like him, even when they supported the crown. The further flung nobility were even less committed: Client kings were always ready to test the new guy's resolve to see what they could get away with. That meant expensive rebellions to put down and pay for. But by whom? Obviously, the rebellious provinces weren't paying tribute, Persian nobility put him in power, so you couldn't really tax them to death either. So, the bill was sent to the non-rebellious non-Persian states and Cambyses ran off to Egypt for a few years to put down the insurrection.

This was easier said than done. The Egyptian campaign ended with new king forcing the Egyptian priestly class to finance their own subjugation, which went down as well as can be expected. While he was at it, he pushed onward into the Libyan desert near modern Benghazi.†

In the absence of the new king and ever-increasing tax burden needed to pay for his campaigns, Baraiya was out in the

---

* The incest thing mightily offended the Egyptians of the day – although later dynasties took to incest like a duck to water.

† I only point this out because Cambyses was the first in a scattered line of foreign invaders that have found themselves near Benghazi thinking, "What in the hell am I doing here?"

east, proving himself a great warlord and excelling in the virtues Persians admired: Looking good on a horse, being a deadly wicked shot and chopping up bumpkins. He also had reportedly suggested tax breaks for everyone. Always a crowd pleaser, no matter what century it is. The gears started turning in the heads of the nobility. This was a legitimate son of Cyrus, as well as the great man's son-in-law. Seditious rumors began to circulate that the likably violent Baraiya would make a better king the current one – who was such a damn ponce.

With the Egyptian rebellion put down, Cambyses caught wind of the nasty rumors and set off for home – but had to stop off in Syria just to let them know he was still boss. There Cambyses poked himself with a sword hilt while dismounting a horse. The wound got infected and a few days later he died of gangrene.

As it was, Baraiya didn't need sedition. He had an airtight claim to the throne, made even more so when he took his brother's surviving widow (yes, his sister) Atossa as his wife. With so much turmoil around the throne, however, he was faced with same transition pickle as his older brother. The provinces were in an uproar, he'd promised tax relief and couldn't very well get it from the nobles who supported him. So, he took it from the nobles who he thought were his enemies, which Baraiya defined as anyone too close to Cambyses. This included a cousin of the royals who had been Cambyses's spear-bearer.* His name was Darius, and he had no intention of being despoiled by the new fellow, so he hatched a bold plan.

---

* This was a great honor at the time, as rank was determined by your physical proximity to the royal person. Whereas to modern ears it sounds like some violent species of golf caddy.

The transfer window may be fraught with peril, but it was also very narrow. If Darius was going to do what he intended to do, he had to do it quick before things settled down. Darius gathered some confederates whose names are very hard to spell and you don't really care.* Later official (and therefore dubious) accounts would claim that Darius was late to the conspiracy, but he was likely the lynchpin from day one.

Baraiya, only a couple of months into his reign, was returning his summer capital, and stopped the night at a roadside fort. The conspirators arrived and, being nobles, waltzed up into the royal camp without being stopped by the guards. If you maintain the proper air of dense self-importance, this wheeze still works (see Introduction). In the royal quarters, they found Baraiya getting it on with his mistress who was, refreshingly, not his sister. The man went out with a bang.

Far be it from me to criticize the father of histories, but Herodotus gives us a very suspect account about what followed. He claimed that the seven confederates discussed the form of government for the empire going forward. Otanes thought a democratic republic (*isomomia*) was a clever idea and had it happened it would have pre-dated the establishment of the Roman republic in 510 BC by about a dozen years. A few other power sharing options were bandied about with Darius himself pushing for a continuation of the established monarchy (one suspects he needed to keep the power-vacuum he'd created to manageable proportions). He won out, but that still left the question of just who was going to be said king. In a world

---

*Oh, all right... Otanes, Intaphrenes, Gobryas, Hydarnes, Megabyzuz, Aspathines.

without a paper-rock-scissors red robin, they opted for the obvious method of gathering on horseback outside the blood-soaked crime scene just prior to sunrise and see whose horse neighed at the rising sun first.

Before the appointed gathering, Darius had his groom, Oebares, rub his hands all over the genitals of a mare that was the favorite of Darius's stallion. As the prospective kings gathered before the rising sun, Oebares passed his unwashed, horse-sexy hands over the nose of the stallion, who got excited and neighed. Apparently even the gods, such as they were, agreed because seconds after the horse neighed, there was thunder and lightning in a divine stamp of approval. It being the olden days, no one bothered to shake hands with Darius' groom.*

A clever story, to be sure, but hardly a foolproof succession plan. The new king quickly married Baraiya's widow, the put-upon Artystonna, making him, posthumously, her third husband and him, like everyone else with royal ambitions, Cyrus the Great's son-in-law. Still, the fact remained that while Darius may have been a high-placed noble, he was not a royal. And now he was a regicide who'd gained the throne through a coup d'état. Darius really needed that not to be the case.

And so… it wasn't.

DARIUS I WAS A powerful, effective leader, even if you didn't really want to go to dinner with the man. Of the many refinements and innovations correctly laid at his feet, two that are rarely mentioned have proved among the most terrifying

---

* Years later, Darius himself admitted to the ruse, claiming that it wasn't fraud, but cunning.

throughout the ages: fake news and holy war. Rumor mills and conspiracy theories have existed since any two people had the power to communicate with each other about any two other people. The in-group has always told itself fantastic lies about the out-group, but Darius wielded it on a scale that would come to define the idea of nationhood. The concept of a holy war, however, was entirely at odds with the times. He hadn't gotten there yet.

What emerged from the scene of the murder from those alive to tell it was a story that must have been incredible even by the standards of the day. According to Herodotus, it wasn't Baraiya who'd been killed that night at all because Baraiya had been dead for several years and was buried somewhere in Egypt. Darius claimed that he had been on campaign with Cambyses, and knew that the king had had Baraiya killed to avoid his messy claim to the throne. Which, given the spirit of the times, was a perfectly rational thing to do to your brother. In one of those overdoses of irony to which royal families are prone, Cambyses then suffered a lethal poke from with the same sword with which he'd killed his brother.

It was then that a magi, a wizarding fellow called Gautama, stepped onto the stage. Through some dark magic Darius was at a loss to explain, Gautama shape-shifted (mostly) into the form of the dead Baraiya to make his move for the throne.* On hearing the news that a man calling himself Baraiya was coming from the east to seize the throne, and Darius set off to depose the pretender. As proof, he offered, it was discovered that while

---

* Although, it seems that merely shape-shifting into King Cambyses would have been the more straightforward play.

65

Gautama had been able to disguise himself as Baraiya, he'd lacked the magical razmataz to complete the royal ears. You see, Darius had personally known the real Baraiya and knew that the prince was a man of ears. This guy calling himself the new king was sans ears. True, Darius and crew had gotten rid of the body so fast that they couldn't share the physical proof, but one of Baraiya's wives (not his sister, but the daughter of one of the conspirators) corroborated the story when she said that one night she'd brushed her sleeping husband's hair back and seen that the ears she'd so admired on their wedding day had indeed gone missing. So there we are.

Not to put too fine a point on it, to stay on top of a pile of bullshit of that magnitude required a bold move. Darius saw the path forward, threading the needle through Cyrus's fine touch with symbolism and simple human vanity. Cyrus had adopted as an imperial symbol the fire sacred to the Zorastrians and with it the notion that he was setting the world right by tending the truth and fighting the lie. Darius took it one step further by declaring that he was the agent of Ahura Mazda, the one uncreated, and so he was appointed to safeguard the truth against the lie. To stand against Darius, therefore, was to stand against the truth, or more to the point, it was to be part of the lie.* And who wanted that? Gautama the magi had been part of the lie, and just look what happened to him.

The simple truth is that the coup d'état rarely settles matters as well as the prevailing plotters thinks it will. Without the legitimacy of the highly predictable, people tend to get restless.

---

* Today's Social Justice Warriors aren't nearly as original as they tell themselves. This is a very old playbook.

Soon the Babylonians revolted and after that Darius had internal uprisings coming out of the sandbox. It was to the south, in Elam (now the Khuzestan province of modern Iran) that Darius conceived of what well may be the noblest sounding bad idea in blood-soaked history of noble sounding bad ideas: Holy War.

The whole idea was completely out of step with the times. Sure, everyone thought that their god or gods were the best, and everyone else's was a little weird, but that was about it. There were lots of gods from which to choose, and being devoted to one didn't change that there were others whirling around in the clouds, trees and inside horses. It was a little like college football, with each school having its team, colors, ridiculous superstitions, traditions and mascots. A Nebraska alum may well sneer at the weird mojo of the LSU fan (or not understand what's being said) but he'd hardly argue that the opposing team doesn't exist. Darius's radical step was to argue that the other gods not only didn't exist, but their cosmically deluded adherents were actively working against the one who did.

The Elamites were no more or less pious than most Persians, but they were the ones on whom Darius decided to make his example as a holy warrior, fighting the lie, and tending the Truth. In this way, he could promise his soldiers the help of the real god to win the battle and, should they fail, paradise would await. The convenient thing about holy war is that whichever human is waging it can offer a pay-scale more glorious than was possible on a muddy, grimy earth.

Across Persia the message was crystal clear, but to forge this notion into a nation, he needed an out-group – anyone would do. He invaded Egypt, then India. Then Eastern Europe, but it isn't entirely clear that the Eastern Europeans were actually aware of this.

By 510 BC, most of the Greek colonies of Asia Minor had succumbed to the Persian rule, accepted their puppet kings and offered up a humbling tribute of Earth and Water to Darius, the King of Kings.

DESPITE THEIR BEST efforts to the contrary, the Greeks had just invented democracy. Or rather the Athenians had, but only as a last resort. While we like to think of the Hellenistic word as the cradle of Western civilization, in Persia it was known as the dodgy end of the known world. You know, bumpkins.

It was Greece's remote isolation that allowed its cities to develop in their own, Greek way. They were, however, as human as everyone else. The lies that they told themselves about where they came from influenced the ways they ordered their societies. The way Cyrus had framed it, he wanted to bring order and light to the world – something any priest or nun might say. Darius took it a step further by proclaiming he was the appointed agent of Ahura Mazda himself, which was inching into messiah territory. He wasn't the first, Ur-Nammu had done it back in Chapter One. The Spartans over in Greece told themselves that they were descended from Hercules, the son of Zeus,* and nursed a long-standing grudge against the continent of Asia over the shabby treatment of one Helen of Troy. Or Helen of Sparta, depending on who you asked. It was a touchy subject.

---

* Although why they didn't claim ancestry of Zeus, King of all the gods, is unclear.

The Spartans had no need for democracy because, they way they saw it, they had no need for individual thought or identity. Although they did have two kings. At one point the Spartan nobility had been famously hedonistic and rapacious, until the inevitable social meltdown produced a sort of militant communism that completely subjected the individual to the state. And because they had subjugated the surrounding population as serfs (or slaves) called helots, they were as paranoid about revolts as slave societies usually are.

To maintain this high-strung civic order, the state needed single-minded, hyper-competitive Spartans. Males were for winning wars, sodomizing adolescents, flexing, etc., and females were for breeding psychotics and emotionally emasculating all the beta male "also rans" with teasing mockery. The Spartans just couldn't reckon why the Athenians keep asking each other their opinion. There was only one opinion, "Go, Spartans!" and it was embodied in the King – or at least the more macho of the two. And until someone stuck a sword in the guy, it was damn-well your opinion too.

The Athenians, who thought the Spartans were wound a little tight, had an altogether more mellow, if sticky, origin story to tell. The goddess Athena was a beautiful virgin so self-possessed that she would allow no one to have her. Of course, an attitude like that drove everyone up on Olympus to lusty distraction, including the crippled Hephaestas, who happened to be her brother. While trying to give his sister a hug (or rape her depending on the version), he popped off on her thigh. She wiped up the mess with some wool and tossed it away. From the heavens, it drifted down and landed on the plains of Attica surrounding Athens making them abundant and fertile. And that toss-rag-of-the-gods business is the origin story the people who invented democracy told about themselves. Anyone who has ever seen democracy in all its glory will find the story perversely fitting.

What we're seeing here is a basic difference in cultural phycology. The Athenians didn't fundamentally see themselves as a people of conquest but people of the soil, on land made forever fertile by their patron. They didn't have a divine lineage, but were just folks making the best of what the gods had tossed their way. Like the Spartans, their Haves screwed the Have-Nots with wild abandon, but when faced with a social melt-down, Athens took a different tack. In one of history's great ironies, democracy wasn't the collective brain-child of the demos rising against the tyrants for their voices to be heard (although that is the way they'd put generations later), but the reform of an elder statesman called Solon who was given complete dictatorial control over the city in crisis. Considered the wisest Athenian by noble, merchant and peasant alike he wasn't a trying to create a revolution, but avoid one. In short, a dictator invented democracy and imposed it without asking anyone.

Solon's brilliant argument was that the peasants were slipping into serfdom due to their debts to the nobility. This was a shame, but more practically, serfs don't generally fight well for the homeland because they've got no skin in the game. No small consideration as the Greeks always were at each other's throats. The Spartans down the way had the helots, but they sure as hell didn't trust them. Solon cancelled the peasant's crushing debts, gave them legal recourse against the abuses of the powerful, and crucially, a vote in the leadership of Athens. He sold this to the nobles by ensuring that while the poor could vote, they couldn't actually hold office.* Thus, the rich still held onto political power, but had to answer to the voters.

Democracy, a government of the people, was pure and brilliant in its simplicity: the administrators were accountable and for the really big issues everyone† just voted and majority ruled. The problem the Greeks ran into was that it was a little *too simple*. In practice, direct democracy just isn't as straight forward as it sounds in theory: It is very hard to get people to agree on anything. As any good administrator knows, the art of management isn't gaining consensus – that's more or less an impossible ideal – it's managing dissent. Direct democracy led to paralysis for the Athenians, and would later turn Muammar Gaddafi into a Libyan Sun King, and lead bankruptcy for California because the mob will always vote itself more services and rarely votes for paying the bill. We'll get to some of that later.

Democracy might not have gone much further than Athens had Solon, seeing his good work, decided to retire and go on a ten-year cruise along the Mediterranean. Before leaving, he decreed that all the laws he'd enacted as head of state remain in place for 100 years. After that, people would just accept that democracy was just the way it was done – it would be the existing cultural groundwork. Why he thought that there wouldn't be a power struggle as soon as he left is one for the gods. The old guy

---

*In Great Britain, Members of Parliament were not paid until 1911 for the same, if more roundabout, reason. George Washington didn't think the President or congress should be paid, either.

†Well, every man. Or, to be precise every Greek male not currently enslaved or too foreign. Perhaps it wasn't a pure as advertised.

had barely sailed out of sight before the old nobility started fighting for the spoils of civil leadership.

The other Greek kings scattered along the peninsula were absolutely offended by the concept of rule by the demos and tried their best to snuff the idea out. Sparta sent an army to Athens to restore the royal status-quo. The Athenians held their own, mostly. With the rest of the Greeks plotting against them, Athens sought help from the only power strong enough to protect them against the Spartans and their Greek allies: Persia.

While the Greeks of the Peloponnese and Attica were free enough to fight each other, the Ionian Greeks of Asia Minor were out on the western edge of the Persian Empire. Knowing full well what royal little brothers could get up to, Darius had sent his, Artaphemes, to the western edge of Ionian to rule. Thinking that they had in with the Big Man, Athens sent a delegation to strike up an alliance with the most powerful empire on earth. This time Artaphemes actually knew who the Spartans were, and agreed to a neighborly alliance with the Athenians. There was just one thing the Persian governor asked in return... a little tribute of Earth and Water. The Athenians didn't exactly know what to make of the request, but if the King of Persia wanted a big jug of Grecian water and some dirt, that seemed harmless enough.

Back home the delegates got a vicious dressing down when it was explained that the whole Earth and Water bit was a ritual humiliation the Persians made vassal states go through as tribute to Persia. It was a concept picked up from the Babylonians, who believed that the world and everything in it was composed, more or less, from Earth and Water. Since all of Babylonia was built of baked mud, they could be forgiven for that one. Knowing the power of symbolism, the Persians demanded some Earth and Water from all its subject states. Now, it was explained to the delegation, the Persians reckoned the Athenians were their vassals. The Athenians, though humiliated, were wary enough of both Sparta and Persia to do anything but let the matter lie.

The knock-on effect was to let Darius know that somewhere in the hairier parts of the world, some damn group of bumpkins were experimenting with turning the ancient concept of monarchy on its head. For a king claiming to anyone who'd listen that he was the agent of Ahura Mazda, anointed to bring the truth to the world, this wouldn't do at all.

While the King of Kings was pondering this, the put-upon Ionians decided that they were sick of their overlords and sent a delegation to Sparta to join in an alliance to throw the Persians out of Ionia and hand themselves over to Sparta. You see, the Ionians explained, once you'd lived among the easterners for a while, you saw that they weren't all that tough - sissies really. They curled their hair. King Cleomenes of Sparta eventually turned the delegation away for a couple of reasons: 1) Everyone in Greece was always plotting some sort of revenge against the Spartans (something of an occupational hazard when you elevate being a hyper-aggressive ass into the pinnacle of civic virtue) and 2) they were pretty sure the Ionian's next stop on the alliance building road-trip was Athens. And why not just see how that alliance turned out first.

Which is exactly what the Ionians did. They headed up the coast to Athens where the nobles thought that the Spartans had had the right idea. The nobles weren't wrong, either; Persia hadn't just found their empire laying under the sofa, they'd hacked it out of the world. Sending their army across the Aegean

Sea would leave Athens wide open to the other rival Greeks –
notably Sparta. Unlike King Cleomenes of Sparta, however, the
Athenian nobles had to deal with the voters.

One structural flaw in democracy does lie in the fact that the
single, fail-safe method of getting the demos on the same page
(whether you like it or not) is war. It is very, very easy to whip a
mob into voting for a war with a soaring narrative – oppressed
Greek brothers, freedom, and most of all saving face after that
Earth and Water gaff. Athens voted to send an army against the
wishes of the nobility.

The revolt in Ionia went well enough at first. Without a
decisive blow to the heart of Persia, which wasn't even remotely
possible, they'd never cripple Darius. They just made him angry.
More Persians arrived to put down the revolt and kept on going
west because Darius was determined to slap some sense into the
Greeks once and for all.

At this point, the all the bickering Greeks finally agreed on
something – they were screwed. Darius sent emissaries through
the Greek mainland demanding all the city-states give tribute of
Earth and Water, and this time the Persians were very clear
about what they meant. Nearly all submitted save Athens* and
Sparta. Athens tried and executed the Persian emissaries.
Sparta's new King Leonidas took a decidedly Spartan approach
and threw them down a well. Reportedly Leonidas told them to
get their own Earth and Water while they were down there.
Which, I think we'll all agree, is pretty quick-witted for a culture
with little to no sense of humor.

---

*They'd caught enough hell the first time they fell for that wheeze.

Now Persia's enraged empire turned its fury toward the fractious city-states in an epic clash of civilizations. No one on either side thought that the Hellenistic world had much of a chance – Persia was the greatest power the world had ever known and the dumpy Greeks were just sitting around the Aegean, arguing with each other and getting up to who knows what with middle-schoolers.

I HAVE TWO BROTHERS and several friends who've run multiple marathons and a daughter who has run a half race. The hell if I know why, but it seems important to them and they generally keep the comments on my hands-on fascination with other people's civil wars to a minimum.

It is worth noting that better than two millennia after the unlikely Greek victory at Marathon against the Persian forces, we still honor the roughly 25* mile route a soldier named Pheidippides ran to shout *Niki!* "Victory!" to some anxious Athenians before falling over dead. I've pointed this out to my racing friends, usually to be told that more than one fellow has been killed doing what I do. Fair point.

The Athenians were elated at the news, although in truth it only staved off the burning of the city by the Persians for a few years. Even down in Sparta, there were unsubstantiated reports of the odd grin down cracking across a sober face.

------

* The first modern marathon was 24 miles, and varied with each race. For the 1908 London Olympics, it was originally 26 miles, but was extended 385 yards to finish in from of the royal viewing box. And there it stayed. It's good to be the king.

How, you well may ask, had they done it? It had less to do with rippling Greek muscles of lore or the righteousness of their cause than you might think.

To avoid having to fight their way down the peninsula, a massive Persian force had sailed down the Attic coast to land on Marathon beach. Hemmed in by marsh and impassable terrain save for two narrow passes out, it was not a good site for an amphibious landing. The Athenians were badly outnumbered, even with minor reinforcements from other cities. They sent Pheidippides – the Usain Bolt of the Hellenistic world – to Sparta to ask for reinforcements. Here, despite their fearsome reputation, the Spartans proved to be more hat than cowboy: They claimed the entire city was taking the month off for the festival of Carneia. No killing during Carnia, you understand. They'd send an army after the next full moon, in about ten days.

What followed at Marathon was five days of stalemate and containment with the heavily armed but badly outnumbered Athenians concentrated at the only two point to get off the beach other than getting back in their ships. There the two forces waited. For the Greeks, if they could wait out the ten days for the Spartans to arrive, they might be able to route the invaders. It would be a close-run thing, but they might just pull it off. Still, there was the niggling fact that the entirety of the Athenian army was at Marathon, leaving the city undefended. Might the Spartans head to a wide open Athens first? Making matters worse, if the Persians found a way to attack the force from behind, that would be it for the army and the city it was trying to protect.

Five days into the stalemate, the Persian cavalry left the beach, possibly to plan an attack from the rear. Without cavalry, though, the main Persian advantage was lost. The Athenians seized their fleeting advantage and charged into the Persian center with two heavy flanks, pressing the invaders in on themselves. With their only outlet being to retreat to the boats, that's what the Persians did. It was a chaotic, disordered retreat.

Pheidippides, having returned from being put off by the Spartans, was then dispatched to bring the news of the Persian retreat to Athens. He did. Then fell over dead and we're still talking about it.

When Darius got wind of the disaster, he vowed to launch another invasion, and this time he'd lead it. He didn't live that long. It was up to his son, Xerxes, to subjugate the Greeks. Ten years later, he certainly tried.

It wasn't until the second Persian invasion when the Spartans actually showed up for the fight. Still they heroically held up the advancing Persians at a narrow mountain pass near Thermopylae for three days before being annihilated. The Persians then ran amok all over Greece and burned Athens.

In "The Art of War", Sun Tzu advises taking the fight to the enemy's ground – because you can eat out their supplies and destroy their country in the process, not yours. While truer words have never been written, the stratagem isn't foolproof. The logistics of expeditionary armies follow the Law of Diminishing Returns: the further an army travels from friendly grounds, the more vulnerable it becomes to garden variety bad luck.

The allied Greek navy regrouped in its home waters at the narrow straits of Salamis and did not come to the aid of Athens specifically to lure the Persian force south. At Salamis, the superior Persian numbers wouldn't matter because the strait was too narrow. Unable to maneuver, the Persian vessels could be picked off by the darting Greek ships. Then a massive storm wrecked the Persian retreat. This affectively ended the second Persian invasion.

The world's only superpower had raised the largest army and navy in history and ran them headlong into that trap that great powers always run into invading unfamiliar and hostile terrain. It happened to the Romans in Germania, the Ottomans in Europe, Brits in America, the French in Vietnam, the Americans in Vietnam - part *deux*, the in Russians in AfGhazistan, the Americans in Afghanistan - part *dva*, the Americans in Iraq.

Which brings us pretty much up to date.

"War can kill all things except bad ideas."

Sensibly repeated Maxim

CHAPTER FIVE:

THE OPPOSITE OF A GOOD IDEA

THE IDEA OF BABYLON seems so ancient to Americans, and probably Europeans as well, that it is easy to forget that in a place like Iraq you still run into Babylonians. The old city is a ruin, and a new, modern city called Hillah sits nearby in province of Babylon. The ICHF model requires qualified volunteers to fly in for its training missions, but the local doctors and nurses who would stay behind were the other crucial piece of the puzzle. One of these surgical resident we'll call Muhammed* a 19-year old kid from Hillah we'll call Muhammed. We'd taken to calling all the Muhammad's by their hometown. No one called him Hillah, he was known as the Babylonian because, wouldn't you?

The town is only about 60 miles from Baghdad, so he knew the capital well. He was born after the first US invasion, and was

---

*I'm not being unoriginal, of the 11 surgical residents attached to the ICHF training program, nine were named Muhammed, and one was a female.

a boy of ten for next one. Without getting into the specifics, his teenage years were a lot livelier than mine. We spoke of the war and his friends who had died. He had a fatalistic frustration that you just don't see in places where the rule of law is a given. His friends hadn't died for a cause – they were, like most Iraqis, collateral damage in a political fight well above their pay grade. They'd died walking to class, or meeting friends out, when a car would explode in an intersection or in a *souk*. "On television you see only the damage…" Mohammad said, "do you watch Al Jezzera?"

"Yes." For the record, while Al Jezzera is rooting for the home team, they are no more lopsided in the coverage of these same events than CNN.

"So, you know. You see the bomb, the *impact*. But that mess is cleaned up a few hours later. Baghdad in a large city, soon there is no sign of it. I've had friends killed, yes. We all have. But you must keep on living, what else can you do?"

That's a fair, if brutal, point. I asked him about Babylon.

"Yes, the ancient city. I'm from Hillah. It's different in the north. Down here it is more… traditional." Muhammed stopped to organize his polite euphemisms, "Well, religion here is *big*. And education is… not emphasized as much. And it is very hot."

"Whose South are we talking about again? Iraq's or America's?"

"Pardon?"

I explained the charms of the American South.

"So," he said, "we understand each other, then?"

"I'd say that we do."

The Bible has almost nothing good to say about Babylon. If you weren't Jewish, however, it appears that the rest of the ancient world was fairly in awe of the place. Herodotus couldn't stop going on about it. It was recognized as a center of both the arts and learning, renowned for its walls and architecture and the hanging gardens, one of the seven wonders of the world. Which no one in the modern word has ever seen, so we have to take their word for it. Even after the Persians took over, and the Ottomans after that, Babylon and then Baghdad were real centers of culture.

Saddam Hussein wanted to dominate the world in the same fashion, but in his rush to modernize the country, he had – excuse the anachronism here - managed to download a lot of whiz-bang apps of the modern world without updating the operating system.

I asked the Babylonian about the Saddam generation. Those dark sleepy eyes just looking at me while he formulated a thought. This was a guy for whom quick, certain answers were immediately suspect. Finally, he sighed and said, "The people who grew up and reached adulthood under Saddam Hussein can't act for themselves. Can't *think* for themselves. They don't know how to act and affect change. They...we...should have gotten rid of Saddam, but we didn't. The factions couldn't act together. America had to do it for us." He stopped and touched his hand over his heart. "America had to fight our war for us."

"So there is no ill-will towards America for the war?"

He smiled and pulled a *now lets not get ahead of ourselves* face. "Getting rid of Saddam was good. This business of letting the army go – 250,000 armed men who are unemployed and trained to kill– I think this was a...I don't want to say a mistake, but a... *miscalculation.*"

"Oh I'd call that a mistake." I said.

"Okay," he laughed, "you said it. It was a BIG mistake." He said giving me the universal *I caught a fish this big* gesture. A lot of communication in these parts is non-verbal. "Now these new men are in power and they still can't act to change the system. They only know how to take orders. They've never seen another way of doing things, and they lack imagination to see it differently."

That unemployed army had been a problem from the moment Saddam was deposed. According to Bob Woodward's account in *State of Denial,* a few days after the Big Man's fall, President George W. Bush was meeting with long-time Saudi Arabia Ambassador to the US and long time Bush family friend Prince Bandar bin Sultan. The administration wanted to clean the place by both dismantling the Ba'ath party and the army. Prince Bandar gave the following advice:

> "Take the top echelon off because of their involvement and their bloody hands. But keep and maintain the integrity of the institutions... and keep, let's say the colonels on down. Somebody has to run things... Take off the top echelon and keep the second line and let them find the bad guys, because those bad guys will know how to find bad guys."

More to the point, they'd be *our* bad guys. Morally ambiguous to be sure, but it does avoid the pitfalls of dismantling entire armies from the officer class to the grunts. The Nazi parallel is as good as any. When the allies dismantled the German Army in 1918, it played hell on a huge number of people who'd come of age in a corporate body that had been brutally forged in the trenches of France. Their whole sense of self was that of a cog in a bigger wheel. Most of combat veterans adjust to civilian life well enough, but still a large number of veterans found the anxieties for being responsible for their actions and decisions crippling. These alienated souls found themselves in either the fascist or communists camps. Because a movement needs a devil, both factions went at each other's throats.

All militaries (the good guys as well as the evil empires) require a certain, intense indoctrination to get its members to subjugate the self to the whole. One reason soldiers appear so strong to civilians is that they are not slaves to the personal whims that constantly needle the rest of us. And that's true enough, they aren't – largely because the decision has already been made. A soldier very well may have a healthy sense of self – and the vast majority of the ones I've met do. The fact remains the military structure; losing the self into a larger body, free from ultimate responsibility, a tight sense of both purpose and belonging does attract a certain sort. A sort seeking, in the words of a young Nazi explaining himself in the run up to the war, "Freedom from Freedom."

In 2004, the Iraqi army wasn't just demobilized but completely dismantled. Within about a year the predominantly Sunni ex-military – stripped of both employment and status - began gathering in large numbers around a man named Abu Musad al-Zarqawi under the banner of al Qaeda in Iraq (AQI). The irony here is that a link between al Qaeda and the Ba'athist was used as the justification for the 2003 invasion of Iraq in the first place. While there was no link before the war, the invasion actually forged one that had not existed before. With the election of Maliki as Prime Minister in 2006, AQI declared war on the Shi'a majority that elected him. When a US strike killed Zarqawi that year, he was replaced by Abu Ayyub al-Masri, who announced in October the creation of the Islamic State of Iraq (ISI). Masari and the declared leader of ISI were killed in a joint US/Iraqi operation, but what we didn't understand at the time was that this wasn't a cult of single personality at the top, but a cult of the corporate body.

Which, I presume is what the Babylonian meant by "a BIG mistake." So, I asked, "Do you have much hope for President Maliki?"

Muhammed had a pained expression and said nothing, taking a long look at a little boy in the ICU. What we both knew, but neither wanted to say, was that this little fellow didn't have a hope without the "Americans*" in scrubs who'd come to the country after the boots had been withdrawn. "I'm afraid," He said soberly, "that we will have to wait for *that* generation to die for things to change." He stopped and let out a grim laugh.

Iraq may be a tragedy, but even the locals will admit that it is a weirdly comic one. Technically speaking, Mohammad and the other doctors, nurses and residents at the Ali Hussein hospital had plenty schooling, but very little of it was applied. The pecking order here is so structured, so jealously guarded by the senior doctors up the chain, that it isn't uncommon for a doctor to have some 20 years of training and almost no practical experience. To be a cardiac surgeon in the West requires upwards of ten years of hands on practice *after* med school. It doesn't matter how many times you read it in a book, hear it in a lecture or watch it on YouTube – despite the swell of confidence this gives us – the fact is humans simply don't learn well in the

---

* It was actually an international team.

abstract. We have to apply knowledge for it to stick in any practical way.

Mohammad was grateful for the opportunity afforded by what they were calling the "Remedy Mission" and it might just make his career. Within the existing system, his opportunity had infuriated his entrenched superiors who thought they should have been picked for the program. There were good reasons why they hadn't been picked. Mohammad didn't really know why he'd been given the opportunity, so I asked him "So what does Iraq need to get its medical infrastructure up to speed?" I asked fully expecting to hear the word "money" bounce back, but like nearly every other assumption about Iraq, I was wrong.

"We need a new system. Entirely. Now there is money being spent on healthcare and equipment and training." He paused for a moment to make sure we were on the same page, then added, "We've got oil – money isn't the problem. Doctors here are relatively well-paid. But we've lost a generation, No one can think for themselves so we don't know what to do with what we've got."

A lost generation. And unlike Gertrude Stein, Mohammad wasn't full of it.

AROUND THE TIME I was summering in Iraq, where the situation had stabilized from total disaster to the standard post-civil war train-wreck, the United States was still trying to wrap up its Middle Eastern adventure in Afghanistan. The two wars weren't exactly equal. What Afghanistan had been calling a government didn't launch an attack on the US, but the people actually running the place sure as hell knew about it and gave cover to the operation. The invasion was justified, but it also highlighted how hard it was to change regimes when the entire state is being run like a protection racket. Ten years after the invasion, an international grab-bag mediators and diplomats from Iran, Turkey and a handful of "helpful" Europeans had gathered to decide on the future of Afghanistan. No one, including the Afghans at the table, had been able to decided anything about its future since the dawn of civilization.

At issue was the Taliban which, despite emerging as the strongest tribe in the area, really did carry on as if they were in fact at the dawn of civilization. They were radically medieval Sunni Muslims that even the ultra-conservative Wahhabis in Saudi Arabia thought were wrapped too tight for their own good. Tribal, warlike, wedded to tradition and harboring an alarming streak of pederasty, the Taliban were the Spartans of Central Asia. And sitting as they did on the border with radically Shi'a Iran, the two visions of Islam were sworn enemies. As Barnett Rubin pointed out in a commentary in *War on the Rocks*, when a European delegate accused Iran of supplying arms to the Taliban, the Iranian diplomat played both indignant and dumb, replying "How could Iran supply aid to its sworn enemy." It was a very Iranian thing to say: not quite a denial, but it did shed light on some 25 centuries of plans within plans…within more plans… US Foreign Policy, on the other hand, relies primarily on the fact that we can throw cash at every problem and when that fails, we can buy the world's biggest hammer: a device ill-suited for shifting through layers.

Rubin replied, "Iranians were not such a simple-minded people that they could have only one enemy or one policy at a time." He's right. Since the rise of the Ottomans, Iran has had neither the money or the hammer to make itself obvious by force. It it less hammer and more chronometer – with gears that appear to be moving in opposite directions until you see the whole thing as a whole. But even then, its got three different faces ticking away on three different tacks.

Most Arab states supported, and some even took part in, the 1991 invasion to get Saddam Hussein out of Kuwait. With few exceptions, the monarchies, emirates, theocracies and Arab socialists hated Saddam. Most Arab states also knew that Iran's stated goal was Islamic revolution throughout the Muslim world and then beyond – with Shi'a Iran as the unquestioned leader. It was a Persian revival of Darius' playbook: "I am the truth therefore anyone who disagrees with me is the lie." Almost from the founding of the Islamic Republic, Iran's Quds force has existed solely to use military means to spread chaos and revolution outside of Iran's borders. Tedious, sure, but when Iran's main occupation was Iraq, this regional meddling was a part-time hobby. By deposing Saddam and leaving Iraq a shambles, the US allowed Iran to turn its full attention to sewing madness throughout the greater Middle East.

Almost on taking office, President Barack Obama embarked on his "tilt to the Muslim world" in an attempt to walk back on some of the more disastrous policies of previous Bush administration. If noble in aspiration, in practice, his Muslim Tilt was not so much a more understanding approach to the Muslim world than a wholesale abandonment of our long-standing allies* in the region in favor of a radical, anti-Western

---

* Terrible as they were, they were on our payroll and therefore somewhat obedient.

political Islam.* The first problem with Obama's policy was that it fell victim to one of the most common fallacies humans run into whenever they decide to change their modus operandi: The unshakable but absurd notion that the opposite of a bad idea must be a good idea. The second was that it lined up precisely with Iran's aggressive foreign policy aims.

In June of 2009, Obama kicked his Muslim Tilt off with a diplomatically ham-handed speech in Cairo that seemed singularly intended to chap our most powerful ally in the region, Egyptian President Hosni Mubarak. Then, a week or so later, pro-democracy crowds hit the streets in Tehran and across Iran to protest an obviously rigged presidential election to keep the incumbent Mahmoud Ahmadinejad in power. With the bloodthirsty revolutionary regime teetering on the brink of implosion, Obama kept his mouth shut in the strange belief that the same the crew taking live-fire shots at the protestors would come clean about their nuclear program if we just stayed mellow about it. All of which had the knock-on effect of leaving Tehran free to monkey around with its neighbors.

IN NASIRIYA, the local government was getting sick of Iran's "help." The Minister of Healthcare had to get the Remedy Program up and running before the government's funding got reshuffled again. In 2011, the year before, Prime Minister Maliki had announced that in accord with the pro-democracy vibe of the Arab Spring, and a lot of behind the scene arm-twisting from the US, that he would not seek a third term in office. Then,

---

* Terrible as they are, they're also on the payroll and yet still trying to kill us.

about the same time as the US draw down, Iraqi's Sunni Vice-President Tariq al-Hashemi was accused of a coup attempt, a bomb attack, and the odd hit-squad hunting down Shi'a politicians. Hashemi fled to Turkey and was sentenced to death *in absentia*. In a fit of paranoia befitting the last Iraqi to run the place, Maliki started going after other Sunni leaders – effectively destroying the precarious balance that the US had thought itself clever enough to engineer.

Practically speaking, whatever was going to happen at the Ali Hussein needed to establish itself quickly. On the outside, the hospital isn't much to look at: a big Bauhaus sandcastle. Inside, the foyer was colorful and well maintained and smelled of stringent disinfectant. To venture further, however, was an exercise in controlled disappointment. Some nine years after the fact, the hospital still looked like US Special Ops guys had played hot potato with a frightened supply clerk the night before. The place was teaming and the elevators slow and clanking. I took the stairs. It was a hospital built by the old regime with absolutely no consideration for the families of the sick, and not much for the sick themselves. Men in dirty white *dishdashahs* and women in black *abayahs*, lolled and snoozed in the hot stairwells, while others played cards on the landing floors. This appeared to be the waiting room.

The only time any of them even took notice of my hopping up the stairs was when I stopped to snap a photo of such pitiable, abject misery. Then they looked at me with… it wasn't hatred, or defiance or even a plead for help. It was a look I remembered from adolescence that said, *You're being rude. Now leave me in peace.* I lowered my camera and gave a lady with a dry cough my fresh water bottle. Then bounded to what I hoped was the correct floor.

As a free-wheeling Westerner, however, I couldn't help but feel that there was something sinister about the way grown women go about town in an *abayah, burkha,* or a drop cloth. Except that – in Iraq at least – there is no law that saying women must dress this way, they just generally do. The one female surgical resident wore jeans, a fitted – but not tight – lab coat and a headscarf with a stylish forelock of hair showing. The only local female I spoke to during my stay didn't see their dress as anything but practical good taste. "I don't want to be leered at." She said.

"Well, not all men *leer.*" I countered.

All those frustrated Arab poets who go on about the beautiful eyes of their desert flowers may be laying it on a bit thick, but they aren't lying. Perhaps because all their other attributes have been slip-covered, Arab women have developed gorgeous and expressive eyes. Hers said: *You're full of shit.*

And as a father, I'm not sure that urging your daughter to err on the side of modesty is any crazier than the American practice of pressing her to dress like a hooker. I would have liked to have gotten a consensus from more ladies on the subject of women in the Arab world, but they are hard to approach. I'm no Jack the Lad, but until I'd come to Iraq I'd never actually had a woman shield her face and scurry away at the sight of me. At least not one who didn't actually know me.

There is something of a first "boy-girl party" in the way even professionals interact. Three female perfusion students asked, through Alem, if their picture could be in the book. I agreed, of course, nothing would make me happier. If I did this I reckoned at some point, they'd have to speak to me. We went down the hall, they took off their surgical masks, I took a few shots, and Alem gave me their names. I only realized afterwards that they all spoke English. Not one word had been exchanged without going through Alem, who, it should be pointed out, was only in the middle of this silly transaction at the insistence of the ladies

Amongst themselves, Arab women are all kisses and caresses. So are the men for that matter. It takes a bit to acclimate yourself to the sight of entirely straight men air-kissing each other and holding hands as they walk down the halls. An embrace between American men is a quick thing followed with a manly swat on the arm or something to re-kindle a comforting level of violence. In the Middle East they linger, even nuzzle.

THE MISSION TEAM was sitting in a mildly air-conditioned conference room that was well-stocked with flies waiting for the surgical residents to show up. To the annoyance of some of the senior doctors, Karen was heading up the meeting. Something of a wanderer, she spoke some Arabic from experience in Saudi Arabia (which presumably Aran's 14-year-old daughter was going to make much more hep). Karen had a strange mix of genuine compassion and almost no emotion. I asked why the earlier mission – only two weeks in duration, had failed. "Every time we show it's like we've never been here. They have no institutional memory."

After 40 minutes the surgical residents showed up to discuss protocols and procedures for the coming year. This didn't take too long because there weren't any.

As a nurse, Karen couldn't shed any light on heart surgery, but that wasn't really the underlying problem – which was set of protocols surrounding the procedure. That is what she was setting out to do, take a hypothetical little boy, Mustafa, through every step from the moment the surgery is scheduled.

The protocol issue started as far back as the patient's initial file. Here is where the knee jerk reaction to hoard all information begins to throw the entire machinery of the system into paralysis. Most notes are kept in the doctor's head and what is written in the file is sent home with the patients. Nasiriya has a female literacy of 30% with the males clocking in at about 50%. Evidently, the patient is supposed to bring the file that they can't read back in with them next time they have heart attack.

The doctors complain that not only do patients forget their files, but they never show up on time. This hardly matters, however, because the doctors don't keep office or consulting hours. Nor do they show up to protocol meetings on time. Getting a patient and doctor together is like kinetic game of whack-a-mole, with the patient trying to waylay whoever pops around the corner in a white coat. The doctors can't keep regular consulting hours because they are being pulled in every direction by desperate patients lying in wait to see *someone*. I trust that you see the problem.

The next pothole couldn't be fixed with a secretary. Like most government bureaucracies, it is impossible to measure quality of service, so everything is reckoned on quantity. The emphasis is on clearing cases off the docket rather than actually fixing the patient. Don't sneer, in the U.S. the VA does more or less the same thing. Even this low bar of patient care gets tricky when the patient's file is at home stuck on the side of the refrigerator.

Obviously, a "system" like this is not equipped to perform complex cardiac cases. It was all so hairy that the surgeries scheduled to start on Monday where all pushed back a day for a process meeting where every step in the process, from pre-op to the ICU was discussed.

As anyone who has traveled in the Middle East knows, it is not in the nature of the culture to come straight to the point. I'm from the South, a place where even the most sneering insults are framed in polite euphemism, and I thought these people overdid it. The simple act of buying a rug is an extended opera involving pronouncements, oaths of friendship, arguing, hand waving, cigarettes, tea and orations from old men who have nothing to do with anything but seem to be to always be wandering in and out of public discourse. Tempers will flare and there is storming out and cursing, which is followed by a return and more tea. Eventually you will agree to terms and shake hands. This is a momentous occasion because it signified that you've just passed the half-way mark in the transaction.

Meetings where something important is discussed are never quite so simple, though. The task of coming up with the protocol for a new heart center in one day was thrown at Karen. Having Karen chair the meeting was a bit of tactical brilliance – it allowed the Big Man, Gascon, to remain cozy with the local Big Men, who could never bring themselves to admit that they were terrified of her. Like a lot of people in the humanitarian trade, she has the odd tattoo. Down the back of her neck was what I thought at first glance were Chinese characters. "It's Urdu." She told me. "It means 'I will remember.'" Which she told me is sort of like a Pakistani au revoir, as well as a private joke to herself regarding her near perfect synesthetic memory. Which was interesting as hell. I wanted to know more, so I asked the characters above the pocket of her scrubs. "Oh that. That *is* Chinese."

"What's it say?"

"Beijing Women's Hospital."

Karen took everyone involved in the program through each step of the process and reckoned the meeting would take two hours. It took five and a half. I recorded the entire episode, but can't bring myself to relive the tapes, so here are my notes. To wit:

Process Meeting/Nasiriya Heart Center/29 July 2012
Bad noise about Turkish Airlines. TA chap in Basra on vacation now. No news on baggage.

The team is an hour late after [Dr.] Sadiq is sent to fetch them. There a lot more than the 11 surgical residents – 35 people file in. 35 departments and, apparently, no secretaries.

After 1.5 hours, we've moved Mustafa to surgery, but are still hung up sharing patient file and center scheduling. Appears to be the root of all evil.

The residents are getting restless, people are starting to get up and leave & we are still griping about getting the proper information to the right Drs. The simple sharing of information seems inconceivable. What happened to these people?

Gascon pounds the table: "Everybody has to know everything!" Still the concept seems slippery.

There are no secretaries – the doctors and nurses do own paperwork. "The Ministry has no facility to hire for secretarial positions."

There is a secretarial school in Nasiriya but the hospital can't hire them because ...why? Because no one does. Really? That's the reason?

The diagnosis of pneumonia in dry climates proves tricky – can't send patients into heart surgery with pneumonic diseases. Fair enough.

X-rays are taken five days before surgery. How does anyone survive this place?

Ten Minute time out.

These aren't expensive problems – issue is not equipment but protocol. It is not about donating money but expertise on systems as well as surgery.

Karen learns that there is only one intensivist,* as the other is going to India. Sadiq cannot see why this is a problem.

Gascon: "If you establish a routine, the chance of forgetting something is zero."

---

* The doctor in charge of the ICU.

Most checklists in NHC have been largely internal & verbal. The wheel is being reinvented with nearly every case.

Karen asks about the WHO [World Health Organization] checklist ICHF sent over 6 months ago. Where is it? Dr. Jabbar admits that is not being used. Boris [anesthesiologist] reckons that in 5 of the last 155 cases performed everything was in proper order.

What happens to the checklist? It needs to be part of the patient's record to cover your ass.

During the meeting Gascon's ability to mentally go through the process of surgery is astounding: picking up ethereal points like replenishing emergency drugs & when to notifying parents, etc., from admission to delivery to the ICU.

Why are all these damn flies in here?

At some point in that brutal marathon, Dr. Sadiq admitted that he, more or less, kept the entire working system of the Ali Hussein surgical department in his head. And this system, while not up to anything we'd call Western standards, did keep the place functioning. A little cumbersome sure, but it can't be written off as stupid, or even lazy for that matter. After a generation of Saddam, war, and UN sanctions – any existing system had been strangled and died off. The Babylonian had been right: There had been a brain drain for the last twenty years and it is by no means over.

There are Iraqis, however, who are fiercely proud of their ancient culture and are determined to salvage its remnants from the truly bad modern ideas that have plagued it. Of these people, the ones with more brains than suicidal bravado, had to keep pretty much everything in their head. In a place run on the political whim of this month's strongman, information *is* gold (or oil), it is power, more so, it is an insurance policy. After 24 years of Saddam, the urge to horde information was irresistible. The Iraqis knew that they had to adopt Western protocols, and why. But habits, personal or institutional, do not change on a dime, and neither can cultures. That instinct to survive – and in this case to survive through some specialized of bit of data – is very hard to break.

We didn't stop for lunch because it never occurred to our hosts too stop for lunch. Finally, late in the afternoon there was a plea for mercy from Dr. Sadiq. "Please Karen, it is Ramadan, we are fasting!"

"I know!" She shouted back, "After eight hours I'm fasting too!"

It is a very serious thing for a political creed or a political party when they are compelled in spite of themselves to hail national misfortunes as a means of advancing their cause.

Sir Winston Churchill

CHAPTER SIX:
SONS OF LESSER GODS

With the Persian threat to the mainland lifted, the Greeks wanted to make sure that it didn't happen again. In 477 BC, the city-states formed a proto-NATO of antiquity called the Delian League (or Confederacy of Delos) to provide for the common defense should the Persians start looking their way again. Athens was the most powerful member of the league, and was affectively running it, but for appearances sake the league dues were kept in the neutral site of the shrine of Apollo at Delos.* The Delian League did not, however, include all of Greece. To the south, the Spartans just kept on being themselves and refused to play second fiddle to Athens. So they formed their own Peloponnesian League. And so the Greek Cold War began.

---

* This is the same reason that the headquarters of NATO is located in Brussels.

In the tense peace that followed, Athenians were left free to follow the thread of their novel little government "of the people" experiment. The Athenian experiment was idealistic, but practically it was the leadership by the most prominent personality in the room. The towering figure of Pericles ushered Athens to its golden age of democracy before getting himself convicted of embezzling government funds. Never one to do things half-way, Pericles had talked the Confederation of Delos into moving the treasury to Athens. He embezzled that too. By this time the "confederacy" of the Delian League was starting to look a lot like an Athenian Empire.

Inevitably things hotted up in 431 when the Delian and Peloponnesian Leagues clashed in a three-war series. The clashes ultimately broke Athens with help from an outbreak of the plague and then by the Persians, of all people. The conflict left a very exhausted Sparta in charge of a wasteland that would be unified about a century later by Philip of Macedonia in 338. Predictably, Sparta was the hold out. A generation later, it too would be conquered by *the boy*.

HE WAS A LITTLE blond creature named Alexander, the son of Philip and his wife Olympia, but there was no telling him that. Apart from having another one of Philip's wives boiled alive, Olympia had a fetish for sacred snakes and kept her sleeping chamber full of them. She said it was out of devotion, but it had the knock-on effect of keeping Philip away at night. All of which would just be lively background color except that Olympia told young Alex that King Philip wasn't his father after all. According to Mom, his real father was none other than Zeus Amon, a Graeco-Egyptian god who carried on in the form of a snake. Any child phycologist worth their salt would argue that after a bombshell like that, Alexander lost any chance of being even remotely normal. Even by royal standards.

According to contemporary accounts, he was an angelic looking lad who was educated by Aristotle after pushing his previous tutor to his death down a pit. Later, Alexander commanded an army under Philip and destroyed the Theban Sacred Band – ferocious shock troops made up of paired homosexual lovers. Not that Alexander was homophobic, and nor was Hephasestan, his lifelong friend and on-campaign tent mate. The Sacred Band was just in his way. Eventually, King Philip was killed by a bodyguard and the boy just kept moving south to lick the Spartans into submission. With all of Greece organized, but still feeling restless so he conquered North Africa and drove into Libya. Why is anyone's guess, it was pretty empty.

His armies cut through Asia like a knife through butter stopping only to establish cities in his name and pick up some local wives to neglect along the way. The only people to give Alexander too much flack were the Pathans of modern Afghanistan – a habit that they've never been able to break. They called him Sucunder and someone managed to shoot him in the lung before they cried crying uncle. Alexander was pretty sporting about the chest shot, and the Pathans married one of their own, an overbearing local diva named Roxanne, to the conquering hero.

The Persian Empire had lost its élan of old under Darius III, who was a textbook example of difference between those who build empires and those who inherit them.* Now deep in the Persian heartland, Alexander faced off with Darius III three times, finally and decisively at the Battle of Issus. After which he found himself in control of the Persian capital, Persapolis, as well as Darius's family; which included a wife, two daughters, 360 royal concubines and 400 eunuchs for crowd control. He wasn't terribly interested in the concubines but married one of Darius's daughters, Statira, and hitched the other, Drypetis, to Hephaeston so that they could be brothers-in-law. Not a terribly devoted husband in the traditional sense, he and Hephaeston just kept going, subduing more of India and Afganistan. Not many people can say that.

When Hephaeston fell ill and died, Alexander was so inconsolable that he had his personal physician crucified for failing to save his friend. This was short sighted, as Alexander himself died of a fever lying about in Babylon in 324 BC, attempting to make the city into his new capital and once more the center of the world. He was not quite 33 years old.

Things went to hell after that, the high-strung Roxanna had sister wife Statira and *her* sister, Drypetis, killed and thrown down a well. Not to be out done, Momma Olympia had Alexander's half-brother killed and forced his widow to hang herself. His domestic situation is as good a metaphor as any for the state of the empire which badly subdivided itself in short order. After that everyone just waited around for the Romans to start feeling expansive.

---

*Machiavelli would warn about this, as well as most people tasked with managing family trust funds.

LIKE THE UNITED STATES, Rome was not a natural to empire. The republic was forced into existence at the intersection of a popular uprising against Tarquin, the city's last king, and the invasion by the Etruscan King Porsena to highjack the uprising for his own ends; namely establishing himself as the next monarch of Rome. For their part, the Romans didn't want a king, foreign or otherwise, and they were violently clear about the matter. Porsena was forced to withdraw. So it was that they established a republic with two annually elected leaders called *consuls*. Records are spotty, but the senate may have existed as an advisory board for the old kings. To maintain a sense of continuity, the institution was kept on in an altered form in the republic.

Even as Rome developed into what we'd call a superpower, it still held republican pride in having thrown off its tyrannical kings to become a nation of free Roman citizens. It *was* a superpower, whether it wanted to be or not, and soon found itself playing the role of the world's policeman. Also like that far-distant ancestor in the Americas, senators were always heading out to trouble spots, along with armies, to "help" small, friendly states against their bigger, hairier neighbors.

Meanwhile, Alexander's empire had come undone. To the east, Persia had been left to one of his generals, Seleucus I Nicator, resulting in the Seleucid Empire consisting of a Greek elite atop the Persian masses. The local Parthians, under Mithridates I began hammering away at the Western-leaning empire.

By 73 BC the Seleucids had been reduced to a mostly Greek enclave clinging on in modern day Syria as Mithridates VI terrified all its neighbors. To manage the situation, a succession of famous Roman senators, beginning with Sulla and ending Pompey Magnus, were sent to the hotspot to keep the peace by killing everyone who looked at them funny. Pompey settled the matter in 63 BC, having chased Mithridates IV up into Armenia and establishing the Roman province of Syria. For its part, Rome most certainly did *not* lose track of the weapons it funneled into the country.

Since Pompey was in the neighborhood, he was asked to weigh-in on a succession dispute in neighboring Judea, a western-leaning province being menaced by the Parthians. The ruling Hasomonean Dynasty had been semi-autonomous rulers under the Seleucids when their Queen Alexandria Salome died, triggering a civil war between her two sons: Hyrcanus and Aristobulus.* Both sons visited Pompey in Damascus begging for help, or more to the point, a favor. He said he'd decide when he visited Jerusalem.

Aristobulus, who wanted Judea to stay vaguely independent, smelled something amiss in the gesture. When Pompey arrived with his army, he refused the senator entrance. Pompey had Aristobulus arrested and Hyrcanus, thinking the matter settled, let Romans in by a gate in the eastern part of the city. Meanwhile, the Temple Mount and City of David closed ranks and prepared to fight the Romans. The siege lasted three months before the Romans broke into the temple district and killed everyone who didn't surrender. The victorious Pompey pressed his point by entering the Holiest of Holies – a ritual desecration, but not a physical one. He left the treasure and funds untouched.

---

*A careful reader might notice that those Greek(ish) names are not remotely Semitic.

The next day he had the temple ritually cleansed and declared Hyrcanus its High Priest. As for the matter of the crown, Pompey decided that if the Jews were going to be fussy about it, no one could have it. Then he went home.

The Romans kept hanging around in the Levant but were never able to make much of a dent further east, where the lands were so rich the Romans called it *Felix Arabia*, "Fortunate Arabia." Unable to do much to shift the frontiers of the Persian Empire, they followed the example of the Greeks by hooking a well-worn path around into Egypt and North Africa. The Romans were good administrators and, like Cyrus the Great, had largely cracked the nut of getting subject peoples to buy into the idea of being part of the imperial whole. They outsourced the bureaucracy to locals where they could, brought technical innovations that improved life in the provinces and tolerated the other fellow's religion. At least that was the plan. This is an easier sell if you are a pagan and believe that there are plenty of gods around for everyone. It is also worth noting that the monotheistic Jews never really stopped giving the Romans a headache.

This global adventurism hid a nasty rot at home. Things had gotten so unstable that the normal course of power in Rome got disrupted under near constant states of emergency. A dictatorship of three – called the Triumvirate – was established between Julius Caesar, Pompey, and Magnus Crassius which lasted from 60-54 BC. The point of the arrangement was that no one man would have absolute power. It was a temporary measure, but it did lasting damage. While free elections make free republics function, they also expose their fragility. Like paper money, peaceful power transitions only work because we all agree that they will.

For the Romans, the dictatorship was a legal, if seldom used, device for when republican politics descended into violence. Akin to an emergency powers act, it was a temporary measure intended to be for six months *or until the crisis had passed*. It was a fatal legal loophole that, once abased, transformed the Republic. When Crassius died the Triumvirate ended, leaving Pompey and Caesar eye-balling each other suspiciously. Caesar was off subjugating Gaul at the time, so he headed back home with his army. For obvious reasons, Roman fighting legions weren't allowed in Italy, the northern border of which was marked by the river Rubicon. When Caesar crossed the Rubicon and brought his armies into Italy, it was a wildly illegal move that was either going to kill him or make him. The gamble paid off when he managed to terrify the senate into making him sole dictator in 49 BC. The crisis, as defined by Caesar, was so broad that it couldn't be settled in six months, or a year. Once in sole command, his dictatorship kept being re-upped by a cowed and spineless senate. He kept claiming that his goal was to restore the Republic, but he never fully explained why he started promenading around the senate chamber in purple boots, the symbol of the old Roman kings. Then in 44 BC, with the senate and the citizenry used to the idea, he declared himself Dictator for Life.

Once Julius Caesar had thrown a rock through that delicate precedent of power transfer, it was very hard to set it straight again. In any event, Julius Caesar didn't restore the Republic before being poked full of holes in the middle of March. At this point, however, it didn't really matter – the norms had been shattered. The assassination was sold as a blow against tyranny, and it was. The larger point is that even if a full restoration of the republic had been managed, the order was always just one hurled stone from shattering again.

Another dictatorship of three - the Second Triumvirate - was established between Caesar's great-nephew Gaius Octavius* - by then called Octavian - along with Mark Antony and Marcus Lepidas. This one ended with Lepidas in exile and Mark Antony committing suicide after being famously stood-up by his girlfriend, Cleopatra, at the Battle of Actium (31 BC), which he then famously lost.

In an effort to shore up a domestic alliance, Octavian married Scribonia, who was either the sister or sister-in-law of the son of the Pompey. Scribonia delivered into the world Octavian's only natural child, Julia. Later that week, Octavian divorced her to marry one Liva Drusilla after pressuring her into a divorce. Liva's son from her first marriage, Tiberius, would marry Julia, and be adopted by the emperor, making the two brother and sister.

By 27 BC Octavian had restored the façade of the old republic to his satisfaction - read: with him in complete control of all of it. While the *Pax Romana* Octavian established was never, strictly speaking, all that peaceful, its far-flung foreign wars of expansion had stabilizing affect at home for the better part of two centuries. Surely, we should rank Augustus Caesar up there with the Cyrus the Great's of the world - he nearly doubled size of the Roman Empire. But to snatch land is one thing, to maintain an empire is another. Cyrus had the creepy foresight to manage imperial succession by marrying his sons to his

---

* The boy changed his name to Gaius Julius Caesar Octavinus when his great-uncle formerly adopted him as his son - Octavian for short. Then later to Augustus.

daughters to shut down any rival claims. Augustus was less clear about his estate planning.

He died in 14 AD – naming Tiberius his heir. After 70 years of stability on the throne, no one thought the republic was coming back. At that point, most Romans didn't even want it to.

NOT MUCH IS KNOWN about Pontius Pilate – his title of Prefect means he was a military governor. Pilate was probably an aristocrat and well-connected – but the fact that the imperium had stuck him out in some sandy pothole suggests that he wasn't that well-connected, or possibly not that good at his job.

Back in 37 BC, the Romans had decided that it was easier to appoint a suggestible local and propped a local fellow called Herod on the throne. Judea didn't really move the needle for most of Romans – apart from the fact that since the country had been annexed, the Jews had been coming to the Rome *en mass*. Pretty tolerant about letting Jews be themselves way over in Judea, the Romans were less mellow when it came to being Jewish down at the forum. Tiberius thought he'd solve at least part of the problem by pressing the Jews of military age into the Roman army. This aggravated things.

Pilate got to his post in Judea only to discover that the Legate of Syria, to whom he reported, hadn't been appointed. It would take six years for the post to be filled. Pilate was at a loss, he was a somewhat adequate cog, not a leader of men. Dropped into a job with no direction, he needed local help to keep the imperial wheels on the gravel so he appointed a High Priest, Caiaphas, for the entirety of his tenure.

Details vary, but it seems that Pilate wildly offended the locals with the promotion of the imperial cult; basically treating ex-emperors as gods. He festooned (the next) Herod's palace with Roman shields inscribed with *divi Agusti fillius* (son of divine Augustus). Reportedly, when Tiberius got word of the stunt he told Pilate to take the damn things down. Then there was an uprising over his using funds from the Temple treasury to build an aqueduct. The Barabbas mentioned in the New Testament may have been connected one of these kerfuffles. Basically, the Jews hated Pilate. King Herod was a Jew, but he was also a Roman lapdog, so they hated him too.

Things were tense when Pilate's local man in the Temple, Caiaphas, came to him with tales of a radical fellow calling the High Priest out on his hypocrisy and, even more dangerous, talking about a world beyond the *divi Augustus*. The hoi polloi was calling him the King of the Jews. The Kings of the Jews, Caiaphas pointed out, was whomever Pilate said it was. And no one wanted another uprising.

Jesus, that guy was stepping on everyone's toes.

FOR ALL THIS BROAD administrative acumen, the Roman Empire had an angry red pustule at the head. Despite 62 years – roughly two generations – into a stable imperial system and there still wasn't a succession plan. The why is an interesting question, but a fair guess is that the empire, while working, went against the grain of the Roman society. They thought of themselves as a republic, and simply found it uncomfortable to think too hard about how emperors came to power. Certainly, after Caligula's lively three and a half years following Tiberius, the senate could be forgiven for not wanting the process set in stone.*

What evolved in practice, more or less, was that a general with enough victories under his belt to be popular with the crowds would be declared emperor by his own men, and then march on Rome to press the point home. After Caesar crossed the Rubicon, this foolishness no longer freaked Romans out. If successful, the new guy would try to get his son appointed successor while praying that some other general wasn't getting too popular. Over the next three centuries, some 29 Roman emperors attempted to establish dynasties and were murdered for their efforts. Mostly by their own Praetorian guard.

Without any real plan for the transfer of power, imperial succession invited either a civil war or the threat of one. Predictably, things went completely haywire: Civil wars, peasant rebellions, coup d'états, plague, Germans, economic depressions, credit bubbles and currency debasement.

Into this mess came a capable soldier of humble birth from Dalmatia (in modern Croatia) called Diocletian. He'd risen through the ranks to become a cavalry officer in the army of Emperor Carus. It was on campaign at the always hairy Persian frontier that both Carus and his son Numarian died. The army declared Diocletian as emperor. Why not? No one in Rome knew Carus was dead, so there would be no counter-claims. The plan seems to have been something along the lines of a victorious army returning home with a new emperor as *fait accompli*. The problem was that no one thought to ask Carus's surviving son,

---

* Americans do this too: Colonies go against the grain of the American psyche, so we informally acquire territories, call them protectorates or territories, and then don't think too hard about it.

Carinus, what he thought about the plan. As it was, Diocletian settled the matter at the Battle of Margus.

The new emperor restored order by both increasing his hold on power and, counter-intuitively, dividing the empire into two regions administered by co-emperors, called "Augusti", in 285. To keep it tight, he named a high-ranking drinking buddy named Maximian as co-emperor. Maximian had a huge head.* The idea was taken further in 294 when each imperial half was further subdivided and ruled by a subordinate "Caesar" – a sort of vice-emperor to learn on the job and succeed as ranking augustus on the death of the old fellow. The rule of four system was called the Tetrarchy.

Perhaps because he had divided his "insoluble" empire into four parts, Diocletian needed to emphasize imperial and cultural unity where he could. He took a page out of the book of Darius about using religion for forge national identity. The caesars all claimed to be descended from the gods, but few but the Roman *plebes* actually believed this – just a bit of fashionable snobbery on the part of the elites who could afford it. Despite the divine family tree, they generally waited until after they were dead to be deified because it tended to end badly when they declared themselves gods while still walking around and apt to be strangled in the bathtub.

Yet Diocletian decided that he was the embodiment of the god Jupiter himself. Great for the ego, and the pagans of the empire didn't think too much of promoting a Caesar a little early - especially one who'd stabilized the empire. Yet Diocletian ran into the same problem of being the embodiment of god that

---

*Not really crucial, but I thought that you should know.

Darius had. Now that the Jews had been drummed out of their homeland after a series of insurrections, his issue was with a radical Jewish sub-cult calling themselves Christians. Like the Jews, they had a deity who was not only *not* part of an ensemble cast of hundreds, but faith in whom erased all other gods. According to the Christians, there was only one God to worship – and it absolutely wasn't Diocletian or Jupiter.

The emperor's reaction to the Christians was so fierce that even the pagan on the street thought the whole thing was over the top. First of all, the average Josephus felt, everyone was entitled to a god or two, so what difference did it make if some weirdos from the backcountry who thought theirs was special? Secondly the worse thing the Christian sect did was tell everyone to pay their taxes and not cheat their neighbors. Regardless, Diocletian killed heaps of Christians and they called him "the Dragon" for it. One of his victims, tied to a wheel and shredded with knives *before being beheaded*, was the son of a friend and a gifted imperial guard whose name, when Anglicized, was George. Not much else is known about St. George, but that does put the legend of his slaying the "dragon" in an entirely new light.

Due to illness, in 305, Diocletian abdicated along with Maximian, who knew who was keeping him in power. Their caesars, Galerius and Constantius the Pale,* were raised to augusti without a hitch and new caesars, engineered by Diocletian, were duly picked. Like all transitions of power, however, it only worked if everyone with the clout to do something about it agreed to the process. And the sons of those

---

*Pretty cruel nickname as the man almost certainly had leukemia.

augusti and caesars did not see why dad was picking anyone but them.

Specifically, the son the Western emperor Constantius, Constantine, had been held as a sort of hostage at court of Diocletian (who hadn't trusted Constantius). Despite the hostage business, he assumed that he'd be appointed caesar. Now Galerius was holding the boy hostage for the same reason and reportedly trying to kill him just to be safe. Obviously, as the son of the other augusti, this was delicate matter. As it was, Constantine escaped to go fight with dad in a vain attempt at keeping Britain Roman. Dad died and then, despite the best laid plans of the Dragon, the army hailed Constantine as Emperor.

Another civil war followed and Constantine reunited the empire. In 324 AD he decided – or to hear him tell it, was told by God – to found a city on a hill over-looking the Bosporus to be "the new capital of the world." Indeed, when Europeans referred to the city nearly 1,000 years later, they still called it "Midgard": the center of the world.

Even in antiquity real estate was reckoned on location, location, location. The well-sited Greek trading town of Byzantion was sitting exactly where Constantine thought the New Capital of the World was supposed to go. In 330, the emperor, in some interesting political double-speak, "refounded" Constantinople by renaming the place after himself, and made it the capital of the Eastern Roman Empire.*

---

*They thought of themselves as Romans, *Romani*. The term "Byzantine" wasn't applied to the empire until the reemergence of Europe, whose elites didn't want to muddle their claim as heirs to the Roman Empire. You and I both think of said power as the Byzantine Empire, so let's just go with that, shall we?

Unlike Diocletian, Constantine was famously tolerant of the other chap's religion, even if he hadn't really said much about it during Diocletian's persecutions. His mother, Helena, was a Christian and after the founding of Constantinople, she invented Christian pilgrimages to Jerusalem, specifically to the spot of the crucifixion, and the future site of the Church of the Holy Sepulcher.

The arrangement worked well enough until the 370s when internal struggles over Christianity and external issues with more Germans caused the Western Empire to begin to sink. In 476 the Germanic king Odoacer sacked Rome and deposed the last Western emperor. In a weirdly polite, but unmistakably final gesture, Odoacer sent the crown and royal threads of the deposed Romulus Augustus to Emperor Zeno in Constantinople.

In 489, an Ostrogoth king by the name of Theoderic was making a bloody mess of the Balkans a little too close to Constantinople. So Zeno told Theoderic that if he could have the western rump of the empire he could keep it. The emperor, assuming that crazy knows its own, reckoned that if he just threw the entirety of the clearly ruined old Rome to the Germans, they'd leave the shiny, eastern half alone.

Still, the dream of a reunification with the old empire remained a dream of Byzantine emperors but it never happened. To the east, however, the old frontier with the Persians still menaced.

In 614, while at war with the Persian Sassanid Empire, Jerusalem got sacked. The city wasn't all that tactical but the gold in the Christian shrines that had sprung in the last couple of hundred was just sitting there. They burned the Church of the Holy Sepulcher and (briefly) appointed a wealthy Jew named

Nehemiah ben Hushiel to govern the city before the Christian citizens revolted at the idea. Returning the favor, the Byzantines invaded and destroyed the temple of the Ahura Mazda to blacken the eye of the Zoroastrians. The fire of Ahura Mazda was dimming as another movement began to take shape in the harsh wastes of Arabia.

"Sensible men are all the same religion."
"And what, pray, is that?"
"Sensible men never tell."

Benjamin Disraeli (1880)

CHAPTER SEVEN:
CONVERSATIONS WITH SENSIBLE MEN

At the time, the situation on the ground in the south of Iraq seemed pretty stable, despite the hotting up of violence in places like Baghdad – but looks can be deceiving. And it is in the nature of terrorism to deceive. You can argue that the German blitz of London, or the Allied fire-bombing of Dresden were either simple, if savage, acts of war, or that they were full-blown war crimes. You can make the same argument about the Japanese over Pearl Harbor, or the United States over Hiroshima and Nagasaki a few years later. The question is certainly up for debate, the term "terrorism" isn't used. Germany was at war with the British and her allies – and knew they were going to punch back. The Japanese launched an unprovoked surprise attack, but it was on a naval base. Later, we actually warned the Japanese about the atom bomb.

What makes terrorism so terrorizing, as the Babylonian had pointed out to me, was the sheer randomness of it. Unless you actually happen to see someone drop a backpack in a crowd or park a car and start running there is no way to know what coming.

There is also no overarching effort to stop it by the Iraqis. The peace was being held in the south by an increasingly fractious group of militias; often co-religionists and theoretically on the same side. But there was no telling them that.

Like mafia families, the militias were staking claims in neighborhoods and business. Which was the reason our escorts that had met us at the Basra Airport never stopped the convoy – moving targets are very hard to hit.

By 2012, small arms and rocket propelled grenades were a dime a dozen throughout the region. In urban warfare where there is no "front" in a traditional sense of the word, this can be very dangerous. Should an argument break out between to pick-up trucks with .50 caliber machine guns tricked out on the bed – you need to remove yourself. Should someone launch a grenade, you need to do it quickly.

Understand that you can't out run a grenade that has been lobbed any more than one that has been fired. Your instinct will be to place as much distance between yourself and the explosive as possible. Which is good thinking, up to a point. While it's counter-intuitive, you are actually better off not running, but taking the longest flying leap you can in the opposite direction. When you hit the ground, stay there and stay flat so that the shrapnel and other flying debris sail over you. Dive away from the grenade so that your head is a far as possible from the explosion. Obviously, this will place your feet about six feet (give or take) closer to the blast than your head. It won't do your arches any favors, but you're are trying to keep yourself alive here, not go out for the NBA. Close your feet together because no one wants to absorb blast like that in the genitals. Pull your elbows in close to the torso for an added layer of protection for your vitals. Cover your head and ears with your hands because the blast can, and probably will, rupture your eardrums. Close your eyes for obvious reasons. Less obvious - open your mouth. If your jaws are locked shut the blast very well might cause your lungs to explode. This will improve your chances with the caveat that the odds diminish rapidly in proximity to the explosive.

When someone gives you instruction along these lines, you tend to listen carefully – replaying likely scenarios in your head and tabulating outcomes. As they say at the SIS, do your calculations beforehand (or words to that effect). It also raises the unsettling question of what affect a life like this has on the people who are forced to take these sort of things as a matter of course.

The deeper issue (and there is always a deeper issue) was not the personal paranoia, but societal. After a couple of generations of self-defeating social behavior enforced by the individual survival instinct in a fundamentally warped system – as Iraq was under Saddam Hussein – habits are formed that are very hard to break even if people know that they are self-defeating. Muhammed the Babylonian's observation that Iraq's middle-aged "lost generation" simply couldn't get their heads around personal initiative and open cooperation wasn't too wide the mark. And research suggests that his theory that the old guard is too old to adapt may not be too far off either.

NOBEL PRIZE WINNING phycologist Daniel Kahneman described the brain as two "systems" that make up the human behavior: "System 1" is automatic and unconscious, responsible for fight or flight type reflexes, hunger, native languages – basically things about which you don't have to consciously decide – and is capable of running interrelated as well as wholly independent computations at the same time. "System 2" is the conscious mind, the reflective, socially calculating and logical processor of which we are aware. Because we know it's there and can follow its logic, we think that the conscious mind it calling the shots. It isn't. The conscious mind is actually only capable of processing about six bytes of data per second – that's not a supercomputer, that's the stuff of vacuum tubes.

Jonathan Haidt puts it more organically as "the rider and the elephant." The elephant is a herd creature, it retreats from uncertainty and reacts positively in the face of reward – but is not inclined to really think things through. Nor can it articulate what it is thinking in a way that the rider can understand. Despite the control the rider assumes he has over the situation, he is actually at a complete loss to stop Tantor once the elephant gets spooked, hungry or horny. Or desperate. Often the best the average rider can do is hold on for the duration of the rampage and afterward develop a plausible sounding post-rationalization that boils down to "I meant to do that." Which is where the conscious brain excels – not in deciding what to do, but in coming up with a plausible story after your unconscious has already decided.

And that's just on a personal level – multiply that by a whole mob of people desperately spooked and things get decidedly hairier. Introduce a massive traumatic shock, or atrophy, to an entire system, and what little control the rider has over the direction of the elephant evaporates almost completely.

So what happened after a two-month foreign army maneuver that put things more or less the way they'd been before that drove Iraq's healthcare backward some 50 years that an eight year ground war that also gained nothing couldn't do? The United Nations Resolution 661 happened. It stated, in part:

The Council therefore decided that states should prevent:

(a) the import of all products and commodities originating in Iraq or Kuwait;

(b) any activities by their nationals or in their territories that would promote the export of products originating in Iraq or Kuwait, as well as the transfer of funds to either country for the purposes of such activities;

Resolution 661 affectively closed the borders of Iraq to all commerce. It was passed to support 660, and was supported in turn by resolutions 662, 664, 665, 667, 669, 670, 674, 677, 678. All passed in 1990, and who says the UN doesn't do anything? In 1991, it was decided to wrap it all up in yet another resolution – 686. And let the matter drop.

The economy starved, but Saddam remained and can't be said to have dropped any weight. In the face of a contracting economy, he moved money that had been going to healthcare to the military and conscripted medical students into the army. Iraq did what all traumatized countries do when cut off from the world, whether by choice or force, it regressed. Twenty years and another invasion later, Iraq had lost a generation of doctors as well as a generation of medical advancement.

It was so obvious that you could almost see it in the halls of the Ali Hussein hospital. But the Arabs aren't the only ones who spook. I'd slipped away from the medical team for a chat in the administrative offices of the hospital when I found myself standing with a doctor, maybe about my age. He seemed friendly enough, and from his body language I could tell that he was framing a thought. He pulled at his chin in that very Arab way and finally said, "If I might ask you a question… American yes?"

"Yes."

"Why are you here?"

Gascon kept going on about not saving lives, but all that was a little too abstract for non-native speakers. "To clean up a mess." I said. "To save lives."

"No. No." He said, "Not you. I mean, why did you – America – come here? Yes yes. You rid us of Saddam." He touched his heart, "But what was your plan? For after?" The man didn't seem angry, just genuinely baffled. The same power that – standing alone after World War II – had developed and maintained a liberal world order which had in a few short years choked the old entrenched imperial system to death. A country that had designed itself along the lines of the Roman republic, whose peasantry had built an empire that surpassed Rome itself, had come into their country, toppled the government and not had a step two. How had we not thought it through?

So, there I was standing in the hospital with a doctor asking a perfectly rational question: "What were you thinking?"

The truth is that we weren't.

Unlike the Romans, we never needed an empire because we have most of a continent. In our glorious isolation and self-sufficiency it's hard for us to fathom the changes a few well-placed and traumatic shocks can make to the psychology of a people. And when the national elephant is spooked it heads for safety – and will crash through almost anything to get it.

The Uncle Sam's elephant had gotten spooked after 9/11 and just gone off and did what it did. Not just to Afghanistan and Iraq, but to ourselves with the excessive powers we signed off the government in the wake of that fright. Although the doctor in the hall likely wasn't thinking that far down the thread either. To him what we'd done was very destructive. What subsequent White House administrations, the State Department and the Pentagon had called "mission creep" was really just the dizzy rider looking at the destruction of his spooked elephant and stammering "I meant to do that."

The logical response to all these foreign policy missteps would be to stop throwing buckets of good money and blood after bad – basically lay off blowing everything to hell – and have ourselves a savage reassessment of the situation. The human response, however, is to ignore the constellation of obvious failings and carry on – because being the bearer of bad news is never great for your career. Better for the mortgage to carry on endorsing billions on weird nation building hacks that only prove that the human brain is baffling even to those who possess one.

Which is not to say that you can't change your destiny it just requires a lot of history falling on your head to do it. The Iraqis are having a dramatic time getting it together after the shock and awe of all our "help." It would be a mistake to assume that they are stupid, or even uneducated. If anything, they fall into that Frenchman's trap of thinking too much. After 50 years of Ba'athist rule where doing would definitely get you killed and talking might, thinking was – for a generation – all that was left.

Imagine living in a world where the boogey man isn't some harmless childhood haint playing squatter under your bed, but the head of state controlling your world for 24 years. A guy who – indirectly if you are lucky and directly if you have opinions – controls your fate, whose mug is on half the walls in the country and on all the crumpled, worthless money. You can't even wander down to the souk to buy some tea without having to look your low-simmering worst fear in the face.

ONE OF THE RELATIVELY few advantages of having a grenade go off in your world is that you don't have to build it back exactly the way you found it. For Nadwa Qaragholi – our Iraqi fixer who seemed capable of massaging the silver out of the darkest cloud – she has no intention of trying to put Iraq back the way it was. She has a vision of how it could be that seems to be to be built out of weapons grade optimism. It is an optimism that is tempered, like everything else around here, with a brutal dose of realism.

Her vision is a tall order – and even a dangerous one as anarchy throws people into a brutish survival mode that exists far away from anything we'd really call aspirational. An elephant on a rampage that isn't even aware of the rider, much less interested in where he might want to go.

There are charities throughout the country, but most of them are religious – in the south that means Shi'a – and is often the case when religion is as much political as spiritual, the help they offer war orphans* comes with strings.

---

*The term "war orphans" in the Arab world, with its lopsided sex roles, includes widows as well.

What Nadwa saw wasn't an Iraq where those wrecked lives were attached and dependent on charity, but that weren't attached to anything, really. "I thought to myself," she told me, "Iraq still has problems. People should be able to move where the work is. What is a completely portable skill? Coding..." So she pestered Iraqi government officials, engineers and coder writers – as well as much less local volunteers in Europe and the USA to create a coding school for war orphans. "We all need a skill. They can take this with them wherever they go."

I'm not certain that she saw it this way, but what she seemed to be cobbling together out of the detritus of a war zone was network of programs that got children off the streets by having them clean said streets up and plant gardens as a price to get into the local soccer or sewing club. That kept them in school to develop relationships with other school children outside their world, which gave them a vision of what a post-war world could look like. Then the kiddos rolled out of grammar school and into computer coding training to give them options unheard of since the war and, for many of these people, before it.

The religious charities, she told me, weren't bad in and of themselves, they just seemed more interested in developing adherents rather than opportunities.

I asked her about her religion. She gave me a vague answer that I won't quote here. However, I will say this: Benjamin Disraeli – author of the epigraph at the beginning of this chapter – would have found it a very sensible answer.

In the end though, Nadwa is just one woman (albeit a formidable one). None of these plans could take root unless the guy on the street was determined to build a country that they could be proud of. There are wrecked buildings around, but a new heart center is being built and the new "dream homes" we drove past where modern McMansion sized domiciles. Instead of trying to cram traditional European elements into contemporary buildings, they were doing the same with traditional Arab flourishes...to roughly the same awkward affect. That, and the houses were walled. Not a walled development, every house was its own fortress.

COULD ANY ATTEMPT at nation building work in the chaotic blast radius of foreign invasion and civil war? Could the Iraqis, or anyone for that matter, resist the pull of a power vacuum created by the dismantling of government apparatus as well as an entire society? Actually, it might if we could just come at things with the right angle. American may be an historical anomaly, but it we did prove that it could be done. If the plan was to build stability around a regional medical center, Iraq didn't just need the endorsement (and protection) of the mercurial government. It needed the buy-in of the citizens. The Babylonian was correct, generally, that money wasn't the problem – but allocation of money was.

Since the invasion, a group community leaders – and that is not a euphemism for warlords - had coalesced in Nasiriya to discuss and plan its future. I was invited, but Gascon warned me not to bring my notebooks. Old habits die hard in a place like Iraq and he reckoned that the invite was really just the government wanting to figure out what I was going to write about them. It turned out the doctor was wrong, although it wasn't bad advice. While there was the odd local politico, it was really a gathering of businessmen, doctors, professors and journalists belonging to the aptly named society

"Communication." It turned out to be a cross between a literary club and a high-minded Chamber of Commerce. At any rate, they really did seem genuine in their efforts to sort the mess out.

In honor of me, I think, we kicked off the discussion with William Faulkner. It wasn't a Southern thing, but an American thing as well as a literary one. I'm not sure any of them knew where Memphis was. After a week in Iraq I could see why they loved that bane of high school American lit students: lofty, stream-of-consciousness perceptions of a violent, hot and sometime barren landscape filled with people incapable of a simple declarative sentence. Faulkner is tricky enough without the language barrier, in Arabic he's really fearsome. Fortunately, it could be argued that Dr. Amir Doshi, the friendly, charming chair of the meeting as well as my translator, spoke better English than I do. They were delighted to learn that Memphis was (the way I framed it) down the road from Oxford, Mississippi. They were especially taken with *The Sound and the Fury*, and the Shakespeare quote from which Faulkner got the title:

Life's but a walking shadow, a poor player
That struts and frets his hour upon the stage
And then is heard no more: it is a tale
Told by an idiot, full of sound and fury,
Signifying nothing.

Given what these people had been through, their affection for Faulkner made perfect sense. We discussed the Russian writer Nabokov, the new heart center and the re-valuation of the Iraqi dinar. But "discussion" in the Middle East is not like the Western mosh pit of conversation. It's more akin to dueling orations. They loved Faulkner, but they rooted for the home team too.

They told me that Nasiriya is set on the Euphrates River, near the biblical city of Ur and there have people living here for over 6,000 years. They told me that, in the Middle East, this place was called the Cradle of Civilization, and did I know that? I tried to answer but that was a gaff. Amir gave me a universal symbol to stop talking, I wasn't supposed to answer the question posed while the man was on a roll.

In the Arabic world – or judge by the company at the tea-houses I'd seen earlier, the middle aged Arab world – puts a great deal of weight on poetry and eloquence. This isn't a society where you can rise to the top one tweet at a time. I have no idea if any of these guys had prepared remarks in advance or if they were all just really good at rhetoric – but their comments were soaring. The fellow who'd asked me about the cradle of civilization sat down and after a beat I realized that they were all starting at me. Amir nudged me to say something.

They seemed astounded to hear that every American student knows about the Tigris, the Euphrates, and calls it the Cradle of Civilization as well. I'm not sure what possessed me to re-read the "Epic of Gilgamesh" before I left the US, but I'm glad I did. And if you aren't forced to read it for class, it is actually pretty riveting stuff. It made them proud. It should.

We talked about war journalism. I protested that I wasn't a war correspondent. That's when they looked at me as if I were insane or very naive. I was a foreign writer who'd flown into the center of a three-way civil war, that made me a war journalist. They had me there. So I quoted Robert E. Lee, of all people, "It is good that war is terrible, lest we grow too fond of it."* The point of journalism, I said, was to keep a conflict in front of the public because no society needs to be too comfortable in a state of war. The United States, for example, was entirely too comfortable with the concept of perpetual conflict because we didn't have to see it. The purpose of a writer in a war zone, is pretty simple if harrowing: Keep people thinking about the death reeked until they'd had to change tack.In a society that was growing dangerously resigned to a forever war on their own turf, this rang a bell.

Then came the glance that I didn't expect. Travel the world, certainly to places off the official tourism for the sane guides, and you will know what it's like to be that global pariah, the American. What I was told was that I had the heart of a poet – which is quite a compliment (and probably due to Mr. Doshi's brilliant translation). I chocked up. At least that made it easy to keep my mouth shut.

These guys traded stories of arrest, kidnapping and torture the way that my friends swap stories of awful summer jobs in high school. Dr. Dosi's own kidnapping was chronicled in the book *American Hostage*, by Micah Garen and Marie Helene Carlton. The situation in Iraq was described to me as waking from a nightmare only to find that the scars were real.

Now they are determined to rebuild their city, and the Nasiriyains had big plans for their heart center. They saw it as an economic driver was well as a medical necessity. Like the regional Director of Healthcare, they wanted to remake their little

---

* The terminally woke can keep their comments to themselves. The quote stands no matter who said it. If you find yourself in the same position and have something better, let me know.

agricultural city on a big river, into a hub of the biomedical industry. A retiring director of the hospital said that Nasiriya didn't really need money to reinvent itself. Bids were going out to explored oil fields in the area, but that the economy needed something other than oil to make it stable. They had a plan: The heart center would bring regional medical conferences, which would bring visitors that would require hotels and restaurants, but it would also bring vendors and biomedical industry – and all those high paying jobs – to the area. Secretaries would have to be employed (assuming, of course, that the Minister of Health could be talking into hiring some) and someone would have to sell cars and build houses for all these new professionals. What they wanted to know was just how the trick was pulled by people who'd done it before. Then to let them do it *their* way.

To circle back to the dad-running-along-side-junior's-bike metaphor – in terms of economic development, they were at Bike with Training Wheels. And this wasn't all that bad in a country that hadn't known a moment's peace in about 40 years and, prior to that, had had a very authoritarian socialist government squeeze all the economic development opportunities from local markets. "Communication" wanted to fill that gap while the gap still existed. In short they were attempting to massage that tricky power vacuum to their advantage. And they were right to do it – they didn't need a Made in America one-size-fits-all solution. "Nothing that we do here will work unless it fits into the existing cultural groundwork."

After the plans for Nasiriya's future were laid out, I was asked what I thought about them. I hope my laughter didn't offend. I told them of course it could work. I told them that was exactly how a place like Memphis had gone from a smallish, single commodity agricultural city on a big river to being an enormous Tier One medical center. And how, a generation or so on, we were sending teams of surgeons crawling over the globe to show others how it was done. If a place like Memphis could manage it, they certainly could, if they were just allowed to.

The meeting broke up in the street outside the office with lots of farewells and hand clasping. Outside we continued chatting, but this was less formal and far livelier, with everyone laughing and talking over each other. Reality outside seemed closer than it had inside those air-conditioned walls. In a courtyard, a weather-beaten reporter asked me my age. He smiled, "I'm the same age as you. I just look older." He laughed a strange laugh. Harsh but not cruel, and not without a cloud of black humor. "I spent some time with Saddam." This was the euphemism for having been arrested and tortured by the old regime. Others slapped his arm and they roared with laughter. Having 'spent some time with Saddam', now that the nightmare was over, was something of a badge of honor. The scars, however, were real.

Except for the politics, there seemed to be no real obstacles to the Iraqi's building a real, functioning heart center and, for that matter, properly functioning society. Politics, certainly political Islam, is a huge 'except', however.

The formula is simple and proven: let the innovators innovate, the commercial interests will follow to distribute the innovation, commerce flourishes and people have both more innovation and money.

The Iraqi's could see the goal, had a plan and were learning how to make it work from people who'd done it before them. They'd contacted the ICHF, not the other way round. Now if they could only keep the factionalism at bay, they'd be looking a pretty bright future. I crossed the street in front of a café feeling pretty confident in these fine people.

A few weeks later, in the same spot I said my final farewell, a car bomb exploded. And like that, I had a smart, dedicated friend who'd been killed in one of those attacks we see on television, but don't pay attention to anymore.

*Mahomet called the Hill to come to him. And when the
Hill stood still, he was neuer a whit abashed, but said; If
the Hill will not come to Mahomet, Mahomet will go to
the hill.*

Francis Bacon (1625)

CHAPTER EIGHT:
FELIX ARABIA

Islam – which simply means 'submission' in the same way
that catholic simply means 'universal' but now it doesn't – has
always been political, but then again, most religions are. Ur-
Nammu gave the priests privileged positions in society in return
for telling anyone who would listen that he was a lesser god
himself. Like Christianity, the state religion of the Persians didn't
start out political but got there eventually. Zoroaster was just at
wandering holy man carrying on about the truth and the lie until
Cyrus saw its potential to forge a cohesive society. The Roman
Imperial religion may have been a many splendored thing – but
all of them were political. According to the Jews, God has
nationalistic impulses.

There are no contemporary accounts of the Prophet
Mohammad's life and there is little to no editorializing in the
Qur'an. Its lessons aren't hung on a narrative, it is more a list

131

rules and best behaviors. It's an elegant, poetic list, but it is a list. Think of the Ten Commandments that Moses took down, just not in bullet form and there are 114 of them. Which isn't a bad simile because in its earliest form Islam wasn't supposed to be a radical destruction of Judaism and Christianity, but a continuing refinement of that common understanding of man's relationship to God.

As happens in cases like these – the fellow monotheists, the People of the Book* – didn't see that their relationship to God needed refinement. Certainly not from a bunch of outsiders, thank you very much. It looked to the other monotheists that the Muslims were confusing what might be called cultural idioms for universal truths. This is important because the medium of a message's delivery affects how a message is received and understood more than we like to think.

Moses' trip up the mountain notwithstanding, most of the lessons of the Bible are interpreted from a narrative of histories and morality tales, rather than expressly laid out regulations. Given inexhaustible genius humans have for hearing only what we want to hear, this narrative form leads to widely different interpretations. Consider for example, the University of the South, in Sewanee, Tennessee was founded as an Episcopalian University, yet depending which direction you head you are only a short drive from an auditorium sized Baptist churches or a one-room snake handling outfits. And those are just the Protestants. Fold in the Greek Orthodox and the Roman Catholics still within a short drive, and you get heaps of Christians all professing the

---

* Muslims, Christians, Jews and Zoroastrians, if you were wondering.

same religion and yet are almost entirely foreign from each other.*

As Alem and I discovered chatting about Ramadan v. Lent, Islam wasn't intended to allow for quite so much human wiggle-room. Although if we're being level-handed, Mohammad's straightforward bullet-point style has been twisted pretty badly of late. Still, the cultural medium leaves its imprint. A declassified British Intelligence report which sought to find predictors of people at risk for Islamic extremism found that the undergraduate degree that produced the most radicals wasn't Islamic studies, but engineering – a profession where even the most creative genius still must adhere to black and white rules. In a chaotic and fearsome world, it does appear that the simple 'freedom from freedom' may offer more phycological sticking power than self-doubting, modern Christians.

Islam did form a vicious split, and quickly, but it didn't have much to do with dogma. Both Sunni and Shi'a sects mainly agree on the set of rules to which the faithful submits. Unlike Martin Luther's dogmatic arguments, but very much like Henry VIII's dynastic concerns, the schism in Islam was more political in nature.

As important as the format in which a message is delivered, is the state of mind of the one receiving it. In its beginning, Christianity was forged as an out-group persecuted by a Roman

---

* Not always, I was raised Catholic and married an Episcopalian, I've been to dueling Easter services *on the same weekend* and can attest that you almost need a theology degree to tease out the differences between the two.

establishment.* Whereas Islam began as a conquering in-group. The shocking speed of Islam's spread meant that the faith was forged in victory, not oppression. Differing schools of thought diverge wildly on what happened next, but there are some broad strokes where a story emerges.

By the end of the seventh century the forces of Islam had broken out of the Arabian Peninsula, first into Mesopotamia and then east to mighty Persia. The Arabs sneered at the monotheist Persians under the wing of Ahura Mazda for worshipping fire. I can assure you that 1,369 years later, Sunni Arabs still make snide comments about Iranian fire fetishes. During the Muslim conquest of Syria, forces again laid siege to city of Jerusalem in 636 until the patriarch of the city submitted to the Caliph six months later.

Old Jerusalem, the biblical city, doesn't date from antiquity, it's been razed too many times for that. A strange honor for a city that has never been the seat of an empire or even much practical strategic importance. Old Jerusalem is a badly maintained medieval city, but it is an exercise in meaning. For modern Jews it is the old capital of historic Israel. For Christians it is where the Passion of Christ played out. It is also the third Holiest place in Islam. Iran's elite expeditionary force – tasked with "exporting revolution" (more to the point – arming and funding every semi-aggrieved Shi'a minority into destabilizing the local government) – is named after the city.

To use the Islamic term, three of the four "People of the Book" may have converged on the city of Jerusalem but they did

---

*Although, once Christianity went "Establishment," it didn't do it half-way.

it in three distinct ways. For the Jews it was simply a matter of a state religion born out of coalescing tribes in the desert. Both Christianity and Islam were effectively urban movements, growing outward from the cities. With more connections and social pass throughs that urban life offers, most mass movements generally are. Christianity, however, took root in the cities of an empire, in opposition of a unified imperial cult, growing along the lines of a secret society until it reached a tipping point.

In Arabia, the forces of Islam had no unified opposition. This was a wilderness of tribes and isolated towns each with its own gods and devils. What Islam offered wasn't in opposition to an empire – it was an empire itself. Like the Romans, it offered something bigger and better to the scattered tribes than a brutal existence of hit and run wars with the neighbors. Whereas the Bible is symbolic poetry containing lessons and truths to be draw out by the reader, the Qur'an reads like the constitution – and that's not by accident. Christians didn't need administrative law, because it was born in an ordered society. In fact, this tension between the temporal and secular worlds has been a central part of its development through the Roman years, the dark ages, the Enlightenment and is enshrined in the US constitution. Islam, on the other hand, offered structure to life and rule of law. Like Cyrus – Mohammad didn't utterly destroy the conquered; he folded them into the movement, gave them a place, gave them some meaning to hold dear and just kept on going.

At the time of Mohammad's death in 632 AD – the movement was still a professed religious movement, but it operated along the lines of an empire – levying taxes and tribute. In short, there was a lot of money and power at stake.*

Like Rome in the first days of the empire – no one had given much thought to succession. The movement had simply moved too fast. Had Mohammad died with a direct male heir, the boy would have likely taken control on the force of dad's personality and that would have been that. As it was, he had a daughter married to a loyal chap named Ali. One faction thought that the son-in-law ought to take the reins and called themselves the Followers of Ali – or *Shiat Ali* – or Shi'a.

The other, larger faction, thought that a college of Islamic elites should choose a new leader, or caliph. They called themselves Sunni, from the Arabic *Sunna* or "Tradition." There was no great dispute over dogma or theology – this was a fight over who got the top job. As it was, the Sunnis won out and named Abu Bakr the first caliph. Things went predictably hairy after that. Ali did manage to become the fourth Caliph (or "Imam" to the Shi'a) after the quick time assassination of the previous two Caliphs. Then, in 661, Ali himself was killed. By the time the sixth Caliph, Yazid I, was named, the Sunnis had established hereditary rule of the Caliphate which, you'll note, is exactly what they were fighting the Shi'a against. *Plus ça change.*

With his power-base in Syria, Yazid's nomination was opposed by the Mecca contingent, but eventually his block won out. To put an end to the business with a small but loud Shi'a faction, he started squeezing the Shi'a in Baghdad hard. They called out for Hussein, the son of the murdered Ali and grandson

---

*In contrast, Peter I might have been the first pope, but he was the leader of a religion that had to hold services in stables for fear of the authoritarian state and gossipy neighbors.

of the Prophet, to help them out. Over in Mecca, Hussein's seat of power, his advisors and followers told him that he should absolutely *not* go to Baghdad. He weighed his options and went anyway, reportedly with some 72 followers and relations.

So it was, in 680, that Hussein led a small band from Mecca to Karbala, between Babylon and Baghdad, to liberate his supporters there. Yazid met Hussein with a Sunni army, reportedly 4,000 strong, and after a ten-day stand-off designed to starve the smaller army out, Hussein was killed with the rest of his contingent, his head lopped off and taken back to Damascus. The ironic part of all this is that the Battle of Karbala was to settle the matter of who would succeed the Prophet once and for all by killing off the last vestiges of said Prophet's family.

Despite its internal divisions, the forces of Islam swept through the region. By 688, the entirety of the Levant was secured for Islam and its forces were spreading across North Africa. In 691, in Jerusalem, construction of the Dome of the Rock was started on the site that had been the Temple of Solomon and the second Hebrew Temple the Romans razed in 70 before turning the Jews out for good.

You'd be forgiven for asking why the Arabs thought Jerusalem was so important. In Islamic tradition, the Prophet rode a flying tiger through the air one night to Jerusalem and then ascended bodily into Heaven from there rather than someplace like Medina or Mecca. Why is unclear and the story doesn't really even appear for discussion until about 50 years after the death of the Prophet when Muslim forces had taken Jerusalem for themselves. A cynical reader might even entertain the theory that, giving the meaning vested into the city by other people, that the story is more political appropriation than strictly theological or historical in nature. The Persians and Romans had done this before, and the Christian were currently doing it over in Germany. Sometimes it's best not to argue.

There is no real doubt that the first wave of converts came at the point of a sword, but the movement really flourished and took root with a series of economic and societal carrots. After 750, the Abbasid caliphs moved the seat of their empire to that erstwhile center of the world, Baghdad, shifting the center of gravity out of the desert peninsula and to a place used to being the administrative center.

According to the Qur'an, Mohammad himself preached religious tolerance, certainly for the People of the Book. So, the ruling caliphs didn't so much persecute religious minorities (not at that point, at any rate) as lay a bunch of tedious "I'm not a Muslim" taxes on them and blackball them from all the best government posts. Like the Romans before them, the caliphs learned the trick of making subject people decide for themselves that it was just easier to be a part of the club.

As Islam spread it folded in the Persians to the east, while Berbers and Moors pushed it west across North Africa. There it made the leap across Gibraltar onto the Iberian peninsula in 711. With alarming speed, Islam spread across Christian Spain. And indeed, to the invaders, the very hand of God seemed to be on their side. They stacked up an alarming number of victories until crossing the Pyrenees into France, where they checked by the forces of Charles Martel. The French took this to mean that God was on *their* side, but couldn't explain the loss of Spain. It is possible that the earthly truth is a little less glorious on both sides: The Pyrenees are not easy mountains to cross, making successful land invasion either direction very tricky.

On the Spanish side of the mountains, the Muslims hung for about 800 years, and - if we can tease politics and religion out of the equation - they really improved the place. Within a couple of centuries, Cordoba, Spain - the seat of the Caliphate of Cordoba was the second largest city in Europe with some 400,000 residents at its peak - even known in Christian Europe as the "Ornament of the World." Without a doubt the city had grown fat and rich, like the Muslim traders that occupied Sicily, on supplying European slaves to the African and Arab slave markets. A morally dubious stability held as administrative systems unheard of in Europe were put in place.

A century on, the Cordoba's elite liked to think they were better than mere slavers, but mere slavers generally do. Cordoba was beautiful, but it lacked the awe-inspiring fortifications of Constantinople. For one thing, it didn't really need them. The local Christians lived in dumpy, scattered villages, either completely aimless or the plaything of some petty Christian warlord. In short, Muslim citizens though that they were only fit for the slave trade. Besides, you might even win a few converts for God among the enslaved.*

Western civilization in the 21st century has had a tendency to look at the Middle East, since the collapse of the Ottoman Empire, and be smugly baffled at the locals inability to pull themselves together. It helps to understand that for the first 1,200 or so years following the collapse of the Roman Empire the peoples of the East – Christian, Jew or Muslim – looked at the West and thought the same damn thing.

---

* This perennially bad argument for slavery is weirdly familiar.

PART TWO:

MIDGARD

ISTANBUL, TURKEY

New opinions are always suspected, and usually opposed, without any other reason but because they are not already common.

John Locke (1632-1704)
"An Essay Concerning Human Understanding"
1690

CHAPTER NINE:
MAGIC CARPET RIDE

There is a marvelous story I first heard when I was in the advertising business, and then again years later when I started doing whatever the hell it is we're calling what I do now. When Mustafa Kemal (later Atatürk) founded the modern, secular Turkish state in 1923, he scrapped Islamic Law, dropped the Arabic script for a stepped-on marriage of the Latin and Cyrillic alphabets, cherry picked civil codes from different European states and outlawed the fezzes then worn by Muslim men with the 1925 Hat Law.* Yet, after all that, the new modern state could never bring itself to ban the traditional headscarf worn by the women. Even the upstanding Mrs. Kemal was often seen at his side wearing the very accoutrement her husband was trying

---

* Leaving them to sole preserve of overweight Shiners on wee motorcycles.

to get women to abandon. Most likely, she saw the political point that he was trying to make, she just didn't care. While fine with crushing male opposition to his Western reforms, Atatürk was terrified of the blowback from irate Turkish women (or at least one of them). No matter how far reaching your political vision, you just can't tell a lady how to wear her hair.

His solution – and it was brilliant – wasn't to prohibit the headscarf, but simply make it compulsory for prostitutes. Which did the ironic trick. Not wanting to look like a harlot, the respectable ladies of the republic started to disregard the modest *hajib* on their own. The story is almost too good to be true, but the fact remains that headscarf was never outlawed until a military coup d'état in 1980, and then only in public jobs and buildings. Even with the force of the army – that bastion of the secular Turkish state – the ban wasn't ever really enforced.

Why, you well may ask, was the man who raised a collapsed empire into a modern state, or the Turkish military for that matter, concerned with the nuances of women's headwear? Since the establishment of a multi-party political system following World War II, elections in Turkey had gotten a trifle too democratic for the tastes of the Kemalist reformers. There had been a persistent fear that the voters just might vote the conservatives (today we'd call them Islamists) into power, wrap their heads on all manner of tradition, and return the country to the Ottoman-era caliphate. Both the Turkish army and the judiciary became the self-appointed protectors of Atatürk's secular reforms. To hear the army tell it, this sacred protection has required a coup d'etat in 1960, a military "decision" in 1971, another coup d'état in 1980*,and yet another military "decision" in 1997.

Shortly after the last "decision", in 1998, the army and judiciary stripped the professional footballer *cum* Mayor of Istanbul, Recep Tayyip Erdogen of his job, threw him in jail and banned him from holding elected office for inciting religious hatred. He'd read a poem. So Erdogan left his Islamist Welfare Party to form the Justice and Development Party (AKP) which tapped into a growing Islamist vibe without being too obvious about it. Erdogan is credited with leading the AKP party to a landslide victory in 2002, despite being unable to hold office himself. So Erdogan had the AKP prime minister (who really did owe him one) lift his political ban and got himself elected prime minister the next year. He became president and started purging the secular military of the secularists. This led to an attempted military coup in 2016.

One of the most basic steps of any coup d'état in the age of mass communication is to seize the newspapers, radio and television stations and announce the operation as a done deal. It puts the public at ease. Unfortunately, for the 21st century plotter, this only works well when the means of communication are somewhat centralized. In a world where everyone is walking around with a global television network in their pants pocket, things are a little trickier. Case and point: the coup looked posed to succeed until the Erdogan made a last-minute comeback when he face-timed the loyalist in the army (and the rest of the country) to fight the action. That, in and of itself, is a game changer.

---

*You'll note this is the year after Khomeini's Islamic revolution in Iran.

Once he got back to the office, Erdogan had some 10,000 soldiers arrested on charges that they had taken part in the fracas and better than 2,700 judges claiming... well he never explained that one. Given the judiciaries self-professed partnership with the military to keep the Islamists in their place* it seems pretty obvious.

I watched the whole thing intently from Memphis. Mrs. M., suspiciously eye-balling my keen interest in the matter. Using her mysterious female powers, she eventually got it out of me that I'd signed on to another errand – this one in Beirut – and the coup in Turkey was playing hell with my travel plans. "You aren't going to Beirut." She said flatly. She'd evidently had enough of my foolishness.

ISTANBUL'S OLD CITY is beautiful crossroads – a cosmopolitan survivor in a world of rising and falling civilizations. It is not a tomb, nor is it one of those modern cities desperately trying to stay on-trend. She has the bearing of those ladies of my grandparent's generation who, when the end of things appeared nigh, dug in her (high) heels, stood up straight to show off grandmother's pearls and said calmly, "No dear, it's not."

The city may no longer be using its maiden name, but has the sort of timeless vibe that can't be manufactured, or at least can't be manufactured in under 1,700 years. The city stood as the seat of the Roman Empire as the western half collapsed and never saw the dark ages that followed in Europe. It lasted almost 1,000 years longer than Rome itself as the reigning power in the

---

*The mosques

world and then as the reduced bulwark of Christianity against a rising tide of Islam. It was the administrative center of the Muslim world, and the home of the first Arab Spring (not the one that spread on Twitter), and a major clandestine battlefield for both World Wars.

It still is the layover for Western travelers heading into the Middle East. The thing that you notice coming in from the US or Europe is how exotic the place seems. Flying back into the city after some time in Iraq, however, and suddenly the same places – cafés, restaurants, shops – sudden seem very Western. Istanbul is a place where, no disrespect to Mr. Kipling, East and West do meet.

Then again maybe I'm not the right person to say. Coming back from a place like Iraq was like waking from a surreal, sandy dream of the sort that you get by mixing booze and sleep medicine. Unlike those strange nightmares of the Iraqis, I didn't wake up with physical scars.

Istanbul's old quarters are well preserved and the cafés that line the streets were filled with chatting, sharp looking people in comically tight jeans branded "Amigo" or "Elvis" worn with pointy Arab shoes. Over the Bosporus in Asia Minor, you see women in *abaya*, but in Istanbul, the women mostly keep it to the traditional headscarf, if that. In truth, the *Istanbulii* have traditionally thought that the word "Turk" is synonymous with "bumpkin." The clothes are excessively trendy (I think) but not racy. You'd see a lot more exposed skin at an American high school.

On the hunt for a Turkish coffee the way it was supposed to be made, I slipped into a café. While the place felt Western, the *ezan* (the call to prayer in Turkish) rang out. In the Old City, the three great historic mosques coordinate the *ezan* in a sort of prayerful round – what Americans would know as holy "Row, Row, Row Your Boat" that is exceedingly beautiful. Or at least it would have been had it not been mingled with American Top 40 music coming from inside the café. I was trying to take in the *ezan* in all its glory when the waiter came up in the middle to ask if I wanted another coffee. Or a beer.

At the time, there were some tension between Turkey, an important NATO ally, over EU membership so I reckoned that I'd do my job and ask the waiter about it. "The EU hates Muslims – it's bigotry!" he said. The French objection to Turkish membership was a little more nuanced that that, but he wasn't entirely wrong either. The kid was, however, selling me a beer at 3:30 on a Friday in the middle of Ramadan so he can't be accused of taking his religious oppression too seriously. "Have you seen the Sultan Ahmet Mosque?" he continued, "It is known as the Blue Mosque." I said that I hadn't but that's was where I was heading after coffee. "It is the second largest mosque outside of Mecca. Most mosques have only four minarets for the *ezan*. Yes, but the Sultan Ahmet has six."

"That's interesting." I said, "Why's that?"

The waiter stared off at the mosque. "Because they wanted six minarets." He seemed baffled by the question. Like a Turkish Nigel Tufnel explaining that 11 is "one louder, iddn't it?"

In France's defense, their objection to Turkish membership to the EU wasn't entirely bigoted. For one thing, most of the country isn't even in Europe. More crucially, the union simply doesn't work unless all hints of the religious division are leeched from the halls of the respective governments. So they are justifiably wary of a mighty injection of political Islam, or any politicized religion for that matter. The Union had created a Europe without internal borders, but held onto the greater external borders of the EU zone. Meaning that while getting into the EU zone required the usual border controls, once inside you could move from Germany to France with complete freedom. Given the titanic upsurge in migrants from Turkey who'd already settled in Germany since the turn of the century, along with its own overwhelming North African migrant issues – France was in no mood to erase the border with Turkey, the main conduit for the stream of refugees and the waves of economic migrants from the Middle East. Nor was it helping that President Erdogen was directing the Turkey's ex-pat communities from Istanbul while managing something of a domestic religious revival at home.

As a wave of political Islam swept across the region, Erdogan began a roll back of aspects of the secular state established by Kemal Atatürk in 1923. No mean feat given that the population regards the man and something of a national hero. Erdogan's particular tack, as a member of NATO and a Muslim nation, was to position Turkey as the leader of a moderate version of political Islam. Everything got a lot trickier when the Arab Spring in Libya turned into the ouster of Muammar Gaddafi and the revolutionary spark jumped to neighboring Syria's ill-fated attempt to overthrow its dentist *cum* despot, Bashar al-Assad. The Kurds of the region, feeling put upon by both the Turks and the Syrians since roughly the beginning of time, saw their chance for freedom if they could only get the arms and the traction.

The sad truth is that dueling mass movements, even in democracies, don't always boil down to the numbers, but rather the sheer volume of noise that can be produced.* And guns produce a lot of noise.

In the summer of 2012 – when I was summering in Iraq – the situation was deteriorating, but the gravitational pull of history was taking events back to that old center of the world. On 6 June, a bomb placed at the gates of the Special Mission Compound in Benghazi had torn a 30-foot hole compound wall. This was in retaliation for a US drone Strike that killed al Qaeda deputy commander Abu Yahya Libi in Waziristan, Afghanistan.

The attack and retaliation illustrate as much as anything a perennial blind spot that Western nations have in dealing with the former Ottoman empire: Namely that the East doesn't share the West's baseline assumption of the nation-state. It exists, and governments certainly go through their nationalist phases, but the stronger cultural ties are to the *Ummah*, the Islamic family, and tribal, ethnic ties. The journo I had tea with in Nasiriya wasn't lying when he said that the Shi'a in Iraq's south didn't fight with their co-religionists in Iran because "We are Iraqis." Still, I was left with the impression that the choice was less Iraq/Iran than Arab/Persian.

A day after the 6 June bombing, the *jihadis*, mostly under the organization of Ansar al-Sharia – a Sunni militia – staged a parade of some 30 brigades from 15 militias to promenade along Benghazi's seafront corniche. A resident of Benghazi who'd spent time in America described the ordeal to me as a sort of perverse version of an American 4th of July parade. What it was, in fact,

---

* If you don't believe me, please see the US Presidential election of 2016 – where most polls pegged some 75-80% of the voting population thought *both* candidates were crooked egomaniacs.

was an open declaration. In Islamic jihad, he explained, infidels are supposed to be warned of an impending attack so that they can convert and avoid bloodshed.* Once in the city, the *jihadis* had planned to just occupy the place, but they started getting too much pushback from secular Libyans who could see where all this was going after the overthrow of Gaddafi - even if the US State Department could not.

A few days later there was an attempt to kill the British Ambassador, Sir Dominic Asquith, with an RPG, followed an attack on the International Red Cross faculty. On 25 June, Libyan Ambassador Chris Stevens sent a detailed cable to Washington regarding the situation of the ground entitled: Libya's Fragile Security Deteriorates as Tribal Rivalries, Power Plays & Extremism Intensifies.

According to a report by the Senate Select Committee on Intelligence,† the CIA had briefed the US Embassy in Tripoli that Ansar al-Sharia and other Sunni militia were in fact getting training and logistics help from none other than vividly Shi'a Iran's Quds Force. They weren't providing weaponry though, they didn't have to. We'd already flooded the country with arms.

In the State Department's defense, it was trying to clean up the spill in the arms pipeline by rounding up what we could and shipping them to Syria via Turkey. Which of course, made the situation crystal clear.

So in August of 2012, they got both when a Libyan fishing boat called the *Al Entiser* docked in Turkish port of Iskenderan with some 40 tons of military hardware shipped in from

---

* Evidently, this perverse mercy is exercised extremely selectively.

† Released January 2014

Benghazi. It was part of what had been dubbed the "Benghazi pipeline" sanctioned by the US State Department its effort at harnessing the Arab Spring to facilitate regime change across the Middle East without looking like that was exactly what we were doing.

The clandestine transfer of arms in Iskenderan began to blow up when an Islamist "charity" in Turkey laid claim to the goods along with the intended recipients, certain brigades of the Free Syrian Army. The whole affair likely would have stayed quiet except that the Libyans making the deliveries were on what can only be described as a "revolution high": Bragging to local journalists that they'd toppled Gaddafi with these same weapons and now they were going to be kingmakers in Syria. They were acting like the children of helicopter parents on their first weekend at college. In short, they were producing a lot of noise. Given the Obama Administration's "tilt" towards political Islam, the Libyans were also pretty confident that even if they didn't have the official approval of both the Unites States and Iran, they certainly were getting a pass to carry on.

MY BRIEF, HOWEVER, was less concerned with the noise making that the resulting burst eardrums. So, I went to church. To be precise, I went to the Blue Mosque to count minarets. At the risk of peddling in stereotypes, saw more carpet sellers on my walk than I'd ever seen in my life. And since my head was in things religious I noted on my approach the mosque that Jesus might have thrown the moneychangers out of the temple, but the Turkish Ministry of Religion allows the carpet cabal to form a tight perimeter around the place.

The Turks aren't stand-offish like the Chinese or the French ,where the locals go to great lengths to let you know that they can't see you. The Turk seeks you out and is not given to reserve. Nor does he care when your flight is leaving. He has not found you out of innocent hospitality, however, much it might appear at first. "You must not go that way." Said a helpful man called Maheb pointing to the grand entrance. "That way is for Turks. Although, you look very Turkish." I don't. I look as Turkish as the Duke of Edinburgh – but he was the heir to the Greek throne, so what do I know? I do know this: No matter where you go in the world, if a strange man comes out of a crowd to compliment your looks he is a) up to something or b) up to something else. I wasn't interested in peaking behind either curtain.

"Well, that's swell, Mebeb, Thanks for the tip." I started to move off towards the correct entrance when I felt Mebeb's hand on my shoulder.

"I will take you to my shop. I sell the best rugs."

"I'm heading into the mosque, but thanks all the same."

"I'll wait."

"No need."

"I'll wait."

"Please don't."

"These rugs are the best."

"I'm not buying a rug."

"These rugs are the best." He said it louder. "They are…"*

---

*This went on for five minutes that I can't bear to relive. If you want the full effect, read the last ten lines until it pisses you off.

"I'm certain your rugs are fit for a Sultan. But lamentably, I am no Sultan." (Not that I ever heard anyone speaking like that in-country, but I was just trying to escape.)

"We have other things."

"I'm going inside."

I went around to the visitors' entrance under a large open-air covered gallery. Istanbul is about the same latitude as Kentucky, but arid, so it was all very comfortable. Here is where shoes are removed, legs are covered and a headscarf is *de rigueur* for the ladies inside a house of prayer despite Atatürk's best efforts. Still, the Blue Mosque is a mosque. Even the most lackluster Christian can be talked into a wearing a necktie on Easter and my Catholic mother covered her head in church well into the 60's. So, I took off my shoes like a good boy. Big blue bed-sheet sized wraps were given to the ladies and the men in shorts to tie around their waists like sarongs, and another sheet to ladies as a head covering.

I'm not proud of it, but in my profession, we are always stumbling around hoping to run into geopolitical metaphor or international incident. So it was with a shameful anticipation that I was eyeballing a trio of aging British hippy women up the queue. The wore baggy shorts with their sensible cropped hair as fully exposed as their sagging knees. Sure, they wanted to see the cultural wonder that is the Blue Mosque, but as they closed in they started loudly disapproving of all this covering-up and, by Goddess, they were getting awful close to being oppressed.

The teenagers of both sexes helping visitors get into the appropriate kit just ignored them and I'm a little embarrassed to admit that I was looking forward to the epic East v. West contest of wills in the twain. It never happened. The showy, indignant resolve of the old hippies melted away completely when they stepped up to the gals handing out the wraps in polite, blinking piety. They covered their heads and their wrinkled knees, walked a few feet and started complaining to themselves about being sexually oppressed.

Inside, the Blue Mosque certainly felt like church – hushed, quiet, safe and old. The floors were carpeted lushly and I suppose I should have been creeped out walking bare foot with a thousand other sweaty bare feet. I wasn't. The place was magnificent. It's very rare to see masses of tourists so affected by the reverence of those who called it home that they maintain a comfortable hush. Just to make me feel at home here on a fallen earth, there was one American woman speaking very loudly and making herself obvious. With all due respect to Mabeb's Turkish comment, she picked me out as a fellow American on sight and started talking at me. I answered her in German and she went on her confused way.*

Outside, my shoes were waiting for me and a little man at a desk called out for donations. Never let it be said that that Ottomans were not great administrators because when I gave him a couple of Turkish lira, he handed me a neat little pre-printed receipt.

And there, waiting for me outside at the bottom of the steps, was Mabeb. He began walking with me, chatting about his rugs. I tried to lose him a couple of times, but my resolve melted away before polite and insistent capitalism. I reckoned I'd better see

---

* The American abroad should always know a little German – useful when it's best not to be an American. In France, speaking German has the knock-on effect of instantly reminding the locals that they actually do, in fact, speak English. It's the one language that they hate worse.

what other things he had or I'd never get rid of him. I followed him to a stall piled with carpet and half a dozen fellows sitting around drinking tiny cups of coffee. "Very good price." He said.

"I'm not buying a rug."

"But we sell rugs." He paused to let the error in my logic sink in. "We ship it anywhere. Why are you here if not to buy a rug? You can put it on a credit card. Very good price, not like in America."

"You told me you sold other things."

"Well, yes. We sell other rugs. See…good price." He showed me another rug.

"How much?"

"Very good price."

"What is that price?"

"Are you telling me that you don't have a place for this tiny rug? To remember our friendship."

"How much?"

The question seemed to come as a shock. He stared at the rug. "This one?"

"Yes, the one that you're holding right now."

"600 American."

"No." The truth is that it was a beautiful rug and from what little I know about these things it was an extremely good price – but I wasn't about to give the man my credit card.

"400? I will lose money."

"No."

"What do you say is a good price?"

"$20." I was being an ass, but I really did need to shut this thing down and be on my way.

"What?! You're being funny now." He glowered at me. "That's not funny."

"Mabeb, thank you, but I have to go."

"But you said—"

"I said I wasn't buying a rug."

"My mistake, I thought you were a real man."

And that did it. "Mabeb, home décor is woman's work."

It was the only time in Istanbul I thought I might get stabbed.

Purity of race does not exist. Europe is a continent of energetic mongrels.

H.A.L. Fisher (1856-1940)
A History of Europe, 1935

CHAPTER TEN:
BAD CRAZINESS AND THE END OF DAYS

EUROPE, AFTER THE FALL of the Roman Empire was one of the largest societal regressions in the very cyclical history of human civilization. Civic institutions and anything any concept we'd call citizenship had collapsed and were replaced with loyalty oaths to the hierarchy of protection rackets.

From that low point, as the first millennium approached things seemed to actually be getting worse. Which hardly seemed possible to the generally wealthy citizens of Christian Constantinople on the edge of the Muslim world, or the glittering Caliphate of Cordoba at the other edge for the Christian world in Spain.

The Byzantine Emperor was still called the Emperor of the Romans, and he lived in one of the richest and most powerful cities on the planet. True, its possessions in the Levant and North Africa were lost, but the empire had never been a military powerhouse like old Rome. It had survived on clever and cunning diplomacy, setting rival powers against each other and keeping markets open. This was possible only because Constantine had chosen the site of the city wisely at the cross-roads between East and West, surrounded by water on three sides, its defenses were seemingly impregnable.

It's hard to calculate just what was lost in Europe with the collapse of the Roman Empire; it is just too big a concept for most of us to get our heads around. I saw a much smaller version of the regression in that protocol meeting in the Ali Hussein hospital in Nasiriya: the information and resources being hoarded, panicked patients overwhelming a system that is only 55% effective on a good day, doctors hiding from patients, everyone out to get what they can before what little is left of the system collapses. Recreate that scene, not just in a single hospital but in all of them, then throughout the entire government. As infrastructure collapses, let the vibrations rattle down through the markets and shops. Dramatic as it sounds, it's not the sort of thing that's easy to detect in your own world until it is too late. Still, the fact that that meeting – frustrating as it was – was even happening was proof that Iraqi society was trying to pull itself back together.

There were attempts to pull it all together in Europe after the collapse – with Charlemagne and the pope conniving a Holy Roman Empire in hopes of rivaling the eastern Empire. Even those two factors, with the legitimacy of both law and religion behind them ran into the same fundamental problems modern states have when attempting a bit of "nation building." You can't just pull new concepts of government and society out of a box. Rome had not, in fact, been built in a day.

It was in the year that we are now calling 949 AD that the Holy Roman Emperor Otto III was openly mocked in front of his court by an emissary of the mighty caliph of Baghdad for not even having a capital. Possibly uncalled for, but the emissary did have a point. Before you can go building capital cities, however, there are smaller details to sort out: like knowing what year it was.

It was decided that all of Christendom would count from the birth of Christ, and that was almost literally the only thing Christians could agree on. The pope often invoked the dream of Rome to establish legitimacy over the fractious kings and chieftains throughout Europe. Yes, these people believed; they believed with a passion and a certainty that modern sensibilities find near lunatic. The fact is that when push comes to shove between your soul and your neck (or stomach), the neck generally wins out. The pope may have laid claim to a higher authority than that of the European kings, but the popes needed kings and their armies for protection, not the other way around. The church claimed to be the binding tissue in the absence of the Roman imperium, but the lights had dimmed. In the ancient, eternal city itself, the old buildings were still there – somewhat - but they were falling over and the streets were choked with weeds. The old ruins were routinely used as ready campsites for Muslim slaving bands.

Protection rackets of the strong replaced government and rule of law. And here *everyone* needed protection. The thing that needs to be understood about the knights and castles of medieval Europe is that in reality they were less Lord Tennyson's King Arthur and more like Al Capone; crime bosses with hired goons exploiting the one industry available in a collapsed society, agriculture, with a protection racket. The barons, dux and counts had multiple sons (multiple wives happened more and lasted longer than you might think, even after conversion to Christianity) and those sons needed to go out and make little fiefs of their own. In the land grab that followed, society had come unglued.

Way back before Christians could agree on what year it was, Augustine of Hippo (a.k.a. Saint Augustine 354-430 AD) had made a prophecy that the anti-Christ would show up 1,000 years after Christ. The average peasant in the field knew about these things, but didn't take it too seriously. It wasn't a lack of faith, but prophecies were considered mostly symbolic at the time because "it wasn't for man to know." Besides, a strict timeline didn't really matter in a world where no one could agree on what year it was. Once the church settled on a standard calendar, people were suddenly aware that they were closing in on 1,000 years since Christ. They started to wonder if Augustine *had* meant it literally. In a superstitious world where the year millennium loomed uncomfortably close, there were portents all over the place, triggering a lively End of Days scare. For one, thing, there was the weather; storms were getting harder and more erratic and out of season. It was getting hotter, the thermometer hadn't been invented, but anyone could see that the tree-lines getting higher on the mountains as the snowcaps retreating a little further each year.*

While it was good for harvests, it wasn't good for the ones tilling the fields. The local lords and thuggish knights grew fat on

---

* The parallels with modern climate change are too obvious not to point out.

the surpluses, and pressed down harder on the peasants and serfs. In their new power they began to solidify control by ringing off once common ground and woods as private property ringed with tolls. What we'd call income equality was growing dangerously way out of whack – even by the barbaric standards of the day. Personal freedoms were melting away.

The end of days was coming – two of them, in fact. One at the turn of the millennium and, when antichrist failed to arrive on cue, another on the 1,000 year anniversary of the Passion of Christ, reckoned to be 1033.

BACK IN WHAT Christians were calling 868 the center of power of the Muslim world had shifted to Egypt under the Fatimids. Had his Christian subjects explained any of this apocalyptic hand-wring to the Fatimid caliph in Egypt, he'd have likely shrugged as the Muslim world was using a completely different calendar.* The Fatimids practiced Ismailism, a subset of Shi'a Islam. Back in Baghdad, the Sunni caliphs (knowing that the center of gravity had shifted) issued the Baghdad Manifesto claiming that the Fatimids were descendants of Jews. Caliph Al-Hakim was certainly rumored to have been born to a Christian slave in dad's harem. It may not have been true, but it was certainly plausible – and then there were his blue eyes flecked with red. Al-Hakim is one of those historical figures who vacillates from the sublime to full-blown maniac depending on who is telling the tale. At the beginning of his reign in 996 he was by all accounts pretty tolerant of the "People of the Book" living

---

* He'd have also done the calculations much faster, as Arabic numerals are much better for math that the Roman sort.

under his protection, so long as they paid the *jizya* – the "I'm not a Muslim" tax. Then things began to change.

Tensions between sects started to strain under wave after wave of European pilgrims. Fueling the migration was the preoccupation with the end of days. The slow trickle turned into a flood of white people into Jerusalem in order to make the trip before end of the world. Pilgrimage to the Holy Land, however, wasn't a matter of finding a cheap flight to Tel Aviv. The sea journey that was both dangerous and expensive but with the subjugation of Hungary, a peasant could just walk. Cheap, yes. The trip was also dangerous as hell, and uncomfortable in the bargain. With their economic horizons narrowing at home, and the end looming large anyway, peasants across Europe began to slip their villages and lords to make the overland journey on foot. Europe was a place where, for most people, if you walked out of sight from the furthest land mark you recognized, you might well never return home. And given the brutal feudal system ossifying on the old rights of the peasantry, many likely didn't even try to return once they'd seen the mighty and glorious walls of Constantinople – a city that, for all its troubles had never seen its light dimmed by a European dark age. Once 1034 came with no second coming (again), many pilgrims simply asked themselves the obvious question: Why go back at all?*

Living under Muslim rule seemed comparatively easy and free from the deranged knights and barons. Pay your *jizya*, and the local strongman was obliged to leave you more or less alone. He wasn't going to offer you a job, but he wouldn't burn your

---

*The parallels with Europe's current wave of migrants moving in the opposite direction almost exactly a millennium later is also too obvious not to point out.

house down either. The Christians may have called themselves pilgrims, but to the local caliphs, they looked like immigrants. To the local guy in the *souk*, they smelled like refugees.

By 1004, the locals were getting agitated, so al-Hakim decreed that neither Christians nor Jews could celebrate certain rights in the caliphate and were also forced to adopt certain dress. Critics claimed al-Hakim came down hard on Christians because, aware of his own mother's faith, he didn't want to appear soft. Whatever the reason, by 1009 he'd had enough of the migrants and destroyed the Church of the Holy Sepulcher built on the site traditionally held to be where Christ had died.

Local Christians – long accustomed to some degree of freedom – were understandably outraged and ran amok. Al-Hakim, in the name of public order, reacted brutally. The bodies started to stack up. Much to the chagrin of the caliph, the Christian pilgrims kept coming, but now they came in armed bands. Bodies continued to stack up.

The next caliph, eager to deescalate the situation, struck a deal with the Byzantine Emperor Constantine IX, to rebuild the Church of the Holy Sepulcher if Constantine would just foot the bill. He duly agreed.

NONE OF THIS played well in Rome, but the pope had closer fish to fry. Despite the uneasy papal alliance with the Frankish, and later Saxon, Holy Roman Emperors, there was still another tribe that needed to be brought to heel. The newly converted settlers in the North of France, the Nord Men – or Normans – were just giving Europe hell. Being converts they didn't normally have multiple wives, but they loved their mistresses. As a result, little Norman bastards were everywhere.

And if they couldn't inherit a title and land, they'd just make their own. Not to put too fine a point on it, the only marketable skill of the new Norman barons was to fight and fuck. It wasn't that they had a problem fighting other Normans, it's just that they were all so good at it. There was lower hanging fruit in the more laid-back south where they wouldn't know what hit them.

The princes of Italy liked to play war as much as the next guy, but because they didn't like getting their uniforms dirty and hired freelancers to do all the bleeding. And there were a lot of bloodthirsty Norman knights who were willing to come south for the money. What the Italian princes didn't understand with their set-piece battles was that the vicious newcomers planned to stay for the land. Whereas the migrant Christians in the Holy land were pathetic, the migrant Normans were really, really mean. All those self-appointed barons back in France had once been knights. And the knights had once been thugs. The Normans also knew that if you got enough ready dough to build a castle – just a stronghold really – and feed the thugs in it, you could declare yourself a count or baron and terrorize the surrounding countryside into being a fair moneymaker. In those hairy days before Burke's Peerage started publishing upper-class stud books, it didn't really matter how legally dubious the title claim was, provided to locals didn't kill you (that's what the fort was for), after a decade or so your pedigree was a *fait accompli*.

The Norman freebooters were laying Italy to waste. In Spain, the Caliphate of Cordoba might have been past its glory days, but the Muslims were still in Sicily and Malta. The Byzantines (they were still Christians, but they were going on about being the New Rome and that chapped the pope over in old Rome) were still in Greece and even had settlers on the Italian peninsula.

Enter one Pope Leo IX. He came to the papacy as a great reformer, but then again most of them do. Leo actually stayed the course, outlawing simony (selling of church offices) and demanding the priests quit setting up house with their mistresses and scattering unholy bastards all over the place (it just looked bad). Naturally, this pissed the clergy off to no end. Fortunately, Leo had a ready-made life-or-death crisis to deflect the haters at home.

Leo decided that the Normans, who looked intent on burning the whole place down, needed to be sent back to France where that sort of thing was *de rigueur*. To do this, the pope made an alliance with the Byzantines in Italy and began collecting Italian princes to rally his cause. To put a polish on the alliance, in 1050 Leo IX did something that no pope had ever done before. Despite the whole "Thou shalt not kill" business and the prohibition of priests welding weapons and the complete lack of precedent in Christianity, Leo blessed an army preparing for battle. Not only that, said army wasn't going up against the Muslims or pagans, but the (theoretically) Christian Normans. As a cherry on top, the pope pulled a page out of Darius the Great and Muhammad's playbook and promised absolution against the crimes of war to all who answered his call, as well as a generous pension in the afterlife should the effort proved fatal.

At first the campaign was a success and the precedent, while dangerous, looked like an anomaly. The retreating Normans managed to trap themselves between the Papal forces and the Byzantines and sued for a truce. Despite all the "forgive those who trespass against you" business, Leo was not in a humor to forgive. While he was telling the surrendering envoys just how fast they could go to Hell, the Norman cavalry regrouped and smashed into the Papal forces, most of whom fled. Being pope, he wasn't supposed to take part in the fighting, so Leo watched the events unfold from the parapets of a nearby town. When the battle turned, the townsfolk – themselves pretty clear on what an army of worked-up almost-Vikings were capable of – saved themselves by offering up Leo to Normans. Fine Christians all.

Accounts from both sides have the whole thing being fairly awkward at this point. Being Christian, the Normans bowed and asked for Papal forgiveness. Being Normans, they held Leo hostage for nine months until he admitted their right by conquest of Italy.

Once released, Leo slunk back to Rome and declared all those who had fallen in the fight against the Normans to be martyrs. Normans just shrugged their shoulders and kept on killing everybody. In their perverse sense of piety, they also started building churches all over Italy. Still chapped about being held hostage, Leo started casting about for another anti-Norman alliance to settle the matter. Henry III, the Holy Roman Emperor, was still dealing with a revolt in Bavaria and so Leo had to regroup with the Byzantines – and not just some colonists in Italy, either. This time he sent an envoy to the home office.

The fateful delegation Leo sent to Constantinople in 1054 was led by his right-hand man, one Cardinal Humbert. This was a bad choice. When the bishops first saw the honey-colored walls of the city sitting impenetrable on the Bosporus they were awe-struck. In Europe, the Caesars and the Glory of Rome were always being invoked, but as the centuries passed and the ruins grew weedier or fell over, the idea of a glorious Rome had grown more abstract. There was nothing abstract about the twelve miles of unbreachable walls on which sentries still stood watch over the Hagia Sophia and its massive gold dome. Emperors still calling themselves Caesars ruled over citizens still calling themselves *Romani* (despite speaking Greek). The Rome that the bishops knew was a tumble down blight. Constantinople was a Rome still standing. Standing alone and isolated, but gloriously standing.

Cardinal Hubert was more intimidated than impressed. Like a prima dona outshone, he dug his heels in, refusing to admit that the Patriarch of Constantinople could ever be the equal to The Bishop of Rome. The whole trip went predictably downhill from there. Pope Leo IX and Emperor Constantine IX both needed a military alliance against the Normans in Europe and the Seljeck Turks marauding all over Asia Minor. Their situations were both dire and their aims closely aligned, so there was no good reason that Rome and Constantinople should not have been on the same team. As it was, Cardinal Humbert and the Patriarch Michael wanted to argue about religion.

The proceedings took on the flavor of an unhappily married couple bickering over where to eat dinner and drift into dredging up every marital grievance and perceived slight of the last decade. Despite both sides desperately needing the alliance to work, the discussions got hung up on matters of just who is boss, as well as every other theological dispute between the factions of East and West manage to get paraded out and spanked on the fanny.

The upshot being that on 16 July 1054, Cardinal Humbert decided that it would be terribly clever thing to march into the Hagia Sophia and slap a papal bull on the altar excommunicating the Patriarch of Constantinople during mass.* His asinine theatrics completed, Humbert then departed for Rome two days later. Like our bickering married couple, they never actually made it to the needed dinner. But they did get a divorce.

As Pope Leo had died prior to the showdown, the Patriarch claimed it wasn't a valid excommunication. By that point, however, it was just splitting hairs. Rome was holding strong in its claim to be the head of the church – but it was paying a heavy price, as said church was now cleaved in two. And there were still Normans running afoul all over the damn place.

Three years (and two popes) later, Stephen IX, who had been called Bishop Frederick when he'd stood there in the Hagia Sophia watching Humbert pull his little stunt, attempted to kiss and make up. It didn't take. On Stephen's death, things got weird.

One Pope Benedict X was elected, but as the Holy Roman Emperor's appointee, he was accused of buying his election. So the College of Cardinals elected their own pope, Nicholas II, and called the other fellow Anti-pope. Obviously, the situation was both hairy and fluid and Nicholas, evidently not convinced the will of God was enough to keep him on the throne, entered into an alliance with those experts in the hairy, fluid and theatrically violent – the Normans. Nicholas II thought it would really look great if he were able to retake Sicily, long a stronghold of the

---

*For the non-Catholic reader, that a fairly sizable turd in the punchbowl.

Muslims, for Christianity.* Not thinking the Italians up to the task (or they'd have already done it), Nicholas first sent the Normans to Galeria where Antipope Benedict was holed up. Once that was taken care of, they then rode south to eat Sicily. The Muslims didn't know what hit them. The Normans, for their part, were on a roll and just sailed on to Malta and took it as well.

Meanwhile, the cold Holy War between Christians and the Muslims was hotting up. The next pope, Alexander II, didn't so much condemn the massacre of Jews, but did praise those who resisted the urge. This low bar of tolerance was lowered further still when he promoted a crusade against the Muslims in Spain with the Crusade of Barbastro. He also sanctioned William the Conqueror's invasion of England in 1066 because it really was just more practical to give the Normans what they wanted. They'd just take it anyway.

A MERE 700 YEARS before the United States enshrined the separation of church and state into its constitution, things were coming to a head over the same between the new Pope Gregory VII and King Henry IV, (but not yet anointed) heir to the title Holy Roman Emperor.

One of Gregory's first reforms was to ensure that the election of new popes was handled entirely through the College of Cardinals. The practical advantages of the sword over the cross had kept the popes playthings to the Holy Roman Emperors. Henry had come to the throne at the age of five, and

---

*The strongholds of Islam in Europe were marked by normal levels of poverty, as opposed to the near total medieval European variety.

had himself been the plaything of various German princes throughout his childhood. When he hit drinking age, he had every intention of exercising every ounce of control he could.

Henry declared that Gregory had forfeited the papacy and appointed another to the throne, Clement III. Gregory excommunicated Henry. This put the king out of sorts with his Italian possessions and then the German princes started to abandon him too. Thinking he was losing his support at home, Henry wrote to Gregory asking for forgiveness. The ever-merciful pope, sensing weakness in his rival, decided to head to Germany to lecture the boy in front of his own court because that would really show him. Realizing some ritual humiliation was needed to get the Pope's forgiveness, Henry put together an entourage to head to Italy to take his dressing down where his friends wouldn't see it. In December, the royal entourage crossed the Alps seeking forgiveness.

Meanwhile, Gregory and entourage was on the way to Germany to deliver his ecclesiastical finger-wagging. His spies came back with word that Henry was coming over the ice-covered mountains and was now in Italy. Naturally Gregory thought Henry was coming to hack his papacy into tiny pieces, so he fled to a nearby castle called Canossa and locked himself inside. Henry, it turned out, was begrudgingly willing to submit to his ritual humiliation and penance outside of Canossa for three days until Gregory let him in to talk. The upshot of the talks was that rule of Europe would be divided into two realms – the temporal and spiritual. Essentially, the two men agreed to keep out of each other's wheelhouses.

They didn't actually do it, you understand, the split was more ideal than practical. Pope Gregory would go on to excommunicate Henry IV twice more and the antipope Clement held on through the death of Gregory and the short reign of his successor, Victor II. Clement was still claiming to be the pope in 1088 when the Gregory's most devoted and high-strung assistant was made Pope Urban II. Since Canossa, the power of the papacy had been growing in a way that surprised even the church itself.

In a trick that would later work for the Mamluks of Egypt, the Ottoman Turks and ironically most of the liberal world's democracies as well as socialist autocracies, the church took control of European affairs not by firing the soul or ideology of the public acclaim. In a mostly illiterate world, they did it through a willingness to do the paperwork. Taking power by revolution or coup d'état makes a hell of a splash, and will get you some flattering statues for your trouble. But these bold moves tend to invite blowback. If you want to take over a realm in a way that no one gives you any static, just volunteer to do the filing and data-entry. They'll never get rid of you, nor will they really know what you are up to because it's all too boring and tedious. And so the church solidified its power in the temporal world without sacrificing its spiritual domain.

It was a great play if you could hold onto your gains and Urban II intended too. He'd been born Odo to noble parents, made Prior of legendary monastery of Cluny* before being snatched up by Pope Gregory to the College of Cardinals. He may have spent most of his adult life in a monastery but Odo had been born in a castle over-looking an expanse of peasantry lovingly exploited by his father's thuggish knights. Unlike the

---

*Then considered the holiest place in Europe.

humble born Gregory, he knew how the nobility of his day worked, and he knew it in his bones.

Meanwhile Henry, the Holy Roman Emperor, made a series of political missteps and Odo, now Pope Urban II, ruthlessly exploited them. The QED being that Henry and his antipope found themselves boxed up somewhere in northern Italy. Urban assessed the situation: The Normans had taken Sicily and Malta back for the church, making the Mediterranean somewhat secure for Christian sea traffic and breaking the back of the Muslim slave trade (at least as far as Europe was concerned). The freeing up of Christian souls was undoubtedly swell, but if you've ever had to move heavy cargo you'll recognize the other advantage that seaport of Sicily and Malta brought to Europe as a whole.

Now Urban was looking east to the holiest place on earth, lost to heretical Constantinople, old Jerusalem was in the hands of the Muslims. That wouldn't do at all. Admittedly, the city still had absolutely no strategic value, but like the armies of Islam had seen a couple of centuries earlier, it had *meaning*. And now, thanks to the Normans of all people, he could get there.

The only things that could make the vision go pear-shaped was that the European neuvo-nobility was still running amok hacking each other to pieces.

SOMEWHAT CONVENIENTLY for Urban, the Eastern Christians were having a tough time of it. For that matter, so were the Arabs. If Europe had had the Normans to contend with, Asia Minor had the Seljuk Turks who'd come out of Central Asia tearing up everything in their path. Like the Normans, they'd been converted to the prevailing religion, even became pious in their own savage way, but it hardly slowed them down. Even the Caliph of Baghdad, once the center of gravity of the Muslim world, had become a servant of the Seljuk Sultan Alp Arslan.

The Byzantines had tried their usual diplomatic tango to avoid pitched battle, but the Seljuks would have none of it. They soundly defeated the Byzantine forces under Emperor Romanus IV Diogens at Manzikert in modern Albania in 1071. Romanus was captured and thrown to the ground before Alp Aslan, who ceremoniously but his foot on the emperor's neck. Ultimately, the sultan decided that he liked the emperor and let him go home after that. Alp was like that.

The humiliation was great fun, but neither Alp Arslan nor his son, Malik Shah, had any real designs of capturing Constantinople. They rode onward to take a swing at the Fatimid's, currently suffering a famine in Egypt. Knowing that it would chap both the Shi'a Fatimids as well as the Christians, the Seljuks stopped off at Jerusalem to wreck the place and hand it over to the now subservient Sunni Caliph of Baghdad. If you're counting, this sounds an awful like the deal the popes had struck with the marauding Normans over Sicily and Malta.

Then in 1085, Malek Shah took Antioch, the richest city in the Levant. To celebrate afterward, Malek dipped his sword ceremoniously into the Mediterranean laying claim to all of it. No one in Europe found this legally binding – just galling. When Malek Shah died in 1091, his kingdom fell into infighting between his sons and nephews and the new Byzantine Emperor Alexius saw his chance to strike back. First, however, he needed to find friends.

His imperial appeal was addressed to Count Robert of Flanders (a Norman and cousin of William the Conqueror) but

Alexius knew that it would be passed on to Pope Urban. It recounted horrible crimes committed against Christians and their holy shrines:

> The enemy has the habit of circumcising young Christians and Christian babies above a baptismal font. In derision of Christ they let the blood flow into the font. Then they are forced to urinate in the font... Those who refuse are tortured and put to death. They carry off noble matrons and their daughters and abuse them like animals... Then too, the Turks shamelessly commit the sin of sodomy on our men of all ages and all ranks... and O misery, something that has never been seen or heard of before, on bishops...

Having captured everyone's attention with sacrilege and all manner of rape, Alexius then mentions the massive wealth of Constantinople:

> And if it should happen that these holy relics should offer no temptation to the pagans, and if they only wanted gold, then they would find in this city more gold than exists in all the rest of the world. The Churches of Constantinople are loaded with a vast treasure of gold and silver, gems and precious stones, mantles and cloths of silk, sufficient to decorate all the churches in the world...
>
> And then, too, there are the treasures in the possession of our noblemen, not to mention the treasure belonging to our merchants who are not noblemen. And what of the treasure belonging to the emperors, our predecessors? ... for it includes not the treasuries of the emperors

but also those of the ancient Roman emperors brought here and concealed in the palace. What more can I say?

The suffering of fellow Christians likely did aggrieve Urban, the man was a true believer, but that mention of gold certainly caught his eye. As the Caliphate of Cordoba collapsed in Spain, the church had made out well on the loot of Muslim gold. And here was the richest city in the world, as well as a rival Cristian center of gravity just there for the taking.

Alexius's letter wraps things back around to the Church of the Holy Sepulcher falling into Turkish hands, before finishing by describing the "beautiful women of the Orient." No record exists of what Urban thought of this last bit.

Were the tales of woe recounted in the letter true? Probably grossly exaggerated, but they likely weren't complete lies, either. Whereas the Arab Muslims and the Christians had learned to co-exist (more or less) in each other's universe, the Turks were usurpers, and like all usurpers, they had something to prove.

So, in 1095, in a field in Clermont, France, Pope Urban II spoke to a gathering of about 300 – some nobles, some commoners. There is no accurate text of the speech, however, just the way chroniclers tended to remember it. Urban struck on a grand idea to keep the princes of Christendom from killing each other: Go kill a bunch of foreign looking outsiders with the inspiring slogan, "God Wills it."*

---

*Modern Theologians, and the religiously sane, debate this. Interestingly, both the Bible and Qur'an advise against trying to divine the will of God. *Plus ça change.*

Pope Urban may have sold the whole operation as an exercise in retaking the Holy Land for God's greater glory, but this was also the foreign distraction needed for European nobles to go fight the Muslims (who appeared to be on the retreat), take a symbolic city of Jerusalem (and its gold), and possibly even strangle Constantinople itself into submission (and take its gold too).

Superficially, Urban's call was to get the nobility to stop their in-fighting and do some fighting someplace else. Urban likely thought that he had landed on a sensible plan until a group of people he'd never really considered glommed onto the idea and things took a wholly different course. As a nobleman, the pope knew all too well that you armed a peasant at your own risk. At best, it wouldn't do you much good, at worst, it just might get you killed. Suddenly, the peasants all started calling out "God wills it", sewing crosses to their shirts. The hoi polloi may have questioned whether or not a great personage as the pope had actually been speaking to them, but in the end, it didn't matter. The dread millennium had come and gone without a fiery and blood-soaked apocalypse, so everyone was feeling expansive.* A fiery preacher called Peter the Hermit assembled an army of peasants and b-list knights and they all just started walking towards Jerusalem.

---

*Don't sneer: it took only 18 months into the next millennium for al-Qaeda to take a completely suicidal swing against the "West", triggering invasions into Muslim Middle East and central Asia, which triggered an ISIS – with the professed mission of triggering the apocalypse. The Millennium is like a full moon on crystal meth.

Caedite eos. Novit enim Dominus qui sunt eius.

"Kill them. For the Lord knows those that are
His own."

CHAPTER ELEVEN:
KILL 'EM ALL, LET GOD SORT 'EM OUT

WESTERN ACCOUNTS tend to mark the speech at
Clermont as the starting bell of the Crusades, but the Muslim
world doesn't see it that way. They mark the beginning about a
century earlier, when all those Christian pilgrims that started
showing up with an annoying habit of hanging around for the
rest of their lives.* Local leaders thought that the migration was
fine for the tax base as long as the *jizya* were paid. The Normans,
on the other hand, were retaking lands Christians had long lost
to conquering Muslims in Sicily and Malta. Since the Caliphate
of Cordoba had fractured, the Christian King Alfonso was giving
the Muslims hell in Spain. An army of what the Arabs called the
Franks, hurling themselves at the civilized environs of the various
caliphates was just the same soup reheated. Despite the religious
rhetoric flying left and right, the whole thing looked a lot like a

---

*An aggravation the Middle East is now repaying Europe in spades.

trade war for control of the Mediterranean. From where the Muslims were sitting, it hardly qualified as a Holy War. Not yet at any rate.

While Europe was wallowing in its dark ages, it bears remembering that the ninth through the 14th centuries are widely regarded as Islam's golden age. The Arab world cultivated centers of art and culture and education: Taking the traditions of Persia, as well as Graeco-Roman thought and philosophy, and refining it still further while the average guy in Europe spent his days trying not to get worked to death, or just murdered, by his landlord. And *his* landlord spent his days trying not to be killed by the other landlords in the neighborhood. And those were the men. The women really had it rough. No wonder the common man glommed onto the call to go someplace else with such regrettable fury. No wonder the People's Crusade had a lot of women in it.

Byzantium also had that Eastern vibe – it was rich, urban and educated. They were Christians but couldn't quite put their finger on why the grand Patriarch of Constantinople or the emperors, who were the continuation of the unbroken line of ancient caesars should submit to a crumbling back-water like Rome. In short, the Byzantines were colossal snobs because they could afford to be.

So, in 1096, when the Peter the Hermit's Peoples Crusade appeared in front of the impregnable walls of Constantinople, the emperor didn't know what to make of them. While there is no way to tell at this distance, but it was likely something along the lines of "ΩΤΦ?"* Was this the army that Rome had sent to

---

* WTF?

rescue Christendom? While he appreciated their enthusiasm, Alexius wasn't about to let a pestilent and hungry beggar mob of refugees into the city. Suggesting instead that they stay put and wait for the real army to arrive.

And there was a real army in the offing. Four of them in fact: Under Raymond of Saint-Gilles, Godfrey of Bouillon, Hugh of Vermandois, and Bohemond of Taranto. Still another army had formed under one Count Emicho, but never made it out of Germany because they got so distracted killing Jews who were a) not at all Muslim and b) no-where near the Holy land.

In his defense, Peter the Hermit, also known as Cucu-Peter, had no way of knowing that the big four had mobilized about the time he'd arrived. Peter would not listen the emperor's calls to hold back because a) he knew whose side God was on, and b) no matter how pious a fellow, if given the choice between being the glorious leader of a divine army of light, and squatting alone in a damp cave, he'll chose glory. The People's Crusade crossed the Bosporus to a camp called Cibotus, where Peter decided that it might actually be a good idea to wait for the main force. Not in a mood to cool their heels, his worked up army relived him of his command and started attacking the surrounding Christian villages killing and looting along the way. They seized an unoccupied fortress and in a fit of blood-soaked piety, praised the Almighty for their victory. Eight days later the Turks arrived and massacred all inside.

Eventually, the four "princely" armies for which Alexius had called did arrive, but they weren't allowed in either. An Army of God is *still* an army, you understand The Emperor, suspicious of the Crusader's ultimate war aims, and knowing full well what Normans, Franks and the like got up to when on road trips, demanded that the Crusaders swear allegiance to him. All but Bohemond refused.* The Franks and the Byzantines didn't like each other, and it wasn't a tight alliance, but they did hold it together long enough to take Nicaea (in modern Iznik, Turkey), the Seljuk Capital in Anatolia in May of 1097.

The Crusader army then moved south to the wealth of Antioch. The siege took about a year, but the city eventually fell. Almost immediately the European princes started arguing about who got to claim the real estate for their portfolio. No one ran this by Alexius, but he needed the alliance to hold, so there he was. In the end it went to Bohemond, who failed to see how this contradicted the oath he was currently ignoring.

Six months after Antioch, the army set out for the main prize: Jerusalem. By now, the Holy City was no longer held by the Seljuk Turks but the Shi'a Fatimid's of Egypt.† In July of 1099, the Franks laid siege to the city and promised protection to its citizens (most were Christian anyway) on surrender. The City was surrendered and the Franks proceeded to kill everyone inside.

Having achieved a couple of quick, if messy victories, and then convincing themselves that it was by the hand of God, the main armies went home. Not all of them, of course, Europe really was a train-wreck at the time. Enough stayed to establish four Crusader States in the Levant: Jerusalem, Edessa (now Urfa in the southeast of modern Turkey, close to the Syrian border),

---

* Bohemond never took his oaths seriously anyway.

† The Crusaders didn't know the difference, they just called them all "Saracens", a term that meant nothing to the Muslims or the Arabs. Then again, the Muslims called all the Europeans "Franks."

Antioch (also in Turkey, but near the Mediterranean coast), and Tripoli (the one in Lebanon, not Libya).

WHILE THE EAST was more culturally and technologically advanced, there was one innovation the Franks would introduce with wild abandon: Building castles everywhere. Once you get used to the idea that the surrounding countryside wants you dead, castles are just something you get good at building. The whole Frankish building spree left both the Seljuk Turks and the Arabs baffled and more than a little offended. By 1130, the Saracens had regrouped and started to hit back.

Annoying, yes, but it wasn't until 1147 when a Seljuk general and governor of Mosul called Zanqi captured the northernmost of the Crusader states, Edessa, that a new call to arms was made in Europe. This was a shock because Christians everywhere had been told that God's verdict in the last war was final.

The Second Crusade of 1147-1149, headed by Louis VII of France and Conrad III of Germany, started badly with a Frankish defeat. The forces regrouped and massed about 50,000 men in Jerusalem. This startled the devil out of the ruler of Damascus, who called on one Nur al-Din (Zanqi's successor in Mosul) for help against the force now moving his direction. Nur al-Din showed up and dealt the Franks another crushing defeat. As usually happens when a weak state calls on a strong force for help, Nur al-Din stayed and took over Damascus as the price for saving the city.

WITH THE SCORE now tied two all – the Kingdom of Jerusalem attempted a two-point conversion by attacking Egypt. So al-Din sent a general, Shirkuh - who you've probably never heard of – and his nephew, Saladin – who you probably have – to go kick the Franks out of Egypt in 1169. Which they promptly did. Nur al-Din died a few years later and Saladin seized power in Mosul and Damascus. After that the man was hard to stop. Yet Saladin's first order of business had nothing to do with the Franks, but to get control of the Sunni - Shi'a spilt that divided his own house before turning his considerable attention to the Crusader Kingdoms.

Saladin is a fascinating figure – even by contemporary Christian accounts. The chroniclers who are generally trusted as well as the letters of those who actually dealt with the man describe him as a master tactical politician, a brilliant soldier and an honorable gentleman in the bargain. He was magnanimous in victory, at least by the brutal standards of the day. During one of several short-term truces with Jerusalem, Saladin provided the city with famine relief in the form of grain supplies. Make no mistake, though, his ultimate goal was always to take the city.

When a political trombone named Guy of Lusigan took over Jerusalem through a convenient marriage and the support of the fanatical Knights Templar, Saladin saw his chance. Guy was a politician, not a warlord, so it was some bad luck he was facing off with one of the best military minds of his generation. He allowed Saladin's forces to wear his cavalry out in the July sun – far away from water or shade. The Crusaders occupied an old lava field at the foot of an extinct volcano called the Horn of Hattin which baked the infantry and rendered the cavalry ineffective on the strange soil. Thus softened up, the forces of Guy of Lusigan were utterly destroyed at Hattin. Saladin while famous for his chivalry, thought the fanatic Knight Templar so dangerous that after the Battle of Hattin, he broke with his long standing habit and ordered all the unmoored Templar prisoners killed.

With the score tied, the third Crusade became a *jihad* tie-breaker. This one was led by the growing powers of Europe that were starting to pull Christendom out of its complete and paralyzing feudalism. Its leading lights were Frederick Barbarossa of Germany, King Philip II of France and his childhood chum and (very likely closeted adult boyfriend), King Richard I of England. For his part, Frederick Barbarossa did not die hacking Muslims to pieces like the fine Christian soldier that he was. After getting overheard in his armor he rode into a stream, and the as the cold water rushed around, it gave him a heart attack and he drowned. Philip, on balance didn't make too fine a showing either – he was pouty by nature. But Richard really made a name for himself. Everyone started calling him "Lionheart."

In September 1191, Richard's forces defeated the Saladin's army at the Battle of Arsuf – the only true engagement of the third Crusade. Having recaptured Jaffa down the coast, Richard managed to re-establish some Christian control in the region, but refused to lay siege to Jerusalem. In September of the next year, Richard and Saladin signed a peace treaty that re-established Jerusalem, but curiously without the City of Jerusalem itself.

Let's call that one a draw, shall we?

THE FOURTH CRUSADE, came violently off brand and suffered what modern MBA's and foreign policy wonks call "Mission Creep." For a modern example of this, check out nearly any aspect of the War on Terror: Osama bin Laden pulled his 9/11 attack and we wanted to kill him. To do this, we reasonably invaded his hide-out in Afghanistan. Then we found him next door in Pakistan living with friends that we thought we'd bought and paid for, and killed the fella in 2011. At of this writing in 2021 – we're still glad-assing around watching our attempts at nation building not work in either Afghanistan or Iraq – which we also invaded despite having nothing to do with al Qaeda, bin Laden, or even political Islam. We then armed the men who'd fought against us in Iraq to overthrow the government in Libya. We *backed* an attempted regime change in Syria, then changed our minds about it and, evidently to help our sworn enemies in Iran, helped keep the last guy in power. While we chew on how fun it'll be to trigger a regime change in Tehran.

Back at the turn of the 13th century, Pope Innocent III called for another crusade in 1203. The Franks, however, had other ideas. The "Glory Be to the Father" stuff was lovely, but down in the dirt business was business. The princes had decided that regime change was needed* – not of the Seljuk's (they were on they were way out anyway) but to swap out the entirely Christian Byzantine emperor in Constantinople for his nephew. The new emperor, knowing exactly who put him on the throne, submitted to the authority in Rome. None of which went down well at street level. Less than a year later the new guy was strangled in a palace coup. In 1204, the Crusaders declared war on quite Christian Constantinople, sacked the city, slaughtered its inhabitants, and basically painted the place in blood. Thus, was established the Latin Kingdom of Constantinople which lasted from 1204 to 1261, when the Byzantines finally got their city back.

---

* See…

As far as the Crusades go, the operations never really regained their focus after that. There was the Albyensian Crusade – fought against a sect of Christians in France. The Crusaders couldn't really tell who to kill because the proper Catholic and the heretics had all been living in the neighborhood since forever. When asked what to do about it. The papal legate reportedly said, *"Caedite eos. Novit enim Dominus qui sunt eius."* For those of who didn't have 12 years of Catholic schooling: "Kill them. For the Lord knows those that are His own." Which translates closely to the gun-nut vernacular as "Kill 'em all, let God sort 'em out."

The Baltic Crusades of 1211-25 were against pagans in Transylvania. The Children's Crusade of 1212 – while famous was completely off the books because only the pope can call a crusade. This one had been whipped up by a 12-year old named Stephen of Cloyes, who claimed to have a letter from Christ telling him to organize a children's crusade. He raised and army of 15,000 to 30,000 children and planned to just walk to the holy land because, per the letter Jesus had sent him, the Mediterranean Sea would part for them *a la* Moses. The army reached Marseilles and the sea did no such thing. Two merchants agreed to take the little rascals free of charge, but once at sea a storm took down two ships and the remaining five turned south to Algiers where the little knee-biters were sold into slavery.

Just before Pope Innocent died in 1216, he tried to take the cause back to its roots by attacking Egypt (where most of the crusader kids had ended up). There the Crusaders were defeated by Saladin's nephew Al-Malik al-Kamil. In 1229, there was a peaceful transfer of Jerusalem, but the treaty expired a decade later. Another crusade was organized by Louis IX in 1248-1254 but it too failed. After two centuries of catastrophic failures and wildly expensive almosts, Europe had lost its taste for crusades and the lost cause of the Holy Land.

Which is not to say things settled down. By 1260, the Middle East was changing: the Seljuks were ousted by invading Mongols who divided Anatolia into manageable emirates. Constantinople still stood in the east, but crippled – ironically, its mortal wound having been delivered by the Catholic Franks rather than the Armies of Islam.

Soon, however, one of those emirates, under a chieftain called Ossman, began to dominate the region. As the Ossomans – called Ottomans in the West – expanded, Constantinople could see the new threat. Despite the bad blood with Rome, Byzantine Emperor John V was still trying to get money out of West when he – while still retaining the official title of *en Christo Autocrator** – agreed to become the vassal of the Ottoman Sultan Mural I in 1373.

If nothing else, the sultan kept John on his throne in a civil war with his son. It wasn't out of the goodness of Mural's heart, though. His own son was also launching a civil war against dad. The two rebellious rascals joined in a joint civil war against their fathers. They were duly crushed.

DESPITE THE NEAR FANATICAL religious devotion of many Europeans, the *Christo Autocrator* subjecting himself to a Muslim sultan didn't move the needle as much as you might think. Europe had grown tired of (for the moment) of its global

---

*Autocrat in Christ. It really doesn't ring well in modern ears.

adventurism and had turned to domestic issues. The rise of Europe had begun, and so had the fight to control it.

In 1328, Charles IV of France had died without brothers or sons and his nearest male relative was Edward III of England. This went down about as well as expected in France,* where the crown was passed to one Philip, Count of Valios. The ensuing zaniness is remembered as the Hundred Years War and it produced a political innovation that gave rise in Europe of the notion of a national identity as opposed to the masses just being mere playthings of the noble families. It is a notion now so ingrained in the Western mind that we can't well conceive of a world without it. The upshot being that we think that this core concept is more universal that it actually is. And in that century lay the seeds of the current disconnect between the West and the Middle East – and the legalistic marker of nation as the paramount marker of identity.

European nobility had been building castles and keeps all over hell's half acre for centuries. Now they really got serious about it. The main technical innovation forged out of the crisis was the building of castles and fortified cities that could withstand the crude artillery now rearing its ugly head across the continent. The last dying heave of the Hundred Years War ended in the defeat of the English with the siege of Castillion in Gascony, in southern France. Happening as it did the same summer as events on the other end of the Mediterranean, it signaled a tectonic shift in both technology and geo-politics. It is hard to overstate the global impact of what happened during the summer of 1453.

---

*They still don't seem to have quite gotten over it.

That was the year Sultan Muhammed (Metmed) II, finally did what all of Europe had been waiting for and breached the walls of Constantinople, the most fortified city in Europe, if not the world. They did it with a standing army of a dedicated military caste – which no king in Europe had or could afford – and new heavy artillery that the Great Powers had better get and figure out a way to afford. What that artillery meant was that all those fortified cities and forts were no longer as impenetrable as once believed.

Huge, stone hurling bombards had breached the walls of Constantinople – famously with a gigantic bastard of one called *bogazkesen,* or more adorably in English "Cutter of Throats." Despite hysterical reports in Europe, it really wasn't a Jericho style razing of the walls. After a lengthy siege, the Ottoman forces managed to punch a big enough hole in the defenses to get into the starving city and rampage through the place until every house, church and most of the streets were slick with blood. Just as the Europeans had expected both the attack and ultimate defeat, they were also aware that given their own policies on mercy and quarter, they wouldn't receive any.

After Turkish victories at Kosovo Polji and in Hungary, this was like the other Muslim shoe dropping on Christendom. The Ottomans started to pose a real threat to Europe as they crawled through the Balkans over the next decades to the far side of the Adriatic, their massive and ominously named bombards ready to pummel fortified walls to rubble.

Just as the Muslim world doesn't see the crusades kicking off in 1095, but a century earlier, they don't see the matter wrapping up in 1254 either. In Muslim eyes, that business Christendom called the Crusades didn't end until the "Romans"were turned out of the Levant altogether.

The summer of 1453 was also a watershed in the way that Europe, and for that matter Christendom, saw itself as a unified people or concept. The medieval mind had put so much truck in Divine Providence that someone's guilt being determined by Trial by Combat was considered a sensible idea supported by the people. And yet, here was a massive defeat at the hands of a Muslim army that was clearly not on the side of the Almighty's true church. All of which raised the alarming question that would be asked on either side of the fight over the centuries: Just whose side was God on?

In light of all this, most European princes politely ignored the new call for yet another crusade to retake Constantinople. Instead they devoted themselves to centralizing governments and building states that could repel looming external threats. The great powers of France and Spain now had to contend with the Ottoman court – called the Sublime Porte – as another member of the club. And that was that.

A century later, under the modestly named Suleiman the Magnificent, the Ottoman Empire included all of what we call the Middle East and North Africa, Greece and the dodgy parts of eastern Europe. It was only in Spain where the Christian kings, united under the banner of *Reconquista*, were able to push back at the Moors, finally defeating the last Muslim kingdom on the peninsula at the Battle of Grenada in 1492.

FOR ALL THE trouble the Crusader kingdoms caused, they were really just some wealthy cities clinging to the coastline. The Muslim world, however, had both western and eastern approaches, nor was Christianity the only religion having a slap fight with itself.

There was a perfectly good reason that Saladin, a Sunni Kurd, got his house in order over the Shia-Sunni spilt. And there is a fair argument to be made that Sunni Islam became dominant because it was the forces of Sunni Islam that knocked out the Franks during the Crusades.*

The forces of Islam came out of Arabia and conquered Persia just prior to the Sunni-Shi'a spilt with the fall of the Sasanian Empire in 651, leading to the rapid decline of the religion of Cyrus and Darius, Zoroastrianism. And even now it's a bit grating to a great many Sunni that so many of the great Sunni poets and thinkers from Islam's Golden Age were, in fact, Persians.

In the summer of 1500, one Ismail I, from the Azerbaijan region of northeastern Iran, started making inroads into the region. Two years later he declared himself the Shah of Iran. By 1508, he had seized Baghdad, whereupon he started, ISIS like, to destroy the Sunni shrines in the city. His Safavid Dynasty was Shi'a, but his suppression of the existing Sunni faith where ever he went was so brutal and absolute that it almost certain that there was more to it than theology. His was an expansionist empire and he was very likely attempting to build an imperial identity completely separate from the Ottomans. A pro-Safavid rebellion in nominally Ottoman Anatolia succeeded until Selim I took the Ottoman throne and took the fight into Iran in 1514.

---

* The Council of Foreign Relations estimates that 85% of the worlds Muslims are Sunni, and the majority of the remaining 15% that are Shi'a live in Iran. The country with the second largest Shi'a population is the United States

Ismail had developed an air and reputation for invincibility, which was tarnished by a pretty decisive loss. The Ottoman's annexed all of Anatolia and Mesopotamia, but left Ismail in charge of Persia. The borders of his empire now set, Ismail set to converting the Mosques to Shi'a only, and adopted a "convert or die" policy without much wiggle room. He was a hard guy. When Selim demanded a ransom for Ismail's kidnapped wife, he refused to pay it.

For all that, Ismail is something of an enigma. The man was actually a well regarded poet who wrote under the pen-name of Hatayi which means something like "One who got it wrong." Ironically for such a religious zealot, he also became something of a drunk in his later days.

Between the Shi'a east and the Christian west, lay the Ottomans in the center of it all. The foreigners who came across the wide frontiers paid the levies, picked up and left ideas and goods, and generally left the place teaming. As a caliphate, the Ottoman Sultan's rule was both temporal and spiritual, so didn't have to contend with the dueling loyalties caused by the agreement in Canossa. While absolute, it was also loosely organized with the different provinces somewhat autonomous. Religious and ethnic minorities were (generally) left alone under the Millet system so long as they paid the "I'm not a Muslim" tax. The autonomy lead to general stability and expansion, but it wasn't exactly equal. Christians in the European provinces were subject to a 20% tax on their sons – creepily called the "Boy Tax."* The little fellas were hauled off to Istanbul where they

---

*It should be noted that the Ottomans were savvy enough administrators to round the figure to the nearest whole boy.

were converted to Islam, trained as slaves to go into either the army or administrative services. Evidently very well trained because a few generations later they were wealthy, powerful and effectively running the bureaucracy of the empire. Hungarian and Serbian parents were bribing authorities to take their little bundles of Christian joy and hammer them into effective Muslim bureaucrats.

It bears repeating the timeless historical lesson here being that if you are angling for regime change, you're better off with a creeping take-over of the Central Budget Office than staging a dramatic palace coup.

Despite the Qur'an's pronouncements that "God hath permitted trade" and, furthermore "Only God can fix prices", the Ottoman Sultans made the same mistake that governments will when they get comfortable: They reasoned that it they grew powerful taxing the trade that came through their gate, they could make so much more owning the trade outright.

This made doing business expensive for the Europeans who hit the sea lanes to get around the Ottoman tariffs. In 1488, a Portuguese sailor named Bartolomeu Dias rounded the Cape of Good Hope around Africa to find an alternate route to the Indian Ocean. Four years later, as the Moors lost their foothold in Spain, Christopher Columbus went west to find India the long way around. Strictly speaking he failed miserably but was way ahead of his time with the all-inclusive Caribbean vacation package. Italy was inventing modern banking and using the great wealth of the Italian states to fund great leaps forward in art, science, exploration and commerce.

As the major power on the block, it was the Ottomans who now waded into European conflicts. In 1522, Sultan Sulieman the Magnificent expanded Ottoman rule into Serbia,* which really freaked out the Holy Roman Emperor and the rest of the Hapsburg dynasty (which is very close to the same thing but not entirely). France, being a rival to the Hapsburg domination of Europe thought that the Ottoman expansion was, well, it wasn't *good*, but it had its uses.

Four years later, Sulieman I defeated the Hungarian King Louis II in an attempt at regime change which led to the inevitable civil war. And this led to the first siege of Vienna in 1529 at the "invitation" of the French. The siege ultimately failed although the Ottomans stayed on as a presence in Hungary, bristling at the borders of the Christian world.

Francis I of France made an alliance with the Ottomans against the Hapsburgs, and was thrown in prison in Madrid for the sin. In 1531, after being sprung from jail, Francis explained his reasoning behind what the rest of Christendom called an unholy alliance to the Venetian ambassador, Giorgio Gritti:

> I cannot deny that I wish to see the Turk all-powerful and ready for war, not for himself – for he is an infidel and we are all Christians – but to weaken the power of the emperor, to compel him to make major expenses, and to reassure all the other governments who are opposed to such a formidable enemy.

Later, during the Italian wars, the French invited the same Muslims the Normans had thrown out of Italy back in. It was messy.

*Those in the modern Middle East griping about the long-lasting damage done by Sykes-Picot at the end of World War I have a painfully valid point. However, Europe is still cleaning up the mess of Ottoman's deciding to eat Serbia.

For the time being, though, Istanbul was still Midgard – the center of the world – and Ottomans were almost everywhere. Not just in Asia and the sunny Mediterranean Sea, either. In 1627, they raided Iceland of all places.

Oh, east is East, and West is West, and never the twain shall meet...

Rudyard Kipling

CHAPTER TWELVE:
NEVER THE TWAIN SHALL MEET

"FUCK THE EU" the waiter had told me over my eggplant, as the *ezan* singing out in my ears. I was plotting an exit strategy from the restaurant that didn't involve my purchasing my freedom with a swell rug. Although, I'm pretty sure that Mrs. M would have thought it was a fair enough trade. The man added, after a bit of reflection, "Although, it would be good for both of us."

At the time, I'll admit, I thought that the problem was simply a trade spat – perhaps with a garnish of same typically Gallic bigotry or a post-Ottoman suspicion by the Frank.*

In the decade since my eggplant got cold overlooking the old city, France has started to rebuild its neglected army in a way that it hasn't since World War II. It's is developing sophisticated cyber capabilities, yet (unlike its British and American counterparts) is

---

* Remember, to hear the Japanese tell it, that attack on Pearl Harbor was a reasonable response to a trade embargo. Stranger things have happened.

also preparing for a muddy, degraded conflict of the sort that happens when the power goes out and internet is knocked offline. The cause for alarm is an increasingly desperate and aggressive Russia. It's upgrading its navy as well – which has more to do with its NATO ally Turkey than the old cold war foe.

France's opposition to Turkey's entry into the EU wasn't entirely racism but it wasn't entirely wide the mark either. For one thing, most of Turkey isn't in Europe. Then there are the flagrant and brutal human rights violations. Most importantly, the Union doesn't work at all unless all hints of religious division are leached from the halls of government. So, the Europeans are justifiably wary of a great whacking injection of political Islam. And Erdogan's brand of moderate political Islam is making some Ottoman era claims in the eastern Mediterranean.

Behind all of *that* there is the undeniable truth that Europe or the West has, for good or ill, one set of rules and East has another. If a society is going to function on the basic level, there needs to be one agreed upon et of cultural assumptions. There has always been a fundamental difference in how the world works between what Niccolò Machiavelli called, back in 1502, the "Frank" and the "Turk." He devoted the better part of a chapter detailing the divergence of political systems, and the affect those assumptions had on the foreign policy of both the West and Ottoman Empire. One cornerstone of those assumptions, even back then, revolved around the issue of property rights.

It was an innovation – the more left-leaning might call it a fetish – that came out of all that European feudalism. The nobility owned their own property and it would literally take an army to change that. On their death, said property stayed in the family. The issue was that a baron's holdings kept getting divided among his all his sons until they realized that the only way to hold onto power over the generations was to give the whole title and estate to the eldest son, marry your daughters off to someone else's eldest son and pack the rest of the boys off with an allowance. This led to a lot of second sons buying their way into Church posts and third sons riding off to take other people's land. The Normans from the last chapter were notorious for having an obscene number of children – and you can draw a fairly straight line between the marauding Norman younger brothers and Europe's expansionist policies of the 12th century.

In a system like this, the fellow with the most land, and therefore the ability to muster the biggest army, gets to be king. The next level down are his vassals and so on because yes, shit does, in fact, roll downhill. In theory the whole process was guided by Divine Right because, like sex, the old "God Will's It" wheeze just sells well. In practice, however, it wasn't as cut and dry as all that. It's one thing have the best army in a head-to-head match-up with another force, but it is the rare king who can out fight all his rivals combined.

The end affect was that a fellow could only be crowned king if the surrounding nobles and princes agreed to it. He could only maintain a realm with their support. This was true for the Holy Roman Emperor over smallish German kings, the king over the French nobility, or even over one of those Italian resort kingdoms. A king could, *in theory,* despoil and confiscate a troublesome baron's property, but that was a risky move. Once you start that sort of foolishness, the other barons, no matter how loyal, all start thinking "Whose next?" Then the entirety of the second tier would all gang up on the top guy and depose his royal highness. The system wasn't built on mutual trust, but a sort of practical distrust that kept everyone in line. With property rights secure (at the top at any rate) a local noble might improve his land and holdings so his eldest son could carry on the legacy of being both pretentious and mean-spirited.

This is the origin of the word *aristocracy*: rule by the land owners. It may not be the best way to do things, but it did tend to provide more stability than investing all the powers of the state in a single person, an autocrat. If you need a case study, just look to the East.

While the Ottoman Empire was loosely administered, there was no doubt who was boss. Political favors and posts were paid for with land and commercial concessions bestowed by the sultan. Unlike Europe, these assets were considered a salary, not a birthright or even a free-hold. And like a salary, it lasted for as long as you held the post. And you held the post at the pleasure of the local Big Man. The structural flaw in the arrangement has to do with capital investment: Who was going to spend their precarious cash flow for a long-term capital outlay on improvements to a franchise or estate that will likely be handed over to the sycophant who makes the emir laugh into his hummus? You wouldn't, any more that you'd got into hock to renovate a house you're renting from someone else.

Which isn't to say that there wasn't private property in the East – there was plenty of it, but it was never held sacrosanct, and it never held your place in society indefinitely.

The way things are run at the top is generally reflected in the entire society. The hang-over of the unmoored paranoia at the top of the Saddam Hussein regime was palpable in that process meeting at the Ali Hussein hospital in Iraq. A good person could do the right thing, but sticking your neck out to build something much beyond your immediate world and circumstances was fool's errand. Those people were in a protection mode, not a growth mode.

Even the relative stability of the Arab Union represents less an alliance of the modern states as the West understands them than the plantations of a few wealthy families. All the capital of the state is funneled to a few royals, who dispense enough favors to keep the business running and spend the excess on handouts and grand monuments to themselves that produce nothing but divine right pretensions.

THE FRENCH MAY be insufferable, but the recent string of Islamist terrorist attacks across country rather proves their point. Waves of refugees and economic migrants have overwhelmed the European immigration apparatus and you can hardly blame the indigenous population – who took the time and trouble to hash out their problems at the intersection of religion and government four hundred years ago – of being a little nervous of the influx.

The way in which humans are governed affects society, but it doesn't change the fact the governed are human. The Pan-European Thirty Years war (1618-1648) started as a spat between Catholics and Protestants – but as these things do, deranged piety was soon outpaced by a vicious political calculus.

In a nut: the extremely Catholic Ferdinand II was elected Holy Roman Emperor and yearned for a religious conformity in his "empire" which at this point was, more or less, what we'd call

Germany.* The Protestants in the realm, fearing that things would get ugly, formed a Protestant Union to press their interests. This was galling for the emperor, but things didn't get out of hand until the Defenestration of Prague in 1618. "Defenestration" means "to throw out the window" which is exactly what the Bohemians did to the imperial representatives. Which raises the question: Which is worse? That they kept hurling people out of castle windows or that the tactic was so unremarkable that they had to come up with a new word for it.

At any rate − like the Persians sent to the bottom of a well in Sparta − this was the sort of stunt designed to start a war. And the Bohemians succeeded beyond their wildest dreams. The original Protestant rebellion was put down without too much fuss, but the aftershocks changed the tack of Europe history, and can still be felt in the tension between East and West today. A Transylvanian prince, a Protestant named Gabriel Bethlen, called on the aid of Ottoman Emperor Ossman II for cavalry (and agreeing to pay the Emperor tribute) to invade Hungary. It had a knock-on effect of dragging in other Protestant, and then Catholic, powers until the fracas sucked up all of Europe. Ossman wisely sidestepped the melee as the Europeans clawed at each other for a generation, killed eight million people and some 20% of the population of Germany.

The hootenanny wrapped up in 1648 with the Treaty of Westphalia and a dramatic sense of "Let's not do that again." The underlying principle of the treaty being that all the powers needed to stop monkeying around in the religious affairs of the

---

* And why not? This wasn't any different from what Darius, the Romans, Saladin, the popes, Ismail had all tried before.

other powers. The King of France could brutalize a few Protestant Huguenots in Orleans – sure – if not what's the point of being king? And the merrye King of England might roast the odd Catholic in Coventry, but those were strictly *internal* affairs. And would the Bohemians please stop throwing people out the window?

The affect was the further imprinting of the concept of nation states existing as a separate sphere from the religious realm that had been hashed out at Canossa while the Holy Roman Emperor and the pope were trying to figure out just who had the advantage. In contrast, Ottoman world view had a Caliphate as the head of both the secular administration as well and temporal. Ottoman provinces like Syria, Egypt or Arabia were just that, provinces. They weren't nations, but different parts of the *ummah*, the Muslim community. With the political and spiritual so tied up, and wanting to expand the *ummah*, the Ottomans took another swing at Vienna in 1683 in yet another attempt to wade into European affairs and, in the process, take all of Hungary for itself.

Like the summer of 1452, the Siege of Vienna in 1683 fundamentally changed relations between East and West that went beyond political mechanics and delved deep into that slippery concept of coercive power. The siege was unsuccessful, the Hapsburgs and their alliance delivered the Ottomans an epic defeat which was *not* the smart bet at the time. As a result, the Ottoman forces were pushed completely out of Hungary and, more psychologically, the most powerful empire on the planet was no longer thought to be invincible. It was a powerful shift that came just as the European powers were developing empires of their own; far way but mostly profitable. Very resentful of the

Ottoman stranglehold on trade routes, and probably more than a little creeped out by the "boy tax" business, thus started a European pile-on that slowly started to chip away at the old empire, causing it to go from the center of life in the 17th century to the "sick man of Europe by the 19th.

THE OLD FRANCO-OTTOMAN alliance, while historic, was never particularly smooth. In the beginning the Ottoman threat kept France from becoming the plaything of the Holy Roman Empire and the Hapsburgs. With the perceived turbaned menace in retreat, the nature of the alliance began to shift. In fact, by the mid 18th century, all things Ottoman went from being a death nell of Christendom to the height of fashion. A new drink, coffee, was introduced in Marseilles, and made its way to Paris where the fashion-conscious French also began to spot that chic precursor to the mu-mu, the kaftan, on the street. Those damn carpets began to show up everywhere.

Now it was the Ottomans who were seeking French help against the growing threats from Russia and Austria. France was glad to help its old friend, of course, but like the old Sultans demanding tribute, they had a price. They were market concessions, not tribute, which salved Ottoman pride. For the Catholic French, to take the sting out of what historian and diplomat Carl Burkhart called "the sacrilegious union of the lily and the crescent," special "capitulations" placed Catholics in Ottoman lands under the protection of France. Just the sort of thing that the Treaty of Westphalia was supposed to end in Europe. Additional capitulations to other European powers where given, originally for the protection of Christians, but eventually leading to a situation where Europeans (read: white people) were not entirely subject to Ottoman Law.

Seeing the rot in the system, Sultan Ahmed III, like Kemal Atatürk would two centuries later, set out to modernize the empire along European lines. Which suited France's objective to maintain the balance of power in Europe as it kept Russia looking south and the Austrians peeking over their shoulder. In the age of Empire, the balance of power in Europe wasn't always played out in Europe. On the far side of the Ottoman lands lay India. And yes, you *could* go around Africa but the way the French saw things, there was an easier way. It was cheaper, faster, to go via the Red Sea.

Best of all, it would piss the Brits off to no end.

UNKNOWN IN EITHER Istanbul or London – and guaranteed to set off fireworks of rage in both, the notion of France taking over the semi-autonomous Ottoman province of Egypt as a colony had been considered since 1777. The timing was pretty good, with Great Britain tied down with its rebellious North American colonies. The point of the exercise was to build a "double port" linking the Red Sea and the Mediterranean, and then not let the British use it to get to India. That, and the French considered Egypt to be the cradle of civilization and so thought it would be a real grin to go in and conquer the place.

The plans came and went. Before its government got around to that little bit of ill-advised adventurism, France was violently derailed by an its own revolution. Again, while inspired by the American Revolution – which changed very little culturally – the French revolutionaries were trying to rewrite an entire society. Maximillian Robespierre, the mastermind behind the revolutionary Committee for Public Safety,* scrapped the Catholic Church. He wasn't even an atheist - or at least saw the need for a god somewhere – so he made his own. Historically, he overstepped the mark set by Hammurabi, Cyrus, Darius et al, merely hitched their royal stars to an existing cult.

Things went predictably off the rails when he established the Cult of the Supreme Being. Robespierre held a launch party for his new religion on 8 June 1794. That's 20 Prairal Year II on the revolutionary calendar, and let's be honest that alone is enough to damn the man. But no, he couldn't leave well enough alone and had a faux mountain constructed on the Champ des Mars from which he descended in a toga declaring a new religion and parading around the 18th century version of a Kardashian he'd hired to play the goddess of Reason. I wasn't there, but can only imagine my French-Catholic mother's reaction to the scene. Some 12 million French Catholic mothers all disapproving at the same time must have been something else. Just short of two months later, on 10 Thermidor (28 July) Robespierre found his own inflated head separated from his shoulders.

The government was taken over by a five-man Directorate that couldn't quite put a lid on the simmering civil unrest at home. The military hero of the Revolution, one General Napoleon Bonaparte, then proposed the time-honored salve for domestic unrest: The foreign adventure, in this case dusting off the old plans to invade Egypt. And it would *still* annoy the hell out of the Brits. And, being Napoleon, he wanted to walk in the footsteps of Alexander the Great.

---

*Which safely protected a great many shoulders from their overbearing heads.

Napoleon and the *Armée d'Orient* landed in Cairo on 1 July 1798 and the adventure lasted until 1801. Strange for his time, and part of his genius, Napoleon stressed that the army to respect the local culture and religion. There were rumors (persistent if unsubstantiated) that Napoleon converted to Islam to win the trust of the local leaders. The army went through the Sinai but was checked by Ottoman forces on its way to invade Syria. Militarily, the whole adventure ended in a French withdrawal but, strangely, the French engineers stayed, and invited leading Egyptians to institutes and universities in Paris.

The Sublime Porte was justifiably furious, but there wasn't much that they could do about it. If the Sultan sent a force to unseat the Khedive of Egypt, the French would come back. The Egyptians, along with a great many of the Ottoman Empire's Arab subjects, didn't like taking a back seat to the Turks and so welcomed the French, and then the English, as liberators. Soon Cairo was modernizing, outpacing the imperial seat in cosmopolitan Istanbul. The massive transfer of technology between Europe and Egypt in the 19th century did come at a price, however. The semi-autonomous Khedeve of Egypt was kept on his throne despite Ottoman sneering and the Suez Canal was eventually built with loans from France and the UK. Then the entire country was, more or less, repossessed by Britain when it defaulted on the loans they couldn't possibly have repaid.

SO LAME WAS THE SICK MAN of Europe that shortly after the turn of the 20th century, Italy even joined in on the pile-on. They started sniffing about getting colonies like the other great European powers without considering the obvious: Italy was not a great European power. Those little princely mini-states that the Normans had terrified had only unified the peninsula into a single nation under the crown of King Victor Emmanuel II in 1861. About the time the US was kicking off its Civil War.

Seventeen years later, still only about 20% of the newly minted Italian population spoke a language that even the most forgiving professor would class as standard Italian. Yet it was at the Congress of Berlin in 1878 that Italy started to stake its claim on the rest of the planet. During the War of 1877/78, in which Russia and the Ottoman Empire had squared off (again), the Turks had gotten their turbans handed to them. The other European powers came in to make sure that Russia didn't take too much from the sick man. Again, this was that very European notion of keeping a balance of power by recognizing that the biggest army might beat any one foe, but not all of them, Italy was invited to the Congress because it seemed like the white thing to do.

At the Congress, it was decided that France would occupy the former Ottoman province of Tunisia and that Great Britain could sun itself in Cyprus. When Italian diplomats started complaining, the French delegation said that Tripolitania was for Italy. The gesture was likely just meant to shut the Italians up, the place wasn't much of a prize: the Assyrians, Persians, Greeks and Romans had all driven into the area only to ponder that timeless question of the ill-advised global adventure: "I'm sorry, what were we going here again?"

No one thought much about the French reply save the Italians – you know how teenagers can be. They got to work playing the big kids off each other, signing secret agreements with both Britain and France to support their claims in North Africa in return for Italian claims on Tripolitania – roughly the place the Romans had called Libya. France and Britain weren't exactly being hustled – they were playing their own games. Both powers were trying to loosen Italy's alliance with Germany.

Practically, Rome didn't do much with its diplomatic coup until 1911, when the Italian press corp whipped up a *cause célèbre* about invading Libya by claiming that it was a mineral rich desert oasis with lovely farmland. It's not true, but Italy was an economic train-wreck at the time and Italians were perfectly willing to relocate. The government just wanted them to emigrate to North Africa. Instead, they were heading in boatloads to the Americas.*

When Italy finally got around to invading the country, Tripoli fell, but the going was slow. After a surge of troops to 20,000, Tobruk, Derna and Khors fell, but Benghazi held out, prompting another surge to 100,000 troops with the British blocking any Ottoman land reinforcements coming through Egypt. The usual atrocities cropped up on both sides – particularly the 1911 Tripoli massacre when Italian troops murdered thousands of (mostly) civilians and burned a mosque with worshipers inside. In a more literate and mass-media age, these sort of crimes were becoming harder to hide. Wide audience newspapers could get updated information through telegram, and it was changing the way in which people perceived the war at home. Other innovations were changing the way wars were being fought abroad. The Italians pioneered the use of the armored car as well as the use of airplanes for reconnaissance.

---

* There is a story of a Piedmontese man who said ,on settling in New York, "I had to come to America to discover I was Italian." Most Italians were without passports, so their papers were stamped W.O.P. (With Out Passport). The name stuck.

More crucially, one *Sottotenente* Giulio Gavotti invented aerial bombing when he lopped four grenades out of his cockpit on the Libyan town of Tajura. Italy annexed Libya with full European support in 1912.

With the Turks on their back feet, other Ottoman provinces in Europe – Greece, Bulgaria, Montenegro and the always helpful Serbia – formed the Balkan League to shake off their overlords with the First Balkan War (1912-13). At the end of which, Serbia refused to withdraw from territory promised their Bulgarian allies, which led to the Second Balkan War later that year. In the aftermath of the second war, Russia, assuming the rest of the region was about to pile-on the Serbs, pledged to back Serbian autonomy in order to calm things down.

It wasn't a bad plan, but what happened was that Serbians, feeling invincible with the neighborhood Big Man behind them, started demanding that the Austro-Hungarian Empire give up its south Slav provinces. As Germany's older cousin, the Austro-Hungarian empire wasn't as easy to push around as the Ottomans, though.

With the above swirling around his head, a young student activist named Gravilo Princip joined a Serbian nationalist group ominously called the Black Hand. At one of their meetings, they struck on the terribly clever idea of murdering the heir to the throne to press their demands. Which proves that student activists have always been too theatrical for their own good. The assassination of Arch-Duke Franz Ferdinand, like most weddings, was one of those operations that came off the rails almost from the start yet somehow landed perfectly on its feet.

The brooding membership of the Black Hand found the archduke's visit to Sarajevo particularly galling. With the route of the motorcade announced in advance, the fellas decided to litter it with assassins. Fortunately, while killing someone is thrilling in fantasy, in reality it can be pretty unnerving. The first assassin stationed along the route chickened out and failed to throw his grenade. The second fellow – Nedeljko Čabrinović – showed more fortitude and actually took his shot. The bomb went long, bouncing off the folded top of the archduke's convertible, hit the pavement and rolled under the next car before exploding. Čabrinović, seeing that he'd blown up the wrong car and knowing that they don't give out revolutionary medals for a cock-up of that magnitude, popped a handy cyanide pill and jumped into the Miljacka river to drown himself. The poison was old and the summer hot, so Čabrinović was found by police vomiting in about six inches of water. Meanwhile, the motorcade roared off at high speed past three more assassins all of whom, including Princip, decided that the whole operation was a bust.

The imperial couple hid out in the fortified Town Hall while they gathered themselves and decided what to do. The pre-planned route was scrapped, yet it was decided that as a show of Imperial unflappability, they'd head to the hospital to visit those injured in the blast.

A dejected Gravilo Princip had, in the meantime, shuffled over to Schiller's deli to pout. That likely would have been the end of the story had the general in the front seat of the imperial car decided at the last minute that heading back down through the city center towards the hospital was a terrible idea. He ordered the car to stop, reverse at turn down the street they'd just passed, and find a side route. And so it was that he car reversed and stopped directly in front of Princip. The youngster stepped onto the running board and shot the arch-duke in the neck and then, his wife in the stomach. In doing so, he rang the starting bell for World War I.

To the people of Libya, however, that was a European mess. While the Ottoman transfer of Libya to Italy was legal, the *Senussi* – a political-religious order of Sunni Muslims based in the eastern part of the country – just didn't care.

"Making war upon insurgents is messy and slow, like eating soup with a knife"

T.E. Lawrence

CHAPTER THIRTEEN:
THE FIRST ARAB SPRING

SHORTLY AFTER the botched British landing at the Gallipoli peninsula in 1915, the forces on both sides had dug into their positions.* During breaks in the carnage, both lines routinely allowed their opposite numbers out into no man's land unmolested to clean up their dead. Neither side knew much about germs or the spread of disease, but Islamic law prescribes burying the dead within 24 hours if possible. The knock-on effect being that putrid disease was *not* spreading through the defending Ottoman positions like it was through the British lines. One day, a 24 year-old from one of the Ottoman Arab units named Mohammad al-Faroki climbed out of his trench carrying a white flag. The British thought he was coming out to pick up dead, but he kept walking across the wrecked field towards the putrid air of the British lines with the white flag hoisted. Then he politely surrendered himself.

---

* "Digging in" was the great, enduring bad idea of World War I.

Al-Faroki said that he was a member of an Arab society within the Ottoman military called *al-Ahd* (The Awakening), with the sole aim of creating a pan-Arab revolt within the army and empire to rid the Arabs of their Turkish overlords. With the European war spreading into Muslim world, the Arabs saw their chance to use the British Empire to liberate themselves. Al Faroki claimed to be the liaison officer between *al-Ahd* and a secret Arab civilian group that was in contact with Emir Hussein, the Sherif of Mecca.* His hosts thought the whole thing was a fantastic, almost unbelievable story. Yet, as al-Faroki was passed up the chain of command the story was proving more and more credible.

At the outbreak of the war, with the rest of the neighborhood picking sides, there was little doubt that the Ottoman Empire would be pulled in to the conflict. Even the Japanese had somehow inserted themselves into the melee. The question was on whose side? The Entente Powers of Great Britain, France and Russia, even newly formed Italy, had more sway in the Ottoman world, but that was precisely the problem. Between Russia fomenting revolution in the Balkans, making Greek independence a European *cause célèbre*, the British repossessing Egypt, the French annexing Algeria and making themselves obvious in Syria, the Italians trying to sell spaghetti in Libya, the Sultan and all the Young Turks in Istanbul thought that the Entente had a little too much sway.

Germany, for its part, was the only European power that had no official presence in the Middle East. Despite being the seat of

---

* As the spiritual leader of both Mecca and Medina, the ancient office of Sherif was somewhere in authority between the pope in Rome and the Archbishop of Canterbury.

the Holy Roman Empire, Germany wasn't a united nation, much less an empire, until 1871, the years after the creation of modern Italy. With France and Britain strutting around the globe with their empires, the German Kaiser (who loved the ridiculous military uniforms of the day – the Qaddafi of the Rhine) thought that he needed an empire before which to strut. In the zero-sum game of European colonial politics, it wasn't enough to open a brewery in Tanzania or sell lederhosen to locals in the Solomon Islands – other empires had to shrink.

The best way to do this, reckoned Count Max von Oppenhiem, the German ambassador to the Sublime Porte in Istanbul, was to dust off the old concept of *jihad*. If the Germans could whip the Muslim populations into a Holy War against Western crusaders, it would wreak havoc through the considerable Muslim populations of the France and British Empires. There wasn't much of a danger of blowback for Germany because they had hadn't colonized any Muslim lands. What's more, they were fighting the colonial-minded Entente in the bargain. So the sickly Ottoman Empire decided to throw its turban in with the spiky-helmeted Axis Powers of Germany and Austria Hungary.

When the Ottomans entered the war on the Axis side, it mustered troops from across the empire, but did so in separate Turkish and Arab units. This was very short-sighted as it made the feared Arab fifth column, suspected even before the war, a lot more plausible.

And here they were, al-Faroki explained to the British. To counter the threat of a fifth column, the sickly caliph in Istanbul tried to unify the army and Arab population with a call to *jihad* of all Muslims against the Christian West. Being caliph, he didn't feel the need to explain why this didn't include the Germans. The call sent justified tremors of terror through the Jewish and Christian subject of the empire. That fear, al-Faroki explained, was misplaced. Emir Hussein was their spiritual leader of Arb Muslims, not some Turkish sultan. And it was Hussein who had ensured the Arab response to the caliph's call to arms lacked fire through the time-honored method of simply ignoring it.

By the summer of 1916, Emir Hussein, had decided that concessions to the British global market was better than an uneasy peace with the devious Ottomans. He sent his eldest son, Abdullah, to meet with Ronald Storrs of the British Oriental Office. Abdullah, in classic big brother style, sent his 20 year old brother, Zeid, to run the errand instead. On 5 June, Zeid met with Storrs and delivered some vague plans for the revolt that, he said, was scheduled to kick off in about five days and, that being the case, made a request for an additional £70,000 in gold to finance/bribe rebel tribesmen.

Being British, Storrs pressed young Zeid on actual strategic details of an actual battlefield engagement that might lead to an actual defeat of Ottoman forces. Being Arab, Zeid replied, "We will summon the Turks to surrender, and shoot them if they refuse."

Still being British, and not terribly impressed by Zeid's total lack of logistics or planning, Storrs told Zeid that he wasn't getting a gold ducat more until the revolt was underway. "Good." Said Zeid, "It started yesterday. The gold please."* Zeid can't be accused of being detail oriented, but he was certainly focused enough for government work.

---

* Or words to that affect.

By popular accounts, that morning his father, the Sharif, had climbed the tower in his palace in Mecca and fired a musket off in the direction of the Turkish fort, signaling the start what we might call the first Arab Spring. Taking the tiny Turkish garrison by surprise, Hussein's rebels took Mecca, and with the help of a British naval bombardment, the city of Jeddah as well. Then the Arabs got overexcited in Medina and stormed a heavily armed to garrison there to disastrous results.

The problem with the Arab revolt in the Hejaz – that long littoral strip along the Red Sea in the south-west of modern Saudi Arabia - was the tricky matter of being allied with largely Christian soldiers. The Qur'an dictates that the holy cities of Mecca and Medina are strictly off limits to infidels and the rest of the Hejaz is only slightly less off-limits. As such Emir Hussein would only allow a tiny group of British logistics officers on the beach and no further. To allow infidels – even the ones without whom you can't win the war – further inland would invite a propaganda blowback from the Turks who'd claim Hussein was not only a traitor to the Ottoman Empire but a traitor to Islam itself.

T.E. LAWRENCE'S book *The Seven Pillars of Wisdom*, (which you probably haven't read) and its movie version *Lawrence of Arabia* (which you really should have seen) aside, it's debatable how effective or wide-spread the Arab Rebellion against the Ottoman Empire in world War I actually was. It's an ingrained myth now, so to some degree the truth doesn't entirely matter. It still colors people's perceptions and, therefore, how they act in the world.*

Before the war, Lawrence had been in the Holy Land digging around in the dirt for an archeology degree and, rare for expat Brits of the time, he'd actually bothered to learn Arabic. So young Ned Lawrence, without a day of military training in his life, found himself mustered into the army intelligence corps as a second lieutenant making maps in Cairo. He didn't stay there.

Given his language skills and understanding of Arab manners, Lawrence found himself the main contact in the diplomatic dance was going on between Faisal – another of the sharif's sons – and the British. Lawrence kept being promoted through the ranks, not through military prowess but as a way of signally to the Arabs that he had more authority than he actually had. The problem with Lawrence, among the clubby British high command, was that the boy was just weird. Or in Winston Churchill's turn of phrase, that he "was not in complete harmony with the normal."

Lawrence's account of the guerrilla army he led through the *Hijaz* and into Damascus is lively, great fun and – according to documents declassified in the 1960s – somewhat full of shit. Plenty of it is true enough, and Lawrence was uniquely qualified to led a guerrilla war in a largely medieval landscape. Contemporary military commanders are often (rightly) accused of fighting the last war, but only the last one. In World War I that

---

*This is a very human thing: French believe that their resistance to the NAZIs as widespread and effective. It was neither. For that matter, outside of South Carolina, you are hard pressed to find anyone who'll admit their family were royalists or even hedging their bets during the American Revolution.

might have been in the Crimea, maybe, but not the Hundred Years War or even the crusades. Which is what makes T.E. Lawrence one of the stranger figures of modern history: His near complete sense of being out of time at the right moment. He had a detailed knowledge of medieval warfare; unmechanized, hit and run fights that could disappear in to the vast emptiness that surrounded walled cities, and moving armies along supplies of food and water. No modern soldier had studied such outdated tactics in a century.* And for good reason.

Despite the assurances of Prince Faisal and Mohammad al-Faroki of *al-Ahd*, very few Arab units actually defected to the Arab Revolt. Until about six years before the outbreak of the war, the Ottoman Empire was a loosely administered as a big, ailing – but reasonably happy – Muslim family with only the occasional slaughter of the its subjects. The elites of the empire came from all ethnic backgrounds; Turks, Arabs, Berbers, the ruler of Egypt in the 1880s, Mehment Ali, was an Albanian. The system was also wildly inefficient and corrupt. When the Young Turks staged their semi-coup in 1908 – keeping the Sultan in charge, but gelding him of real power. They started to transform the empire from what its subjects thought of as Ottoman into a Turkish one with a Turkish ruling class. It's likely that at the kick off of the war, the Arab Street had hardly even noticed the change, much less become so enraged as to revolt. For the Arab elites, the local pashas and the rural tribal leaders, however,

---

*This is a reoccurring problem. ISIS and other jihadist groups may be a whiz at recruiting on social media, and the lone wolf wannabes tend to get picked up in online chat rooms. The real tactics, however, are done in face to face meetings or the lowly letter. Communication that modern surveillance has a hard time picking up.

alarm bells were ringing; they were about to lose their privileged positions. And from a religious point of view, there was no higher ranking local than Hussein, Sharif of Mecca and Medina.

A descendent of the prophet, Hussein was a member of the Hashemite tribe and the guardian of the holiest sites in Islam. As such, he was in control of the very lucrative yearly pilgrimage to Mecca, the *haj*, that all Muslims are required to take once in the lives. He could see that the centralization of a Turkish elite – certainly one trying to create a secular and modern state – in which his loyal Bedouin tribesmen would hardly have a spot.

Not that the British, fighting for their lives in France, cared too much about Arab independence. They were trying to open up another front through Ottoman territory in order to strike at Austria-Hungary from the east. In that light, the Arab Rebellion was useful to harry the Ottoman troops with wild goose chases through the desert, wrecked rail lines and cut off garrisons. The main Allied thrust on the Ottoman front was the British Indian Army, after a disastrous defeat at Kut (in Iraq), marching through from Basra. Meanwhile dominion troops from Australia fought through the Sinai towards Damascus. It worked.

Australian troops had largely cleared Damascus of the Turks prior to Lawrence and Faisal's "taking" the city. Still, the War Office in London saw the advantage of letting Faisal have his triumph. The cause of Arab nationalism was expedient to the British war effort, and the British war effort was expedient to the cause of Arab nationalism.

The looming problem was that the politicos in Whitehall had managed to weave an 800 thread count sheet of mutually exclusive promises to nearly every non-German on the planet. In 1915, after the Ottomans hitched their star to with the Axis powers, the alliance between Great Britain and France was becoming frayed over post-war spoils to the victors of the war they hadn't won yet. Sir Mark Sykes, the British government's expert on the Middle East, told the Prime Minister at a cabinet meeting, "I feel we ought to settle with France as soon as possible, and get a diplomatic understanding about Syria." Here, reportedly, Sykes drew a literal line across the map on the table and continued, "I should like to draw a line from the 'e' in Acre, to the last 'k' in Kirkuk." He proposed that Britain run everything south of said line and the French north of it.

The Brits had also famously promised the Hashemite Sharif of Mecca the throne of Arabia – which the old guy took to mean that lands of the Arabs, not just the Arabia peninsula. Without waiting for clarification, Faisal pulled off a *fait accompli* by occupying Damascus and proclaiming himself (with a great deal of popular support) as the King of Syria. He held the throne for four months before the French complained to the British that they'd been promised Syria on the perfectly reasonable grounds that it was north of the 'e' in Acre in the colonial office map room. They wanted a colony, and colonies don't have kings.

Given that France (like Britain) was more or less on its knees at the end of the war and (unlike Britain) had done nothing in the Mediterranean, their stance on the great loot is pretty, well, Italian. Not to whitewash British imperial aims (and they were mighty) but after the war the Brits weren't interested in colonizing Mesopotamia. According to Winston Churchill, the newly appointed Secretary of State for the Colonies, the government was more interested in saving money than expanding the empire at Ottoman expense. The Sykes-Picot agreement has gone down in history as an example of British and French greed, but a lot of the discussion *at the time* doesn't bear this out.* As Churchill's voluminous correspondence points out, the British couldn't afford colonies in Mesopotamia – now being called Iraq – even if it had wanted them. Unaware of the huge untapped oil potential in Mosul, even a staunch imperialist like Churchill was trying to get British troops *out* of Iraq in 1920. He wrote about the situation in away that, with the odd tweek, could have been written last week:

> It is an extraordinary thing that the British civil administration should have succeeded in such a short time in alienating the whole country to such an extent that the Arabs have laid aside blood feuds that they have nursed for centuries and that the Suni [*sic*] and Shiah [*sic*] tribes are working together. We have been advised locally that the best way to get our supplies up the river would be to fly the Turkish flag, which would be respected by the tribesmen.

Basically, like the United States eighty years later, Britain couldn't afford to rule Iraq, they couldn't have them acting on their own account, either. And to do that they had to install their men on the various thrones.

The French couldn't afford to take on colonies either, they just wouldn't admit it. The French Empire of the late 19th century had become something of a political masterclass of self-delusion. In 1848, they'd annexed Algeria, not as a colony but a department (equivalent to a state in the US) of France. De Gaulle would later say that the Mediterranean runs through

---

*Not entirely at any rate. It was still pretty damn greedy and imperialistic.

France the way the Seine runs through Paris. No one bothered to ask the Algerians what they thought of this. It's no weirder than what we did to Hawaii, but we had the common decency to grant the people living there citizenship. The French annexed Algeria and excluded the Algerians from citizenship. And they really wanted to get their hands on Syria.

Sykes-Picot was ultimately been scrapped, but Syria had been promised to the French and a promise was a promise. At least between white people, at any rate. So, the Brits stood around with their hands in their pockets while the French ejected Faisal's Arab government out of Syria for a French colonial government.[*]

This left King Faisal without a throne. The Brits had already placed one older brother, Adullah, on the throne of Transjordan (now Jordan) where the family still rules a population that is massively Sunni and Arab. The whole thing was getting awkward so the Brits, who do not do awkward well, installed Faisal as King of Iraq.

Iraq, however, was full of Kurds in the north who, while Sunni, aren't Arabs. The Kurds were under the impression that the British had promised them a Kurdish state that extended from the hinterlands of modern Turkey, the northern third of Iraq, and smallish slice of Iran. The Kurds were under this impression because the American President Woodrow Wilson had said something about "self-determination" before getting

---

[*]The locals spent the next generation trying to eject *that* government out of Syria until the Germans ejected the French government out of France. The British had to then eject the Germans out of Syria and give it back to the French who, without a blessing from the US, had to give it back to the Syrians.

tired of foreign policy and going home. In the middle of Iraq you have a mostly Sunni Arab population that probably would have been happier as a part of Syria, with Faisal as the king. Baghdad was the seat of the Assyrian Empire after all. The Brits, however, weren't about to give the French the satisfaction. Roughly the southern half of the country, and the majority of the Sunni king's subjects, were Arabs, but they were Shi'a.

Any further south you ran into the British protectorate of Kuwait, which dated back to 1899 and was off the table for discussion. Over in the Arabian peninsula, the old King Hussein wasn't fairing so well. But this had to do with yet *another* mutually exclusive promise London had made.

AS THE 19TH CENTURY rolled over to the 20th, America had grown into its long pants. The only real spook we'd ever had was a self-inflicted civil war and, within a generation of it, the United States was the world's richest country, it's largest consumer market with no realistic foreign threats and almost completely self-sufficient. Victory in the Spanish-American war made the US the power in the hemisphere. As such, in 1907 President Teddy Roosevelt sent the United States Naval Fleet – now the third largest in the world – around the globe to show off the "Great White Fleet."* Domestically, Roosevelt kept speaking softly about his big swingin' stick. Why not? It worked for Sargon the Great.

The drawback to telling everyone that you are a world power is that you tend to get pulled into global conflicts whether you

---

*This isn't as racist as it sounds, the hulls had painted stark white because, with the glare of sun off water, it made them hard to target.

want to or not. Even if you are elected, as Woodrow Wilson was, promising to stay out of a European war, things are bound to get out of hand. Which is how Wilson, president of a nation shy of formal alliances, a domestic market protected by some of the highest tariffs in the world and a deep suspicion of international institutions, found himself at the victor's table at the end of World War I. The Europeans kept askingWilson what he thought about the shape of post-war Europe and a sliced up Middle East. Likely, the man had never thought about it before.

Winston Churchill, who did have opinions, by then Great Britain's Secretary of State for War. He argued for putting Kaiser Wilhelm's nephew on the German throne in a clipped constitutional monarchy modeled on Britain's. His reasoning was that shifting instantly from an overbearing king to a democratic republic might invite a citizenry unfamiliar with popular politics to do something rash. Perhaps wanting to make a bold showing, Wilson would hear none of it. From afar, he'd made a 14-point list for how he'd decided the world should work and was married to the wonderfully worded slogan "make the world safe for democracy." Wilson was convinced, and most Americans still are, that the shift from monarchy to free republic is a smooth one so long as you're properly philosophical about it. Eventually, Churchill lost the argument and Germany became a republic.

What few opinions Wilson expressed about the Middle East echoed the same philosophy, but he didn't think that the region mattered enough to needle Churchill about it and went home. The League of Nations may have been championed by the president, but in the end, the American people weren't having any of it. They just wanted to be left alone.

It's not that Wilson was an idiot. He was tedious to be sure, and being president of Princeton is also pretty damning, but he wasn't some slobbering mouth-breather either. It's just that Americans have a pleasantly warped impression of revolutionary upheaval based on our own survivor's bias. True, the American Revolution was revolutionary conceptually in the broad sense. On a more practical level, however, our break with the British Empire had about the same impact on daily life as a corporate spin-off does for the branch office: You change the logo on the stationary and quit filing paperwork with HQ, but that's about it. Because the colonies had long been effectively self-running as long as the taxes were paid, the same well-connected, wig-wearing fancy boys in the colonial assemblies all got themselves elected to congress after the war. George Washington was a revolutionary in that he led an army in a successful colonial revolt. He was not a radical. The man was about as establishment as you could get.

The French Revolution was more typical of the breed: First, they guillotined everyone with an education or spare investment capital, then they re-wrote property rights, government bodies, harassed the peasants for not being woke, deep-sixed the church, declared a sassy prostitute "the Goddess of Reason", adopted different weights and measures,* and a new calendar entirely divorced from nature. These reforms didn't go over very well so the new government of the people had to kill a lot of said people to make the new ideas stick. By the end of the decade, the entire

---

*In their defense, this was the metric system and it really does make more sense that measurements based on a dead king's feet.

country was hankering for the mellowing effects of a guy like Napoleon.

We can never know what a post-World War I Middle East would have looked like if the British had kept their promises, or for that matter, what constitutional German monarchy would have done with itself. To be clear, counter-factuals are always the rubber-chickens of the historian's gumbo. The fact remains that in a restored and clipped German monarchy, the path to power for house-painting, pseudo-intellectual Austrian psychopaths narrows considerably.

DEPENDING ON WHICH SIDE of the matter you ask, the Jews either started their mass emigration to Palestine, or their return to their Promised Land, in the mid 19th century. Whatever you call it, the reason was fairly obvious: yet *another* rise in perennially fashionable European anti-Semitism. Facing hostility back home, European Jews had a perverse incentive to emigrate to Ottoman lands and yet retain their European passports. Under the old Ottoman capitulations, European citizens enjoyed a protection of their governments back home that made them largely beyond the reach of Ottoman law. So, to be clear, in the Middle East, European Jews were protected from Ottoman abuse by the same governments who'd likely be abusing them eight ways from Sunday had they stayed at home.

Once in Palestine, the Jewish *emigres* were instantly hated by their neighbors for decidedly un-religious reasons: We all hate anyone who is above the law. The situation chaffed like an unreachable rash because the Jews, with European education and supported by European money, also lived better than their Arab neighbors. Most of the Arabs considered themselves superior to the Jews – who didn't even have a homeland – and here they were strutting around in a Muslim country being all obvious about it.

Empire hungry though they were, Britain absolutely did *not* want to add a Jewish homeland in the Middle East to their unwieldy colonial possessions. By the turn of the 20th Century, the British Empire had grown into a constellation of formal and informal colonies that were surprisingly autonomous. India, that jewel of the Imperial Crown (referred to administratively by its summer capital, Simla) controlled its own domestic policy and, to a shocking degree, carried on its own foreign policy. Simla considered the Arabian Peninsula to be its sphere of influence and didn't care that the Arab war had been run from Cairo or that they backed the Hashemites. Simla had its own man, none other than Ibn al-Sa'ud, who'd teamed up with the tribe of fundamentalist true believers called Wahhabis. The QED being a low key civil war in Arabia between Cairo's man, King Hussein, and Simla's, Ibn al-Su'ad.

What finally settled the matter in favor of Saud was Israel. London just couldn't get Hussein - who thought the area had been promised to the Hashemite dynasty – to mellow out on the Jewish question. And so it was that Al-Sa'ud, who took the throne in 1924, and created Saudi Arabia.

This left he space on the map now being called Iraq with an empty throne and Faisal nowhere to sit. After his Syrian adventure, the French were adamantly opposed to putting Faisal on the throne. So that's exactly what the British did and thus was created the first King of Iraq.

Faisal knew good and well who put him on the throne, and who was paying his stipend too, so never tried to eat Kuwait like his successors. Iraq gained formal independence from Great Britain in 1932, and Faisal died a year later. He was succeeded by his only son Ghazi, who was on the throne in 1938 when Kuwait actually tried to vote itself *into* Iraq. The Brits put down the uprising (and the vote) and told Ghazi that they'd carve out a proper Kurdistan, take Mosul, and stop his allowance if they heard any more about it.

In 1958, as the Arab Nationalist movement spread across the Middle East, one General Abd al-Karim Qasim overthrew the third and final King of Iraq, Faisal II, for being a British stooge. And he undoubtedly was. Qasim was one of those mini- Gamal Nassers that were cropping up across the Middle East in those days and all calling themselves the Free Officers Corp. Qasim's coup was supported by the local Ba'athist party – which promoted a mix of Arab nationalist and socialism that was born in neighboring Syria. Qasim's infatuation with Nasser, however, had its limits. He drew the line at Nasser's proposed pan-Arab army and refused to join the short-lived United Arab Republic of Egypt and Syria. It was an awkward country anyway, you couldn't get from one end to the other without going through Israel and Lebanon.

This put Qasim out of sorts with the Ba'athists, so naturally they decided to kill the man. The hit squad included a young fellow called Saddam Hussein who loved guns and was eager to try his hand a killing people. According to some (unofficial reports) young Saddam was a little *too* eager because he popped off a bit quick. The driver was killed and Qasim got away with a bullet in the arm. Saddam thought it prudent to flee to Syria and had to finish up high school in Egypt.*

Any strongman worth his salt, after being shot in the arm by some teenager from the local Young Ba'athist Club, must reestablish his swagger. In 1961, with the British protectorate in Kuwait over, Qasim announced an invasion. The Kuwaitis, forgetting the 1938 vote, promptly asked the Brits back to save them. Qasim then tried to nationalize the Iraq Petroleum Company (owned by a consortium of Americans and Brits) like Nasser had done in Suez and Mossadegh had done in Iran. So, President Kennedy threw a bunch of money at Qasim's rivals in the Ba'ath party, who overthrew him in 1963.

Saddam came back home just in time to ingratiate himself in the assassination plot of the next strongman and got himself arrested. After the next coup, in 1968, Saddam managed to get in good with President Ahmed Hassan al-Bakr (they were from the same hometown). Eventually Saddam rose to vice-president and was put in control of the country's internal security apparatus. As Bakr's health faded, Saddam found himself running the country until he was formally made president in July of 1979.

---

* I have no high school monkey shines to rival this.

I never dared to be radical when young
For fear it would make me conservative when old.
Robert Frost (1874-1963)
Precaution (1936)

CHAPTER FOURTEEN:
DARIUS ISN'T MAD, HE'S JUST DISAPPOINTED

IN 1974, THE SHAH OF IRAN threw a 25th Centennial party of the Iranian Monarchy – known as the Peacock Throne. That's not 250 years, understand, but 2,500. Dynasties had come and gone through its long history, but the monarchy had remained an unbroken thread. Yet five years later, it was all over and the entire world saw it coming. I'm getting slightly ahead of myself.

The results of the first uprising in 1915 were a mixed bag for the Arabs. True, the Ottoman Empire had been reduced to a very un-imperial Turkey, but the old provinces now found themselves either dominated by the UK or outright ruled from France. Iran had spent the last couple centuries bullied and dominated by the Ottomans, had not been a part of the empire and so had not been part of the "Great Loot" after World War I. The Peacock Throne still stood – Iran had merely toggled between domineering foreign powers. But they were used to that.

In the heady days of the Great Game between Russian and Great Britain in Central Asia – Persia had found itself wedged uncomfortably between expansionist Russia and British India. Moscow harbored dreams of annexing the area for the imperial glory of Mother Russia. The British Empire, head and shoulders above the rest in the empire game and ruling the seas in the bargain, were entertaining an entirely different approach. They saw a mismanaged country of bumpkins who lacked modern education in both the industrial and the financial: They didn't want to rule it, they just wanted to pick the place clean.

In truth, the Persians weren't any more a bunch of bumpkins that any other group. High Persian culture – from art and poetry to math and science – is some rarified air, if you've ever had the pleasure. The Brits were right about one thing, the management of the country was corrupt and incompetent and had been for a century. The end of the 19th century saw the uneasy but practical alliance between the Shi'a mullahs of traditional Persian culture and the liberal minded *bazaari* (merchant class) against the corrupt and incompetent reign of the autocratic Shahs..

The shahs well knew that the only thing keeping them on the Peacock Throne was tradition, so it was best to be very traditionally minded. And traditionally the court and its hangers-on wanted to go play on the Rivera and use the treasury as their own personal piggy bank. In its pre-oil days, there was only so much you could squeeze out of the backwater the country had become, so to keep up with the other royals, they needed to modernize the country. They just didn't know how to go about it, or more to the point, pay for it. So the shah outsourced the entire operation, giving over most of the government to a pair of nearby Western powers – the UK and Russia – who'd do all the heavy lifting in return for dominating the commercial and strategic interests the country.

To wit, the case of a British socialite named William Knox D'arcy, who sweet talked the shah into the resulting Anglo-Persian (later Anglo-Iranian) Oil Company which effectively controlled Iran's oil industry while paying the Shah a royalty of a meager 16% of profits.

The *bazaaris*, Western leaning though they were, thought this approach was as terrible as it sounded. They wanted to modernize, yes, but not give the commercial and vital interests of the country over to foreigners. They wanted a liberal democracy and just let common sense and sound laws take their course.* To do that, the *bazaaris* needed to curb the power of the shah before he gave the show away to the Europeans. The mullahs, on the other hand, just wanted to *stop* the Shah from modernizing as would almost certainly end with the clergy losing its privileged positions. They too needed to curb the powers of the shah, if for completely opposed reasons. And so, under the doctrine of "the enemy of my enemy is my friend" the mullahs and the *bazaari*'s established an uneasy alliance.

In 1909, the corrupt shah was overthrown in a constitutionalist revolution and replaced with his 12-year-old son who the reformers could push around. The first thing they needed to do is pay off the massive debts incurred by the monarchy which put them, ironically, in need of foreign help.†

---

* It is truly baffling to the historian just how much push-back this idea consistently gets.

† It's an overlooked footnote of history is how many coup d'états tend to trigger margin calls from your banker.

They couldn't stomach going to the British or the Russians, so instead opted for the Swedes and that new anti-imperial upstart, the United States. The American in charge of finances, William Morgan Shuster, attempted to play Britain and Russia off each other, but the new kid was out of his depth here.

To explain to Shuster exactly what the score was, Russia invaded Persia in 1911. The British quietly put their blessing on the adventure while buying up 51% of Anglo-Iranian shares, affectively nationalizing Persia's oil industry for Britain. With crown support, the shah effectively reestablished control over the country until he was overthrown in 1921 by a warlord called Raza Pahlavi, who named himself shah in 1925.

Reza Shah launched an ambitious reform of the country along the lines of what Kemal Atatürk was doing in Turkey, like changing the name of the country to Iran. Like Atatürk, he zeroed in on headwear and introduced a compulsory, a broad brimmed European style chapeau called a Pahlavi hat. For men, of course. Reza Shah wasn't that fashionable, but wearing the hat made it impossible for a good Muslim to say his prayers, as he couldn't touch his head to the prayer mat. The clergy was so outraged that they openly cried foul, prompting the shah to make a special trip to the holy city of Qom to beat the tar out of a local ayatollah in front of a Shi'a shrine. He then had the ayatollah dragged away by his beard to show everyone who was boss. His pious, traditional-minded subjects did not find this spectacle particularly endearing. It should come as no surprise that Reza Shah was forced to abdicate in the chaos following the Anglo-Soviet invasion during World War II – his son became the last Shah of Iran.

The Iranian experience with Americans during World War II was typical but not all that damning. Britain and the Soviets established a Persian Corridor to supply the eastern front with Iranian oil and American supplies. So, there we were too. Sure, the Iranians thought the American's were big and loud and completely lacking in style – but so did everyone else. On balance, Iranians had a positive view of the United States: Here was a Western power that seemed openly hostile to the idea of empire and contented itself not with sending armies all over Hell's half acre (the war not withstanding), but missionaries armed with textbooks, plumbing fixtures and shoes for the kids. Granted, to the pious rural Muslim, the missionaries were a little tedious with all that *Our Lord and Savior* business, but that clean water sure was refreshing, and it didn't kill you anymore either.

The Americans baffled the Iranians even further when, with the war over and won, they simply... left. For their part, the Soviets established an army of occupation in the northern Iran and, being Russian, claimed that they weren't actually there and that wasn't at all what they were doing anyway. The British, still in charge of the Anglo-Iranian Oil Company, stayed around as well. Not with an army, but with a brigade of engineers and accountants. And thus the new world order dawned.

Reza Shah's rule, however, had not been entirely about hats a fuzzy beards. Back in the 30's Reza Shah had attempted to negotiate upping the 16% Iranian royalties on the AIOC up to a whopping 25%. He leveraged the offer with a threat that if the Brits didn't grant the rise, he'd demand 50%. Somehow the Brits – and you almost have to admire them for it – talked the Reza Shah down to 12.5%, along with some other goodies they'd pull out the books that the Iranian government wasn't allowed to see.

This put the Iranian share of the profits about where it started, if the London was to be believed. Then, in December of 1950, much to the horror of the Brits, the American-Arabian Oil Company negotiated a 50/50 profit spilt with Saudi Arabia.

Enter Mohammad Mossadegh. He was a popular nationalist politician – the locals found him charming and charismatic, the West thought he was a flighty hypochondriac. He'd founded the National Front to rally for the nationalization of the AIOC. And it wasn't just the money, either. AIOC hired thousands of Iranians, but not in the good jobs. The housing for the locals was awful and all the decent water-fountains read "Not for Iranians." When news of the American-Arabian deal reached Tehran, Mossadegh pushed the issue past the tipping point. In April of 1951 the *Majlis* (Iranian parliament) overwhelmingly voted for nationalization. The legislative victory was so total that the Shah reluctantly put his name to the order to maintain the appearance of actually running the place.

It was Mossadegh's crowning moment – almost literally. The next month there was a watershed event in 2,500 years of Iranian history: A fair and legal election.* Mohammad Mossadegh was elected prime minister. The United States actually had, despite itself, made Iran safe for democracy. We should have been pleased. The British were furious. Their immediate reaction was to mobilize an invasion of some 70,000 troops to secure the AIOC properties and Iran's southern oil fields. Mossadegh may have been a hypochondriac, but he was a wily one. Most likely he thought that the British would default to

---

*They hadn't had many elections to begin with, and the ones that had been held were problematic. Hell, even Darius the Great rigged the election by neighing horse, and that was *after* he'd killed the real king.

invasion and force the hand of the United States, whose main goal was Soviet containment rather than propping up Britain's informal empire. And he was mostly right. For the Truman administration, the timing was terrible. The administration believed that a British action would provoke a Soviet invasion from the north to "liberate" the country in the name of international communism. If that weren't bad enough, Truman needed Britain's support in Korea. He talked the British off the ledge by offering to negotiate with Mossadegh himself.

The US mediation resulted in something along the lines of "Christ, it's their oil, just give them half." Historical accounts differ widely on just who rejected the offer. From the British point of view, it didn't matter how lopsided the contract was, it was a contract. And Mossadegh, having pulled of a *fait accompli* with nationalization saw no reason to go back to a 50/50 spilt.

It was a great political victory for Mossadegh, but a grim practical reality loomed. Extracting and refining oil isn't like weeding the garden. The British boycotted Iranian oil – not only did they refuse to buy it, but they refused to extract or refine it. The Iranians now owed their oil, but didn't know how to get the stuff and therefore couldn't sell it to anyone. As oil revenue made up two-thirds of the country's foreign exchange this crippled the economy. Still, Mossadegh refused to budge and his defiance was like nothing the people had ever seen before. It was intoxicating. His support was so strong that he appeared to be more powerful than the shah himself – who actually considered resigning in the face of events.

As the standoff ground on, however, the economy cratered. As law and order broke down Mossadegh became increasingly authoritarian to keep a lid on the anarchy with decrees, cancelling the *Majlis* and challenging the Shah's authority to rule.

President Truman thought Mossadegh was tedious, but he was the duly elected prime minister. Eisenhower, however, was less impressed. He thought power had gone to the man's head. The 50/50 split Truman had negotiated seemed perfectly reasonable to Ike. The Eisenhower administration was in favor of full independence for the Middle Eastern countries, but wanted to slow the process down. He thought that too rapid a withdrawal by France and Great Britain might lead to the new governments to orient themselves towards the Soviet Bloc – which offered great sounding political solutions that only work if the listener knows nothing about economics, simple math and basic human psychology.

Winston Churchill, again back in 10 Downing Street, was enough of a politician to know that he needed to forget percentages and profits when selling the Mossadegh situation to his old war-time buddy Ike. The man probably wasn't a full-blown Red, Churchill conceded, but he *was* losing control of the country and stirring up hatred of the West in Tehran. So if things got out of hand as they looked like they were going to, it could trigger a Soviet take over. Eisenhower didn't really care about an Anglo-Iranian trade deal, but that Red Menace business struck a cord. He needed NATO allies to contain the Soviets in Europe – and those nations needed to be supplied with relatively cheap oil to keep them warm and happy. From that point of view, the US had to keep the supply chain open as well as keep Iranian oil on the free market. So something had to be done.

LET'S CLARIFY our terms when discussing the lively recent histories of Iraq and Iran. While one often follows in the other's footsteps, there is a difference between the coup d'état and the revolution. Coup d'état is one of those French words that was too good to not leech into English – it means a "stroke against the state," or more literally means "blow to state." And for the outgoing chief executive it really does blow. Unlike revolutions – which are broad based, involve howling mobs, and a generally very bloody on a national scale – the coup d'état comes from within the existing power structure. They are as often as not bloodless, or at any rate spill just enough blood for the odd assassination. Among the wonks who study this sort of thing there is an actual marker for determining whether or not a coup is successful: It stays in power for an entire week. Which seems to be a pretty low bar.

The coup is also fairly cheap and, baffling to most Americans, triggering one in a foreign country isn't all that involved. Tricky, yes and the chances of whole operation going tits up are astronomical, to be sure. Provided you are operating in a country where this sort of thing has happened before, however, it really isn't all that complicated if you know what you are doing.

The CIA called the joint mission it conducted with the British Operation AJAX. MI6 called scheme to give Mossadegh the boot Operation BOOT.* The CIA sent a man named Kermit Roosevelt, the grandson of President "Big Stick" Roosevelt, to head up the operation. He immediately set about recruiting pro-Western army officers to the cause which in a society fraying

---

*Again, the code-name "Boot" was just bad tradecraft. "Ajax" was – given the social make-up of the CIA of the time, probably just snobby racism, but it sheds no light on the nature of the operation.

under a crippled economy, wasn't difficult. Certainly not if you are throwing a lot of money around. He even delivered $10,000 to Ayatollah Abulgasim Kashani – a one-time supporter of Mossadegh who'd been jailed by the British for being pro-Nazi and had been in exile for being involved in a plot to kill the shah. Time, and CIA money, had evidently had mellowed the man as he was trying to distance himself from his erstwhile protégé, Ruhollah Khomeini.

Mohammad Shah was informed of the plot to rid him of the troublesome prime minister. While no fan of Mossadegh, the shah was indecisive to the idea of the coup. He wasn't opposed to the idea of foreign influence, you understand, he was used to that. It's that the man was just congenitally indecisive to *everything*. The Brits sent their man in Rome to get his twin to go back home and talk some sense into the shah. Had any logic been applied to the Iranian succession, his twin would have ascended to the Peacock Throne, as she was the smart, decisive and headstrong one. But Princess Ashraf *was* a she and traditional Asians are can be prickly about that sort of thing. So strong willed was Princess Ashraf that she was – not in exile really – but it had been strongly suggested she decamp to Rome, where the Italians were used to loud women.

At first, she refused to speak to her brother about the coup. True to form – and you really do have to admire her for it – she bilked Her Majesty's treasury for a huge bribe and a mink coat before agreeing to brow beat her milquetoast twin, the Shah of Iran, into submission.

Back in Tehran, Roosevelt was throwing money around to organize the trade unionists, the police, clergy and thugs-about-town into coordinated anti-government protests designed to throw the capital into chaos. If we are going to get down to brass tacks, a burst of blindsiding chaos is really the active ingredient in successful coup d'état. It's the yeast that caused the bread to rise, as it were. Only in this case, the yeast was nitroglycerin.

While all that was proofing,* Mohammad Shah signed some legally dubious decrees deposing Mossadegh and appointing a CIA/MI6 picked successor. Word, as it will, got out. Mossadegh caught wind of the plot and had one of the officers involved arrested. The gambit so spooked the fearless shah that he fled the country to Rome.

Showing a stick-to-itivness that would have made grand-dad proud, Roosevelt pressed on with the plan. On 9 August 1953 the anti-government rallies went off as scheduled – that $10,000 to Khomeini's mentor had been paid the day before – and the city went into chaos. Pro-Western army officers seized the parliament building and the radio station and sent soldiers crawling through town to round up Mossadegh and his supporters. Mossadegh himself tried to escape by climbing over the wall of his back garden, but was eventually captured.

The news of the ouster reached Mohammad Shah while he was having breakfast at the Excelsior Hotel in Rome. He reportedly said to his wife, "I knew it! I knew they loved me!" His Imperial Majesty hopped on a plane back to Tehran to "take control" of the situation and formally appoint the prime minister that Kermit Roosevelt had told him he was going to appoint.

So it was that the first, and last, fairly elected leader of Iran was deposed by the government of a foreign country built on fairly elected leaders. As for the nationalization of AIOC, it

---

*See what I did with the metaphor there...

remained in a formal sense. To revoke it would have looked so bad it would likely have sparked a popular revolution. A face-saving compromise was reached: The nationalization of Iranian oil stood, but the concession to extract, refine and sell it went back to the British. And the United States. And *those* profits were split 50/50. The British were miffed about it, but it was the price of admission. What's more, the shah was now solidly in Uncle Sam's deep pockets. He reported said to Kermit Roosevelt, "I owe my throne to God, my people, my army and you."

The ever-helpful Roosevelt continued to work with the shah, setting up a highly, even brutally, effective intelligence operation designed to sniff out communists. In 1957, this became known officially as the National Security and Intelligence Organizations, or SAVAK. Oil revenue boomed, which the shah now spent on a shiny new Army and Air Force bought from the United States.

In light of the grand plan to contain the Soviet Union, the United States had its man in Tehran on the southern border of Russia and it was very important to the US that he remain there. For that matter, it was very important to the shah that he remain there as well. He'd had quite enough of a free and lively democracy, and so stepped on the throat of the Iranian people. Hard.

All things considered, it was a very short-sighted victory for US foreign policy. Having been introduced to the *Fedayeen-e Islam* (Fighters of Islam), Iran's first Islamic terrorist group, by Ayatollah Kashani, Ruhollah Khomeini moved closer to the radicals as his former mentor moved away on a raft of CIA money. Khomeini wasn't just chapped about US support of the dread shah either. The country supposedly built on self-determination of indigenous people was, to the Muslim point of view, supporting the efforts of a bunch of European refugees carve a wholly new country out of Palestine. At the time, the plight of the Jewish refugees did trigger sympathy from the majority of the population, but Muslims couldn't see why they had to give them a country just because the Germans had been insufferable. Although Khomeini wasn't that mellow about it – his mentor had been a Nazi sympathizer.

What's more, Jerusalem was a holy city in Islam as well. Didn't they know that? Was the Muslim world looking down the barrel of another European Crusade over the Holy Land? In short, Ruhollah Khomeini was developing and very grumpy world view.

The fact is that the average man's love of liberty is nine-tenths imaginary, exactly like his love of sense, justice and truth.

HL Menkin
Baltimore Evening Sun (12 February 1923)

CHAPTER FIFTEEN:
THE MULLAH IN THE MOON

UNTIL HIS ARRIVAL IN PARIS in 1978, Ayatollah Rudollah Khomeini had been an obscure cleric howling at the moon in exile since the 1960's for criticizing the Shah's iron-fisted rule. Although, being iron-fisted was never strictly offensive to the man. What he really objected to was the regime's attempt at modernization, or more to the point, secularization. And her e Khomeini's medieval fears weren't completely wrong. Under the shah, the country had developed a modern middle class that wanted a greater say in how the country was run. And society *was* more secular – causing Khomeini to fear that the old, uneasy alliance between the *bazaari* and the clerics was shifting to leave the traditional-minded mullah out of the loop.

Khomeini's exile wasn't helping. Forced to leave that Iranian center of Theology in Qom, Khomeini studied and taught among the Shi'a in neighboring Iran and in Lebanon, gathering

241

students and followers. And not much else, at least that's the way it seemed.

The ayatollah preached an intoxicating cocktail with a Great Satan of the United States, a measure of self-important victimization, and garnished with a vision of a glorious past. It was a simple, if harsh, solution: Return to the type of Islam that used to make the West tremble and tremble they would. If we're going to be completely honest (or even remotely self-aware) Khomeini's hatred of America, while a tad unhinged, *was* grounded in a legitimate grievance. And not some century old blood feud either. We'd managed to knock over Iran's first democratically elected prime minister in 1953 when Khomeini was well into middle age. And it was the aftershock of that adventure that caused Khomeini to go into exile. And a lot of Iranians agreed with him.

It was all very thrilling, but in practice, even some of his student followers thought that the man was wound a little tight. As his contacts in Qom let him know that the domestic situation for the shah was worsening, Khomeini started referring to himself as "Imam": a loaded term in the Muslim world that had been out of general usage for hundreds of years.* The educated, religious elite didn't approve of his using it. Iran's left-leaning urban seculars didn't really care. For the pious, superstitious rural population, however, the word meant something in a world that hadn't meant much to them in years. They would have taken the term as a reference to the 12th Imam: Islam's final Shi'a Imam who disappeared in the 10th century and, it was said, would return at the end of days. Heady stuff.

_____

*It gets tossed around pretty willy-nilly these days.

It was in these rural hinterlands where audio cassette tapes of Khomeini's sermons were circulated. Whether he intended to or not, it was a masterstroke, as it pulled the large, and largely ignored, rural population behind him without much blowback from the urban elite. In a pre-streaming world, he could tell both factions whatever they wanted to hear without much danger of the two segments ever actually running into each other, much less swapping cassette tapes.

To put things in context – this religious revival wasn't just taking place in the Iranian countryside, it was pan-Arab in nature.* After a generation of mini-Nassers had swept through the region preaching secular socialism, the Arab world was disillusioned and feeling morally empty. While the shah was rarely accused of having his fingers on the pulse of his nation, he could see it too. He was growing increasingly paranoid that the *bazaari* who'd benefitted so much from the country's modernization schemes just might return to that bad marriage with the mullahs. If Khomeini had a particular political talent, it was his long game. The man could be very patient with bad marriages.

By October of 1978, Khomeini moved to Paris at the invitation of one Abol Hassam Bani-Sadr; an interesting figure in the anti-shah movement. He came from a prominent religious family, his father was an ayatollah who knew Khomeini, yet he had received a middle-class secular education. In his decade in Paris, Bani-Sadr had gone native with the Left Bank intellectuals who'd joined with the unions in May 1968 to wreck the

---

*The West had its revivals as well – even President Carter was something of a Big Tent guy.

government of Charles De Gaulle. Bani-Sadr had learned a trick or two.

"May 68" was violent and disruptive enough to bring the French economy to its knees. President De Gaulle, fearing for his personal security during the crisis, fled to Germany along the Historical Irony Highway. After the government agreed to pay raises for the unions and everyone went back to work, De Gaulle returned to France, declared himself the winner and was promptly re-elected.*

In the last decade, Bani-Sadr had written some books railing against the shah and thought that the gathering protests against the regime a decade later as a repeat of the May 68, despite the fact that De Gaulle had not been deposed. Which may tell us something about both Bani-Sadr as well as the ayatollah.

Khomeini was no left-leaning intellectual, certainly not a French one – but he was playing revolutionary chess while the rest of Iran was playing constitutional checkers. When Khomeini arrived at Ban-Sadr's Paris apartment he was mobbed by exiled Shi'a fans. The ruckus chapped the badly lapsed Catholicism of his neighbors, who kept calling the police until the cleric moved out to the country. Still, Bani-Sadr kept him connected with events unfolding in Tehran as the French government provided for his security. France, appreciative to the United States for bailing them out of two world wars and taking over their far-east colonial conflict for them, made a point of taking any geopolitical position that was opposite any stance taken by the

---

*And why not? It had worked in 1945.

United States. As such, they were willing to house some cleric wailing against the shah favored by the British and the US.*

No one outside the Iranian or regional Shi'a communities really cared what he was carrying on about while encamped in some dusty town in southern Iraq. In Paris, however, the ever-grateful French press started to give his anti-US stance an airing. This was a goldmine for the Soviet directed active measures campaign (basically the trade name for what we now call fake news) designed to drive a wedge between the Western allies. The East German STASI were stoking the anti-nuclear protests rolling through Europe, and with a little help, they could keep Khomeini in the international spotlight indefinitely.

Khomeini was gaining recognition on the international stage as radical head of the "movement" against the shah. Using first world technology like decent phone lines, he exploited contacts still in Iraq where he continued to work with exiled Iranian student groups now scattered across Lebanon, Europe and America.

Most of these far-flung groups didn't care that much about the religious element of the ayatollah's ramblings, only that some popular figure was emerging as the opposition focal point to the shah's regime. The liberal, secular arm of the movement had decided that they'd hold their noses, win the fight, and (hopefully) sort out the details later.

In Tehran, the Mohammad Shah watched events with growing alarm. Always at his best when the chips were up, the

---

*France's foreign policy throughout the 20th century has always had the mentality of an indignant middle-school pout. Although, in the 21st century, their infatuation with anti-American political Islam has somewhat faded.

shah was unreliable on his best days. And these were not his best days – he was holded up in his palace dying of cancer. If he was praying for a miracle he likely thought it would come in the form of another one of Teddy Roosevelt's offspring. What he got was Jimmy Carter.

The truth is that very little of this moved the needle in Washington until matters passed the tipping point. The White House's Iran policy was scattered. The Secretary of State, Cyrus Vance, was advising the shah to create a coalition government with the loyal opposition. Meanwhile, Carter's National Security Advisor Zbigniew Brzeninski, who could have taught a masterclass in revolution, argued the Machiavellian point that if you give the radicals an inch, they'll demand a mile. And probably your head.* Ergo, just crush them and be done with it.

As for Carter himself, he said that he was putting the US policy of blanket support for the shah's repressive regime under "moral review." In light of declassified documents relating to Iran, its more likely that the moral review business was just something he thought voters wanted to hear.

The timing was bad. With crucial White House support now in question, protests against the shah were growing and the Iranian government was now opining about letting people decide for themselves what government they wanted. In effect, the US was responsible for discontent with the shah reaching its tipping point, leading to the first Persian Spring or Green movement. And because no good deed goes unpunished, also the fanatical jihadism that has led to the never-ending War on Terror.

---

*It's not my place to get into the morals of the maneuver, but it appears that Mac is correct here.

It wasn't until November of 1978 that Carter turned his attention to the White House's scattered Iran policy and gave it some focus. He sent a message to William Sullivan, US Ambassador to Iran, to tell the shah that he did have Carter's full support but that there was a "need for decisive action and leadership to restore order and his own authority."

Disconnected from his subjects as he was, the shah still had a better read on the situation on the ground that Carter. According to Sullivan's own report, the shah asked the ambassador why Carter thought that a military government would be successful as it would only trigger a *fatwa* from Khomeini calling for *jihad* in the midst of a religious revival. If that happened, the shah was pretty certain that parts of the army would answer the call despite orders to the contrary. It would be, in the words of the shah, a "bloodbath."

Carter may have sold himself as a Sunday school hippie to the voters, but his papers show a ruthless schemer at work. The two angles created a fateful blind spot for the president in Iran so that he couldn't see that a crack-down to restore order and the reform the regime desperately needed were mutually exclusive operations.

Just as Khomeini's cassette tapes had galvanized the rural areas, his contacts with the political class back home revealed that the cleric also had a Machiavellian grasp of the *realpolitik*. He was assuring the existing power structure in Tehran that not only he was the obvious choice to replace the shah, but once he'd come to power, that he'd work within the existing power structure. Khomeini was a true believer, but he was a practical one. He even called the head of SAVAK, the shah's terrifying secret police, to discuss job openings in a post-Shah Iran.

What happened next had absolutely nothing to do with US foreign policy. Some old granny in southern Iraq claimed that she'd had a dream that all would be able to see the very face of Rudallah Khomeini in the full moon on 27 November 1978. The genius of the rumor was that only the "just" would be able to see it. Ne'er-do-wells, thieves and the generally regrettable would be blind to the holy apparition. Suddenly, on the night of the 27th, *everyone* could see the face in the moon. Or at least no one would admit that they hadn't seen it. To describe the face in the full moon as a mass hallucination, or even delusion, is overselling it. Just a garden variety collective lie carried on a wave crushing public opinion simply because no one wanted to admit to *not* seeing it. From the point of view of the shah, this made his main opposition magic, which is never a good thing. It also meant that, on the off-chance Khomeini *was* the 12th Imam, the end of the world was in the offing.

By the first week of January 1979 even the shah himself could see that the momentum against him was unstoppable. He went on television in a last-minute effort to make himself seem reasonable, and said: "As the Shah of Iran and an Iranian citizen, I cannot but approve of your revolution." The military tried to restore order by arresting a gaggle of government officials while scores more fled the country. Like his father before him; Mohammad Reza Shah Pahlavi, the last Shah of Iran - who just four years earlier had celebrated 2,500 years of the Iranian Monarchy - fled the country.

Carter sent General Robert Huyser, of US European Command, to but some steal the spines of the Iranian general for a military takeover. What Huyser discovered was that they were already busy plotting cushy retirements in exile to really care what the Carter thought about it.

IN FEBRUARY OF 1979, Ayatollah Khomeini, now the popular face of the movement, returned to Iran to take control of the coup d'état and drove it headlong into the revolution that he'd envisioned all along. Here Khomeini was channeling the greatest of Persian usurpers – Darius I – in declaring himself the holy protector of the truth, and therefore all his opponents devotees of the lie. He even bested the old guard by letting people believe looking down from the moon to check who was naughty or nice. Khomeini had carefully chosen to call himself "Imam' without ever saying that he was the 12th – that would have been heresy. Could he help it if the people filled in the blanks for themselves? The end result was the same: Anyone who opposed the ayatollah opposed Islam. This put the secular moderates who'd supported Khomeini in a squeeze because no one wanted to be on record opposing Islam. Soon events outpaced ideology.

On 11 February 1979, the Peacock Throne was deposed after what was left of the army had been overwhelmed in street fighting. That same day General Huyser received a call from Brzezinski, the deputy Secretary of defense, and the chairman of the joint chiefs of staff about Huyser's willingness to stage the military take over. Despite what you see on television, it is almost inconceivable that the call wasn't a direct order from Carter. Huyser agreed only if the White House would agree to a 10,000 troops force. Whereupon, the call lapsed into silence and ended quietly.

Three days later, the Organization of Iranian Peoples had stormed the US Embassy in Tehran and taken a US Marine, Kenneth Krous, hostage. The US State Department contacted the Iranian foreign minister and the embassy was cleared in a couple of hours. Although it took Krous – tortured and sentenced to death in the interim – six days to be returned to US authorities. It was called the Valentine's Day Open House.

In the resulting power vacuum, Ayatollah Khomeini spied a chance to enact his wildest fantasy of an Islamic republic: a Muslim citizenry who would be free to elect a national assembly that would duly be ignored by the untouchable group of clerics actually running the place. This wasn't a revolution of freedom, but one of ideological purity. To get the masses on board for something like that you've really got to beat them eight ways from Sunday. Or, in these parts, Friday. By referendum, Khomeini was elected as supreme leader on 1 April 1979.

The problem was that to get himself seen as the popular head of the movement *cum* revolution, he'd had to make a lot of promises to a lot of moderate forces who he privately thought needed to, quite literally, go to hell. Bani-Sadr, the Francophile moderate with his pesky attachment to 'democracy' became the Islamic Republic's first president. The powers of the office in those days were strangely vague in light of Khomeini's early insistence that the clergy should not be involved in politics, and yet should have control of everything. The ayatollah set about trying to act as a moderator between the mullahs and President Bani-Sadr by undermining the president, vaguely grousing to the clergy and entreating to courts to kill everyone on the street who seemed likely to vote for the Bani-Sadr.

I REMEMBER WATCHING the actual footage of the student groups in Tehran when I was a kid. I didn't realize what was going on, and I certainly wasn't aware that students were ever allowed to lock-up adults in a closet. Sister Nora-Rita, whom if I recall correctly was nine and a half feet tall, would have beaten me whacky with a yardstick for a stunt like that. What I could see, however, was that dad was pissed.

That a group of mostly secularly educated students called themselves "Muslim Student Followers of the Imam's Line" tells us a lot about the events of November 1979, events that many refer to as the opening shot of the War on Terror. Khomeini had made lots of promises to the left-leaning liberals about this new Islam-flavored democracy in January, and ten months later, the shape of things to come were becoming clear. First of all, there was going to be nothing democratic about it. The SAVAK, the old shah's secret eyes and ears, had changed its name as well as its targets, but not its purpose – or even much of its staff. Like the Chinese revolution, the Russian one before that and the French earlier still, mass executions of enemies of the revolution were still taking place in an old school courtyard as the definition of "enemies" seemed to become more and more fluid.

For all its fury, student activism never really pushes events quite like youthful protestors tell themselves it does down at the Student Union or on social media. What the kids are very good at – eerily so – is sniffing out existing social movements just as they tip into the mainstream. Then the kids pile on a fashionable bandwagon and tell everyone that they were there from the beginning. While their middle-aged counterparts, saddled as they are with actual worries like paying for Jr.'s four-year college fantasy camp, are standing around until well after the fact saying things like, "What the hell? Is *that* a thing now?"

A crazy old cleric might be a radical choice for a student movement, but Bernie Sanders happened state-side, so you never can tell. Given the conditions on the ground in Tehran, it was a safest option. In light of the Valentine's Day Open House, what they did to curry favor with the old guy wasn't particularly original. According to an Iranian student called Ebrahim Asgharzadeh, one of five at the first meeting of Muslim Student Followers in September, the original plan was to storm the Soviet Embassy to protest their meddling in Afghanistan. For the record, the United States was also against Russia's Great Game shenanigans. The Soviet Embassy sit-in was voted down on the (probably correct) theory that the students would get a lot more bang for their media buck by storming the US Embassy,* as the Soviets were likely to shoot them and then just sit on the story. Since the students didn't really have any concrete beef with America other than Khomeini's Great Satan business, the idea was to have a sit-in, detain some diplomats while they made some revolutionary demands to the international press that no one thought would actually be met. Revolutionary credentials thus established, they'd wrap things up in a couple of days or a week at the outside.

It wasn't a bad plan: It had been tried before, was incredibly annoying but mostly non-violent, and was as good a hedge as any against having some deranged cleric order you before a death squad. And yet, between planning and execution, what should

---

* Before every loon on the planet had their own YouTube Channel to steal a bit of media coverage was a big deal.

have been a completely irrelevant detail in the opera changed the course of events of the revolution – and US relations with Muslim world going forward.

Since fleeing Iran in January ahead of Khomeini's grand entrance,* the old shah had moved around in plush exile in semi-fabulous places until he eventually landed in Mexico. His cancer had by now progressed to a point where his only hope for treatment was the United States – or turn out the lights. President Carter's advisors tried to talk him into barring the shah from entering the country and, practically speaking, he should have listened. Carter, showing another blind spot – this one for massive, fairly obvious, geopolitical metaphors – was determined to be moral about it. In November of 1979, the shah flew to John Hopkins in Baltimore for treatment.

The student activists, with their keen grasp of the theatrical, if extraneous, posturing suddenly decided that the US was "harboring" the hated shah. They staged their sit-in. The truth was that US Embassy officials, thinking the children would make themselves obvious for few hours like the last group did, allowed them to come on in and called the Iranian foreign minister.

Meanwhile Khomeini was cultivating a mysterious mystique that included not having a phone, along with the fiction that he had no interest in politics. He was conducting the revolution from that seat of Shi'a learning, the city of Qom, where he was certain the cancer-riddled shah would not show up to drag him around by the beard.

---

* For those counting, this is the second time this Shah had fled the country ahead of a coup.

His foreign minister, Ibrahim Yazdi, drove down from Tehran to tell Khomeini about the student activities. The ayatollah didn't know who the students were or why they'd done it and told Yazdi to head back to Tehran and "go kick them out."

After Yazdi left, Khomeini turned on the radio. The press had gotten wind of things and was reporting on scenes of happy crowds outside the embassy in revolutionary euphoria. Yazdi was still on the road back to Tehran when he heard Khomeini's voice on the radio calling the seizure of the US embassy a "second revolution" against the American spy den in Tehran. Now the students, encouraged by the ayatollah's words, started parading the hostages around in front of the cameras. The whole story had a great underdog against the tyrant feel that played well in the Muslim world. And played really well in Iran a mere twenty years after that Mossadegh business. Sensitive to the symbolism of the action, the students – conveniently forgetting the Muslim slave trade – released the African-Americans saying that they'd been oppressed enough by America. They also released the females, citing "the special place of women in Islam." Which appears to be about three paces behind the men of Islam.

CIA documents show that the agency thought Khomeini was behind the seizure. Combing through the company's own timeline, however, leaves open the possibility that the old guy just knew a good opportunity when he saw one and, despite his unswept mystique, he did know where to find a phone. Even in Qom.

As things that haven't been thought through will, the whole ordeal took on a life of its own. The student crowds were demanding the return of the shah so that they could kill the man before the cancer took all the fun out of it. By December, the old guy had left America anyway and flew to very Muslim Egypt, whose diplomats went about Tehran curiously unmolested. Later that same month, the Soviets upped their meddling in neighboring Afghanistan into a full-blown invasion. The US strenuously opposed the move and started supplying the Muslim Afghans the means to resist. Were someone to take the dangerous step of applying logic to the situation, this would (again) completely align the aims of the US and Iran against the USSR – but the mob had spoken. At this point, reality would only take the zing out of things.

That same month, Carter issued a presidential finding ordering the CIA to:

> ...conduct propaganda and political and economic operations to encourage the establishment of a responsible and democratic regime in Iran; make contacts with Iranian opposition leaders and interested governments in order to encourage interactions that could lead to a broad pro-Western front capable of forming an alternative government.

To be charitable about it, Carter didn't just give up and roll over on Iran as is widely believed by his critics. Less charitably, he arrogant enough to keep believing that he could will his own ill-defined reality on Iran if, like Eisenhower before him, he just kept monkeying around with the army to crush the will of the people he intended to help. Which is not something his fans want to believe either.

For its part, the CIA's own assessment was that the issue might just fix itself. According its own (now declassified) documents:"Khomeini's attempt to rule a semi-developed state of the late twentieth century by the standards of a tenth century theocracy will ultimately fail." Their logic isn't bad, really, but one suspects that Carter knew a little more about the effects of those big tent religious revivals that the boys from Langley. The company was pretty Ivy League back then.

When the Shah died in Egypt six months later in July of 1980, no one, least of all Khomeini, seemed to really know *why* the American diplomats were still being held, except sour grapes about a rescue effort called Operation Eagle Claw* that had failed when the helicopter crashed in a Tehran neighborhood.

Any sneering the Iranians got from the failed rescue operation, however, was tamped down by the success in late June of a joint US-Canadian effort to rescue six diplomats that had managed to evade getting held hostage. The wheeze was to pose as a Canadian film crew making a sci-fi movie. The operation was code-named ARGO: which had the advantage not letting on what the ultimate objective was as well as making a really cool name for a movie.

AS IRAN WAS DESCENDING into something close to a civil war, Khomeini was savvy enough to know that he needed a foreign devil to stabilize the domestic situation. Despite the caterwauling of student activists, that "America the Great Satan" business was pretty abstract, so Khomeini started eyeballing the Ba'athists next door. He called on the oppressed Iraqi Shi'a population to rise up against their secular government for the cause of Shi'a Islam and the Kurds to rise up as that would be irritating for the secular Iraqi regime. This wasn't just hot air,

---

*Covert operation code names are supposed to give no hint of the operational objectives. Seriously, that's just Tradecraft 101. The helicopter crash was pretty conspicuous as well.

either. A radical ally of Khomeini, cleric Mohammad al-Sadr, threw a three-day holiday in Najif, Iraq to celebrate the return of the ayatollah's to Tehran.

In Baghdad, then Vice-President Saddam Hussein – head of that country's paranoid security establishment – watched these events with growing alarm. With President Bakr in ailing health, Saddam had been de facto running the country, but before things got too far in the Shi'a south, he needed formal control of the country. It would be a stretch to say that Saddam Hussein came to power legally, but it wasn't really a coup either. More like a strongly worded suggestion to his former mentor that the old man was rather past his gone-off date. Five months after Khomeini's return to Iran, Saddam Hussein was formally President of Iraq and barking about liberating the Arabs living in Iran from Persian rule.* Then both sides started assassinating each other's ministers. Saddam, never one for half measures started murdering Iraqis as well in a paranoid purge. Mohammad al-Sadr, Khomeini's friend and Iraqi cheerleader was one of them. Two generations later al-Sadr's grandson would continue the family business by running around making himself obvious in the insurgency in Iraq.

Like the strongmen of Mesopotamia and Persia, the two leaders hated each other as much as two neighbors can. It was a hatred rooted more in their similarities than their differences. Both men had a vision of themselves dominating the world – which isn't a Bond villianish as it sounds. Saddam still clung to

---

*Most Arabs think Iranians *are* Arab, but are just being difficult. When the Iranians start talking revolution – the Arabs call them "Persians." Iranians really hate this. The Turks, in my experience, find the whole thing hilarious.

the dream of heading a mostly secular pan-Arab bloc to counter the West, as well as the Soviet bloc, while taking money from both. Khomeini was tapping into the growing feeling in the Muslim world that Western secularization was leaving people without a sense of purpose – a society without a rudder. Both wanted to dominate, and they were going to do it with the "Oil Weapon."

The Middle East, through OPEC, had already learned to use the oil weapon with devastating effect on the world's economies. Both Iran and Iraq realized that they could dominate the world simply by dominating the Middle East – still a fractious sphere of quarreling petty rulers who'd never quite found their level since the dissolution of the Ottoman Empire and the subsequent European carve up.

Both men had visions of long faded empires: old Assyrian splendor once again radiating from Baghdad, and the glories of Cyrus riding out of Persia once again to bring order to the world. True, neither man was even remotely equipped to pull off such grand designs, but there was no telling them that.

AS SADDAM WELL KNEW, power changes are tricky times. Khomeini may have been in charge of the revolution, but now that the Shah was gone, he wasn't exactly in charge of the government. Iran's military had been entirely supplied by the US – which it had now completely alienated. This posed a military problem. War is very tough on even military grade equipment, and it is very hard to fight an engagement when your military's only spare parts provider hates you.

In September of 1980, Iraq bombed the airport in Tehran and invaded. The hope was that the Arab population living in the oil rich region of Khuzestan (once known as Arabistan) would rise up and push the invading Arabs forward. The gambit didn't work and, while the Iraqis managed to hold their territorial gains, the front got badly bogged down. As it was, the U.S. did not invade Iran in tandem in 1980 to prop some pro-US rube up on the Peacock Throne is something for which we've never quite forgiven Jimmy Carter. The hostages were released in 20 Jan 1981 – the first day of Ronald Regan's presidency.

What resulted is what the West calls the First Persian Gulf *War*, but what Saddam inexplicably called the Whirlwind War, despite clocking in as the longest conventional war of the 20th century. Military historians often draw comparisons with this conflict and World War I, citing the use of trench warfare, barbed wire, and a general lack of progress on either side. There was also the heavy-handed use of chemical warfare – so heavy handed that Saddam used them on his own people, Kurdish Iraqis.

Some aspects of the war were more like the Crusades. The Iranians called it a Human Wave – consisting of using children walk across to mine fields in order to clear them. Appalling as the tactic was, it actually worked. The Iraqis were pushed back across the border. Here, many in Tehran wanted Khomeini to stop, but the ayatollah wanted to return Shi'a's holiest shrines located in southern Iraq, to the care of Shi'a Muslims. He also hoped, as Saddam had about the Iranian Arabs, that the Iraqi Shi'a would rise up when he took the war into southern Iraq. Like the Iranian Arabs, the Iraqi Shi'a stayed loyal. The war promptly got bogged down into a stalemate again.

Eventually the UN brokered a cease fire that more or less said that no one got anything, and would you all please kindly go home and take your balls with you. To this hard fought stalemate, Saddam commissioned his victory triumph, the "Martyr's Monument" – a pair of glazed blue half domes called "the tits" by the US Army.

Saddam learned his lesson: Picking on someone your own size was a good way to get punched in the mouth. If you want to feel like a Big Man, you've got to pick on a runt. So he invaded Kuwait. The Iraqi forces ran amok until US led coalition forces chased them back to Nasiriya. Which got the Shia population all worked up thinking that this was the end of Saddam. They were more than a little upset that the US left them to deal with their own political lunatics.

PART THREE:

BAD HAIR AND THE CREEPING APOCALYPSE

BENGHAZI, LIBYA

We ought not fight them at all unless we determine to fight them forever.

John Adams
on the Barbary Pirates

CHAPTER SIXTEEN:
MAKING THE WORLD SAFE FOR ... SOMETHING
PARIS, FRANCE

THE CHARLES DE GAULLE airport in Paris is about as good a representation for modern France as there is: Beautifully designed, on trend and incredibly inefficient. I wasn't actually running through the country's grand metaphor because that's a good way to get yourself stopped by the submachine gun wielding *gendarmerie*. They seem pretty easy going, but then again, they always do until it's too late. I was doing that airport trot of the semi-panicked traveler because I was trying to find *the bag*.

The airport is dotted with those wide, one way moving sidewalks down each side of the expansive corridors. Like America, the sidewalk rules are simple enough: Travelers who are letting the technology do all the work stand on the one side of the belt and the ones who want to use the thing to keep going at super-sonic double time, go down the other. I slung my satchel and bag behind me and barreled down the left side. The only thing I had in my hand was the manila folder with my Libyan visa and documents for that damn 55 kilo bag I'd been responsible for since I'd left Memphis yesterday morning. At this point, I literally didn't know where in the world it was.

I'd made it about half-way down the moving sidewalk when I was blocked by five teenagers – two guys showing off to three gals – leaning against the rails and yet somehow taking up the whole passage. I wheeled up, nodded politely and offered a slightly winded and sympathetic, "*Excusez-moi.*"

The guy slouching against the rail in my way gave me the once over, turned back to gang with a shrug of the shoulders and snickered. I don't know if he was mocking me – it sounded mocking, but the language seems to have been designed that way. The girls didn't move either. In a country of very nearly pacifists, I suppose you have to put up with that sort of foolishness, but I don't come from a country of pacifists. I was on a mission that had nothing to do with how cool this pair of Lotharios thought they needed to look in front of the girls. So, I rolled the manila folder in my hand and swatted one of the boys across in the side of the head. He popped up, indignant. He was still in my way so, for the first and only time in my life, I gave someone the back of my hand.

The trick to a maneuver like this – certainly in public - is to not to throw it out like a challenge inviting further hostilities. Don't blow out the chest or try to look fierce – at my age it would look ridiculous. All you need is a headmasters air of finality. I repeated myself pleasantly, "*Excusez moi. Je peux passer?*" And motioned to pass as the boys lined up on the other side of the sidewalk, giving me the sink-eye as I barreled onward.

Confident I'd improved the manners of the average French teenager just a bit, I arrived at the Air France desk where I found a pretty lady in an airline uniform and a stylish scarf tied at her throat. *"Excusez-moi."* I said and really thought I was getting the accent down by now.

Evidently not. "I speak English." She replied with a smile that said *Your French hurts my ears.*

"I have a question about some baggage."

"Your luggage?"

"No. Not really. There is a bag coming from the United States, originally in Memphis, Tennessee and headed for Istanbul, then ultimately to Benghazi…"

A light went on behind her eyes, she smiled beautifully. "Ahh, *oui monsieur.* That bag!"

Yes. That bag. The ICHF was more than willing to let me tag-along with their operations but they'd make me work. I'd been fairly used to humping nondescript duffels into South America, Iraq, and Ukraine and it hadn't been too much trouble. But the monster I was attempting to get to Benghazi had been causing a lot of bad noise from the start. First of all, it was huge. Yesterday morning, Delta airlines had charged me $100 for the overweight. Which I paid only to discover that my outbound flight from Memphis was running so late that there was no way to catch my connection to Paris. "Well," said Larry at the Delta desk, "we'll just have to get you on a later flight." With that *these things happen and screw your connection* vibe that airline employees always affect.

"Look," I told Larry, "I have a job to do, but honestly, it's not all that important if I don't make my flight. I'm not that crucial in the great scheme of the operation. The problem is the gigantic bag I've already checked. It has to get to Benghazi on schedule."

He stared at me and said, slowly. "Okay, I'll bite. What so important about that bag that it has to get to... did you say Benghazi?" The news was still playing that footage of the burning mission every night.

Well I didn't say I was headed to Katmandu! I explained to Larry at the Delta desk what was in the massive bag and why – all things considered – it was much more important than the one carrying it. This was pediatric heart surgery, kids in North Africa whose only chance for survival was in the hands of gifted surgeons and nurses from across the world meeting to donate time and skill. But there was literally nothing they could do without the donated surgical supplies in that bag. A strange grin crept across Larry's face as I spoke and then he just stared at me for a long moment that I couldn't read. Airline employees take a perverse pride in saying things like "Yes, I get this all the time" in an exasperated calm before telling you to go away. I was fairly certain that he hadn't heard this one before.

Larry took a breath and said, "I had three open-heart surgeries by the time I was twelve. So I'm pro-pediatric heart surgery. You'll have your bag." He started working both the desk phone and his mobile. I tried to help by offering more information but he gave me the kill sign to shut the hell up. Finally, after burning up both lines a couple of times, he hung up both phones and said. "You're gonna to have to run."

I did and only barely made it to that far gate to catch a flight to Minneapolis which, for the record, was not at all where that damn bag was heading. After landing, the plane had only just rolled up to the gate when a stewardess came up to me and said,

"Mr. Murff? Get your bags, they're holding the plane for you." I made another mad dash through the airport. When I turned into the gate the seating area was completely empty save a single attendant standing by the open door to the ramp. "Mr. Murff?" she called.

"Yes." I heaved.

The airplane was backing out of the gate about twelve minutes later. Anyone who has ever actually run through an airport knows that you may catch a flight by the skin of your teeth, but the luggage never does. This was the thought that kept me from sleeping over the next eight hours.

The next morning, the pretty lady Air France desk had the smile of a minor adventure well played. "Yes. That bag! It is in Paris and marked through to Istanbul. There you will need to retrieve it and recheck it onto Turkish Airlines for Benghazi."

"*Mon Dieu.*" I said, "*Merci. Merci.*"*

"You're very welcome." She said. It was a lovely smile but she didn't have much patience for me butchering her mother tongue.

In American airports, restaurants, cafés and bars all have the feel of a shopping mall food court. The coffee kiosk in Charles de Gaulle looked like a slick sidewalk café plopped down in the middle of a terminal, which it basically was. I ordered a cup of good coffee at an astronomical price and read a letter that Mrs. M had slipped into my bag the morning before, which now seemed like a week ago. Next time I was in Paris, she wrote, she'd

---

*Larry at the Delta desk, I owe you big, and I'm not the only one, either. There are children that are alive because of you as surely as the surgeons and nurses who cared for them. Thank you.

be at my side and we'd leave the airport to stay in the city as opposed to flying on to some civil war. Still, I had to do what I had to do, and for that, she was proud of me.

It was a good letter, and on balance, a good morning. In a couple of hours I'd be on a plane to that anti-chamber of the Near East, Istanbul, for an overnight layover. The bag was accounted for, I like Istanbul and so things were looking good. Beyond those little pleasantries, the world was getting hairier.

Being a certain sort of Southerner, the charming Mrs. M and I had discussed my travel for work in a hurricane of euphemism that allowed us to politely ignore what was happening in Libya. There is, however, only so much that you can hide under a pile of charming misdirection. Before I'd left, I suggested a dinner and a movie, as you do. Which is how we came to be – two days before hopping on a plane to Benghazi where the US Special Mission was still a blackened husk – staring at images of Iranians having a grand ole time killing Americans and taking them hostage. It didn't matter that *Argo* is a pretty good movie, or that things always get more harrowing in the retelling, or even that a hunky Ben Affleck would save the day in the end: I am still the most tone-deaf man still currently married.

IRAN'S 1979 CONSTITUTION specifically mentions exporting revolution throughout the Muslim world and, eventually, the globe. Revolutionary constitutions, though, tend to be more ideological than practical. The United States' 1789 Constitution, on the other hand, being affectively a second draft of the erstwhile Articles of Confederation is a little more pragmatic. It is also famously vague about who gets to do what when it comes to foreign policy. This makes a certain degree of sense as the whole idea of the United States was conceived by people who'd high-tailed it to the other side of the planet in an attempt to render foreign policy moot.

George Washington's Farewell Address to a Grateful Nation, written in 1796 on his refusal of a third term, breathes practical authority on the subject. Indeed, for about a century, his farewell was more widely reprinted and read than the actual constitution. What he has to say about foreign entanglements is simple and straightforward: Don't you do it.

Washington was wary about these entanglements for a couple of very sound reasons. The first was that he'd had enough domestic trouble that he didn't need any more: He'd had to put down a "Whiskey Rebellion" in Pennsylvania, and the secession of the yodelin' parts of North Carolina and what's now Tennessee into the Republic of Franklin. He also knew that if you did get help from a foreign actor, payback was hell. Within a decade of taking enough French support and loans to actually win our revolution, we'd been dragged into defending France's Caribbean territories in the War of the First Coalition against Britain and the Netherlands. Which is not at all what US thought would happen when we were taking all that French money.

Faced with a budget pinch, Washington's solution was to argue that France just wasn't its old self after the 1793 execution of Louis XVI and all treaties in His Majesties name were now void. Congress passed the 1794 Neutrality Act which cancelled all military obligations. The French Republic seemed to accept this until we quit repaying out revolutionary war debt on the same grounds. At that point, France went full repo and started seizing American ships trading with the British. This led to the Quasi-War with France which wrapped up in 1800 with a treaty that had France not repaying our shipping losses and our not repaying our loans. Everyone called it a draw.

The problem here was two-fold, now no longer under the protection of either the British or French governments, and the US government having largely disbanded the navy after the revolution, American commercial shipping was ripe for piracy. As a tiny nation of exiles perched way over at the end of the world, barely recognized by the great powers of the day, the United States entered into one of its first international treaties of friendship – with Morocco. Basically, the sultans and pashas of the Barbary Coast – roughly three semi-autonomous provinces of the Ottoman Empire – Tripoli (the capital of the Ottoman province of Tripolitania – now the western chunk of Libya) Algiers, and Tunis, and independent Morocco were running a protection racket where ships plying the Mediterranean either paid tribute to the Sultan or the ships were seized, the goods sold and the crew either ransomed or auctioned off into slavery.

Congress just decided that it was cheaper to pay the sultans off rather than built and maintain a proper navy. Until it wasn't. George Washington eventually urged the building of six frigates that would form the US Navy. The old bastard may have been against foreign entanglements, but he wasn't afraid to throw hands either.

By 1797, with John Adams president, the United States would pay $1.25 million – nearly 20% of the national budget – to the Barbary States for safe passage. During the presidential election of 1800, Thomas Jefferson argued fervently against subjecting the United States to "the spoliations of foreign cruisers."

Years before, in 1786, both Jefferson and Adams had been sent together to negotiate with Tripoli's envoy over what amounts to protection money. Jefferson asked the envoy on what grounds the Barbary States made war "...upon nations who had done them no injury." According to Jefferson, the envoy replied:

> It was written in their Koran, that all nations which had not acknowledged the Prophet were sinners, whom it was the right and duty of the faithful to plunder and enslave; and that every mussulman who was slain in this warfare was sure to go to paradise. He said, also, that the man who was the first to board a vessel had one slave over and above his share, and that when they sprang to the deck of an enemy's ship, every sailor held a dagger in each hand and a third in his mouth; which usually struck such terror into the foe that they cried out for quarter at once.

Jefferson found this grating and always maintained (correctly it turned out), that paying ransom money to pirates would only lead to more piracy. On Jefferson's inauguration, Yusuf Karamanli, the Pasha of Tripoli demanded $225,000 (equivalent of about $4.5 billion 2020 dollars) from the administration. The new president refused. First of all, he didn't have the money, secondly, Yusef wasn't the rightful pasha anyway, but had usurped the throne from his older brother Hamet, now in exile in Egypt. The pasha sent some goons out to cut down the flagpole in front of the US consulate in Tripoli – which was his way of declaring war. Things moved slower back then, and other than a bit of fist shaking, it wasn't until 1802 that the United States sent ships to patrol the area (the hold up being was to get Ferdinand

IV of Naples to let the US Navy use Sicily and Syracuse as a base).

And so it was that the United States, with a government barely a dozen years old, got involved in its first foreign war just down the beach from our oldest ally – in what is now Libya. Being Americans, we tried to whip up a coalition so we hitched our wagon to Sweden's star. The war didn't amount to a lot more than pale Protestant sailors turning a violent shade of pink cruising the Riviera and giving the brown Muslim sailors the hairy eyeball in passing.

It was while pursuing a pirate corsair, the *USS Philadelphia* ran aground on a reef about two miles out from Tripoli harbor. Attempts to float the ship only pushed her further aground. The next day the crew threw all the provisions and cannon overboard in an attempt to lighten the load, but she was stuck. The captain ordered holes drilled into the hull that that no one could float her and surrendered. He and his men became slaves of the pasha. The Libyans used the *Philadelphia* as a gun battery against further US attacks.

In a daring mission, US marines took a captured Berber ketch and sailed up to the *Philadelphia*, overpowered the Ottoman sailors on board and, since the ship was no longer seaworthy, and torched it.

American's first experiment with global adventurism was finally wrapped up when one Lieutenant William Easton lead a force made up of marines, and a lot more Greek and Arab mercenaries, on a 500+ mile forced march from Alexandria, Egypt to Derna in the capital of Cyrenaica (now the eastern chunk of Libya). It was in Alexandria that Eaton had hatched a plan with Yusef's older brother, the exiled Hamet, to seize the throne from his little brother. The plan was to re-provision in Derna and move westward toward Tripoli where we'd have a spot of regime change and install someone grateful to the home team. Tensions got so bad on the 50-day trek that the Marine detachment had to use their one cannon on the Arab mercenaries trying to make off with the chuck wagon.

On 26 April 1805, Eaton (who'd declared himself general of the force because, evidently, the military was much more mellow about that sort of thing back then) asked for safe passage and supplies from the Mustafa Bey, governor of Derna. According to legend, Mustafa responded "Your head or mine!" Which is, even today, a terrible thing to say to a marine. The navy bombarded the city from their end and Eaton launched an attack from his end.

By the end of the day, the American flag flew over a city on the far end of the Atlantic Ocean. Over in Tripoli, Yusef Pasha sent a force to retake the city, but failed. With the city secure Lt. "General" Eaton set out for Tripoli. In the meantime, however, Yusef Pasha has cried "Uncle Sam" to US pressure and agreed to cut out all the piracy and ransom and the rest of it. Eaton was told to go back to Egypt and take to Hamet with him. Eaton was furious, but probably not as angry as the Arab mercenaries, who were never paid.

So the Marine's Hymn kicks off with:

From the Halls of Monetezuma
To the shores of Tripoli

It's a swell hook, but the fact of the matter is that the marines never made it to the shores of Tripoli. And nowhere in the hymn does it mention a sleazy diplomat making a side deal with a creep who, three weeks earlier had been a sworn enemy, or the massive unpaid bill at the end of the beach maneuver. *Plus ça change.*

None of this completely stopped the piracy, of course. With all of Europe in the clutch of the Napoleonic Wars, the Barbary pirates correctly decided that white people were too busy to notice the odd shake down on merchant shipping. Over on the edge of the world, in the Americas, European foreign policy was still running amok in the Western hemisphere with the War of 1812. Once that was wrapped up, the US turned its attention to North African piracy again with the Second Barbary War in 1815. This time we were on the same side as the UK – sort of. Great Britain wanted to stop the piracy, but was also putting a hi-sheen gloss on the issue by angling for the release of all Christian slaves. London had abolished the slave trade in the empire in 1807, and would outlaw it all together in another 18 years. Meanwhile, the position of the US government was that while slavery was an awful thing to do to a white fella, it really just wanted its stuff back.

In 1823, President James Monroe warned the European powers that they had to stay out of the Western hemisphere and we'd stay out of Europe. What's more, now that Portugal and (mostly) Spain had been thrown out of their colonies, Europe could no longer push Latin America around. From now on, only *we* could push Latin America around. This was called the Monroe Doctrine and it was well enough received to get a quasi-religious sheen applied in the form of "Manifest Destiny." To prove it, we invaded Mexico. To hear the Mexicans tell it, we haven't left. They do have a point.

Based on these evolving addresses, doctrines and destinies, US foreign policy has always been like the government's New

Year's Resolutions: We know what's good for us, we know what is the right thing to do, but sometimes an irresistible urge hits and you just *have* to tidy up the sides of that chocolate cake. Or invade Iraq.

IT IS IMPOSSIBLE to really understand our 21st century foreign policy or all its ill-advised global adventurism without the havoc let loose by the briefly mentioned house-painting, pseudo-intellectual Austrian psychopath from Chapter 13. Or more to the point, the post-war settlement. In 1918, the interested victors had negotiated a self-serving deal between allies and the losers just had to take it. In 1945, however the post-war settlement wasn't negotiated at all but simply dictated by the one power that hadn't been razed half-way back to 1452. What was so remarkable was that the same deal was offered to our crippled allies as to the vanquished foes. And it didn't take place in the gilded halls in London or Paris, but at an off-season ski resort in in Bretton Woods, New Hampshire.

The main purpose of the imperial navies of the past – French, British, Spanish, Japanese – had been to keep markets and supply chains open between the home country and the colonies. Obviously, this sounded boring as hell so it was sold as Imperial Glory to the respective publics. When a power was feeling expansive, it went off to wreck the markets and supply chains of a rival and called it Imperial Expansion for the Greater Glory of ... He didn't know it at the time but Darius the Great, that shifty bastard, had really hit on something.

The American revolution was a political anomaly as well as a geographical one: We didn't need an empire because we had a continent, and after that Manifest Destiny business, we had the run of a hemisphere. And it looked like things would stay that way. The old Spanish colonies had envisioned a "United States of South America," but in the resulting power vacuum* the center didn't hold. We didn't have to fight for access to the sea lanes because we had an ocean on either side of us. Our two neighbors who might stage a land invasion were so economically tied into *our* markets as to make the very idea of hostilities not only impossible but aggressively unprofitable. In fact, the only way to invade the United States was an imperial-sized navy. And in 1945, despite efforts to the contrary by the Japanese, we had the only one still floating. And because the US had the only industrial centers of note that hadn't been bombed to rubble, we were the only country capable of maintaining one. When the allied powers met at Bretton Woods, the American economy accounted for a third of the global total.

The QED being that the United States didn't have to negotiate at Bretton Woods, but could dictate terms. And for all you Americans out there poor-mouthing your country, the terms were so generous as to be entirely without historical precedent. To the victorious but brutalized allies, the terms seemed almost non-sensical, even baffling. The United States navy would keep all the markets and global supply chains open. Not only for the allies, but for the defeated Axis as well. Under the new American system, a country could have access to the American market but, unlike the old Imperial system, you didn't even have to do business with America. All you had to do to gain access to the largest free market system in the world, under the protection of the largest naval power, was play by the rules.

---

*With which the North American colonies didn't have to contend.

The liberal rules-based global market ushered in the greatest period of peace and longest, most sustained growth in wealth and standards of living since Ur-Nammu dictated that the price of a turn with a working girl was a piglet. Like Cyrus, and later the Romans, we persuaded most of the world with a better system. It worked on a greater scale than Cyrus the Great's attempts to bring order to the world, and outstripping either the Pax Romana or Pax Britannia.

It wasn't as altruistic as that. Not really. The new system was designed with the US at the top. Still, there was the knock-on effect. Navies, while glorious, are incredibly expensive. No government would splash out on one unless they felt they had to, and now, at least for our allies, they didn't have to. The point of the American system was to contain and put pressure on those powers that had not signed up for the US led free market. As has already been pointed out, where foreign policy from maintaining the greater order to forcing smaller powers to sign onto the system, was where we made a mess. And there was another option, developing a post-war bloc of its own: The Soviets.

This modern world needed oil so both blocs were eager to have the Muslim world sign with their team. The Muslim world, for its part, was sick to death of the Great Game. After the collapse of the Ottoman Empire, President Wilson had made Germany safe for democracy but left the Arab world to their kings and European colonial overlords. And then there was the matter of Palestine *cum* Israel. Again, the feeling in the Muslim world was one of general sympathy to the plight of the Jews at the hands of Nazi Germany. They failed to see, exactly, a Muslim country in the Levant should largely erase itself to give a homeland to the refugees. The Germans had caused the war, why not carve a homeland out of Bavaria?

To the Arabs, the Cold War brewing between the West and the Soviets looked like just more of the same and began seeking a third way – *nonalignment* – which might have worked if the post-war world had not gotten rich enough to buy all those cars. But the West *did* get rich enough to buy all those cars. Suddenly all those people that the West had declared too backward to rule found themselves with a very, very big hand to play.

The hand included feelings of nationalism and self-determination and in Iran all of this was embodied in the AIOC. After the First World War, when the Europeans came in with their "mandates" crawling all over the place looking for oil and screwing the locals, the Arab world barely had a standing army, much less navy. Now with Europe on its back, they struck back. Which put the US on a strange footing with its European allies. We wanted, even needed, the old imperial systems to collapse. We just wanted the old system to collapse in the right way.

And that's the tricky part, isn't it?

Richard Murff

If you treat them like dogs, they will follow you like dogs.
Particularly terrifying Libyan proverb

CHAPTER SEVENTEEN:
BEHOLD THE HAIR AND TREMBLE

THE SEATS ON Turkish Airlines are wildly uncomfortable, but the food is surprisingly good. I had some local cheese, fruit, yogurt that wasn't trying to be ice cream and a glass of wine that was wasn't terrible for an airline. By that I mean never had the urge to ask the stewardess if I was being punished. Of course, it may have just been the altitude, you never can tell. Earlier that morning, I'd wriggled through Istanbul's Atatürk Airport security by acting like such and insufferable ass that security figured I had to be someone important. This was no small feat of acting on my part because, as I'd explained to Larry at the Delta counter, I really was the least important part of the equation. After my performance with Turkish airport security, I'd have quaffed a cup of prison toilet moonshine if I thought it would take the edge off.

Flying into Benghazi was as good a place as any to consider the difference between states, as Machiavelli put it, "acquired with the arms of others" and those "acquired with one's own abilities." It is a world of difference that colors politics long after the war is settled, each with their own raft of troubles. It was a matter that had made George Washington nervous enough to get into an almost war with France. The immediate question when I'd arrived in November of 2012, in that hopeful twilight between revolution and civil war, was just who had acquired the state, and just what in the hell had they acquired?

I was seated next to a Libyan eye doctor I'll call Ahmed, heading home for his brother's funeral. He lived and worked in Ireland and had been home twice since the previous year's revolution. Ahmed seemed to think that the situation was stable enough to bring his son along, a lad of about seven or eight with a nose pressed into an iPad. It made me wonder if that landing on the moon sense of foreignness I'd had when first arriving in Iraq would be erased in a generation or two with all the world's little ones having the same digital babysitter.

Ahmed was seemed pleasantly bored, so I struck up a conversation. He had opinions. "Gaddafi had been a good ruler at first." he told me. "And the monarchy was corrupt and inefficient." As a lieutenant, Gaddafi was known to consort with a group calling themselves the Free Officer Corp, named after the clique Gamal Nasser mooned around with before taking over Egypt a generation earlier. There was revolution in the air, so much so that the CIA was closely monitoring a gang of also-rans called the Black Boot Revolutionaries. Possibly Gaddafi's Free Officer Corp was discounted because they hadn't come up with an original revolutionary name. At any rate, with King Idris traveling abroad in Turkey, the Free Officer Corp saw their chance. It was a standard coup d'etat MO: Take over airports, barracks and the radio station so you could tell everyone about it before you arrest the crown prince and force him to relinquish any royal claims. Even King Idris wasn't terribly surprised. Reportedly, when told about Lieutenant Gaddafi's power grab, the old fella simply asked if the usurpers were Libyans. When he was told that they were, Idris said, more or less, O*kay fine, carry on.* Not actually waiting for permission, Gaddafi declared a republic and promoted himself to Colonel - just like Nasser.*

According the Ahmed in the next seat over, the troubles didn't start until mid-seventies. Then, being a man of science, the doctor pinned it down closer. "It was 1977, after a visit from Castro."

"What happened after Castro's visit?" I asked.

He threw his hands up in the air, "He surrounded himself with his own tribe."

Tea with Castro aside, what happened in 1977[†] was Colonel Gaddafi's Third Universal Theory – published in his *Green Book*. He dissolved the republic and replaced it with j*amahiriya*, meaning "state of the masses." It was billed as an experiment in direct democracy where the citizens voted directly on issues without the corrupting influence of elected representatives. But these direct democracies never really seem to work out in practice because the masses are rarely accused of anything that we'd call long-term vision. In this particular case, the colonel was the one counting the votes, so the immediate effect was to turn him into something of a Libyan Sun King – he was the state.

---

*Muammar seems to have had a bit of a man-crush on the dreamy Gamal Nasser.

[†]Mohammad Ali Bara, a 37-year veteran of Gaddafi's diplomatic corps and former ambassador to Switzerland and Kuwait, puts it earlier. He told Luke Harding of the *Guardian*, "Up until 1975 he was very good. After that he was like Hitler."

Ahmed leaned over like he was telling me a secret. "He wasn't Libyan you know."

"I did *not* know that."

"The hair." he said, "You can tell by the hair. It wasn't Libyan."

"His *hair?*"

Ahmed nodded quietly.

"I thought he was a member of the Quadhadhfa tribe." I said.

"He was *raised* by them." he explained.

"His *hair?*"

He nodded agreeably to the truth of it. "After he came to power, he surrounded himself with family." Ahmed continued. "By 1977, he was cut off from the people. Then he started going out into the wilderness. He spent too much time in the desert. These places are dangerous." The doctor pointed to the side of his skull. "Do you know the *jinn?*"

I know that it's where we get the term "genie." Where I saw a cuddly wish-granting cartoon or an adorable blonde in intriguing loungewear, in official Muslim tradition a *jinn* is a treacherous spirit, largely invisible and made of fire. They can be loners, or group in tribes with leaders; picture mean-spirited saints with standing armies. Meditations out in the desert may seem all deep and introspective to Westerners trying to annoy their parents, but many North Africans think that those places are the haunts the *jinn* as well as the flesh-eating and shapeshifting *ghūl*. They look askance at anyone spending too much time among that crew.

The doctor, a scientist living and working for the last decade in a secular, modern European country, was telling me – while his son squirmed on an iPad – that a haunted race of invisible creatures made of fire and up to no good were, in effect, the root cause of Libya's political exile from the global stage. The empirical evidence behind his theory was obvious and irrefutable: The colonel's really bad haircut.

AMERICAN REVOLUTIONARIES, on the other hand, just wore silly wigs. A more relevant point to the success of the American revolution was that, again, it was more of a bureaucratic revolution than some fool attempt by self-absorbed intellectuals to rewrite an entire society. Ironically, up until the eleventh hour, the American colonists were attempting a legislative solution to specific rights and goals while remaining *within* the British Empire, standing silly wig to silly wig with the mothership. As such they'd taken the time to think through items and rules *that could be implemented* in order to achieve those goals. Thomas Jefferson's high-flown rhetoric aside, the leaders of the American revolution had a pretty good idea how a post-imperial United States could actually function. This also makes the operation such an anomaly among revolutions.

Robespierre, Lenin, Ayatollah Khomeini, and Muammar Gaddafi* all wanted to strip society back the beams and rebuild it in their image. None of the them had more than the barest grasp on the details of how it would be done. The practical less being that you can fight a revolution on a slogan, but you can't build a government on one, much less a society.

Muammar Gaddafi's particular brand of terrorism had been the socialist revolution along the Soviet model. Yes, he was a

---

*And the typical American undergrad.

Muslim, and a bit of a puritan in the bargain, but Gaddafi never favored the Sharia law that would come into fashion a few years later. Perhaps it was simply that the man was a product of his generation and that Islamist reawakening hadn't come into vogue when he seized power in 1969. The way Gaddafi himself explained it, "God doesn't need to be consulted regarding municipal waste disposal." More likely, given his *jamahiriya* business, he just didn't want to share power with elected representatives or a bunch of mullahs playing the well-worn "God wills it" card.

Fortunately, King Idris had done most of the centralizing for Gaddafi when he'd abolished the federal system in 1963. Until then the three provinces of Tripolitania, Cyrenaica and Fezzan had their own legislative bodies. Pretty much the whole country was Sunni, so there wasn't any religious factionalism, just garden variety ethnic and class snobbery. The rich coastal provinces of Tripolitania and Cyrenaica were mostly Arab who spent their time sneering at the mostly Bedouin population out in the landlocked interior. Although, by Gaddafi's day, there wasn't all that much at which to sneer. By most estimates, the Italians killed about half the Bedouin population between the world wars.

When Gaddafi came to power seven years after the federal system had been scrapped for ten districts, there was still no strong sense of a Libyan nation. His political power base was in Tripoli near(ish) to his hometown of Sirte. As for the formerly privileged eastern part of the country, Cyrenaica – which includes Benghazi, Derna and Tobruk – Gaddafi kept them poor by striking a balance of too weak to launch an effective opposition, but not so desperate to do it anyway.

It is possible that Gaddafi got the idea of *jamahiriya* – with himself as the anchor – from Castro, but it's more likely that it was a *realpolitik* reaction to events on the ground, As the 1970's wore on, he could see from his secular socialist utopia in Libya the spread of political Islam throughout the greater region. By 1979, Iran was firmly in the grips of what Christopher Hitchens would later call "Islamofascism" and it was quickly becoming their number one export. Gaddafi needed to export his own political vision which, through *jamahiriya*, had managed to veer to the left of even the Soviets.

Whether you peg it to 1975, or like our doctor in the next seat, 1977, what is clear is that by the 1980, nearly everyone not actually on Gaddafi's payroll pretty much hated the man. Given the Arab fondness for nicknames, they dubbed the man *Abu Shafshula* – or Father Fizzyhead.* To counter that sort of hatred at home, you need some shiny foreign adventures.

The lessons that Khomeini learned from the Iran/Iraq War was that a far-flung proxy war was a lot more efficient and a lot less painful that one fought in your own yard. Generals throughout history have long seen the advantage of taking the fight to the enemy in order to "eat them out" – read: feed your armies on the enemies supplies and resources. What Tehran figured out with its newly formed Quds force was that if the state in question was screwed up enough you could actually recruit an entire army from the enemy's own citizens and direct it against the offending state.

---

*It's hard to explain how badly the man's hair offended the Libyan on the street.

Post-colonial Lebanon, for example, was absolutely screwed up enough. The country had been a mandate of the French until – well neither Germany nor Britain really intended to liberate the place during World War II, but that's what happened. When the UN officially came into existence on 24 October 1945, Lebanon was one of the organization's founding states, which is pretty official as these things go. In an attempt to make completing groups happy, Lebanon became the government that Identity Politics built: Where representation was figured not on population or geography, but a modern sectarian tribalism. It worked as well as someone over 35 might think.

In 1975, a civil war broke out in Lebanon between almost every ideology, religion or neighborhood with enough adherents to vote on a flag and club by-laws. After a couple of UN cease fires had failed, and no end in sight, a multinational force (including US Marines, the French, a few Brits and even fewer Italians) arrived in August of 1982. They withdrew about 20 days later, but were back later that same month after a local Christian militia started massacring Palestinian refugees. Not to be outdone, Iran sent its Quds force into the area with much less fanfare. The end result was a snappy little model for global adventurism that has, unfortunately, stood the test of time: Hezbollah. They bombed the US and French Embassies in April 1983. In October of the same year the barracks of the US and French forces were attacked with a car bomb – killing 241 Americans and 61 French. By early 1984, Ronald Reagan was announcing the withdrawal of US troops from the region. Under the direction of Tehran, Hezbollah recruited local Shi'a to give the thing a grass-roots feel and soon they were punching well above their weight, and evolving into a state within a state that is, more or less, loyal to Tehran.

Gaddafi was watching all of this from Tripoli. If someone was going to get credit for scaring the devil out of the West enough to clear it out of the neighborhood, it was going to be him. So, in March of 1986, that Gaddafi drew a line along the mouth of the Gulf of Sidra – from Misrata (outside of Tripoli) to Benghazi – and declared this invisible boundary his "Line of Death." He dared any power to violate the line and face his wrath. Understand that international law stipulates territorial waters extend 12 miles from the coastline. By drawing the line from Tripoli to Benghazi, Gaddafi was enclosing better than 70 miles of international waters and claiming them in the most cartoonish way possible.

Gaddafi's carrying on prompted President Ronald Reagan to order Operation PRAIRIE FIRE: Three battle carrier groups consisting of 225 aircraft and some 30 warships entered the Gulf of Sidra but stayed well within the globally recognized international waters. There was no real reason for us to be there, other than some blow-hard told us that we couldn't come in. Nevertheless, there we were. Colonel Qaddafi sent out Libyan naval forces to meet the American threat. US forces knocked some Libyans out of the air and sank some ships, but that was about it. No US casualties.

The colonial vowed revenge. On 2 April 1986 the Abu Nadal terrorist group – based in Libya and funded by Qaddafi – planted a semtex bomb on a TWA flight 840 blowing a hole in the fuselage, killing four Americans. Despite the damage, pilot Pete Peterson managed to safely land the plane in Athens.

Three days later another semtex bomb, this one packed with shrapnel, went off at the La Belle discotheque in West Berlin – popular with American GIs - exploded killing four and injuring 230.*

Gaddafi denied any part in the attacks, but US intelligence had recordings of calls he'd made in Tripoli to the Libyan embassy in East Berlin giving the order. Having had quite enough of this, a week later President Reagan ordered Operation: ELDORADO CANYON — airstrikes on Libyan military barracks and the personal family compounds of Gaddafi.

The strikes didn't actually kill Fizzy-head, but is sure as hell pissed off the Europeans, who took a break from praying that the US would save them from the Soviet creep to come out in mass protests in Germany, Italy and Spain against the American intervention. In West Berlin alone – where the last attack happened, some 20,000 West Berliners protested the US action.

Just how much of this Euro-fury was homegrown is hard to say. As with earlier anti-US, it can partly be explained by resentment to an overbearing neighbor - but there was also that whiff of an East German active measures campaign. A split Germany meant that a communist East could "leak" damaging forgeries regarding US foreign policy, nuclear armaments and future aggression into West German papers without translation

---

*After the collapse of the Soviet Union, Václav Havel of Czechoslovakia announced to the world in March of 1990 that the former Soviet government had sold some 1,000 tons of Semtex to the Libyans. In the end it turned out to be closer to 700 tons, but at that point does it really matter?

or even cultural idiomatic issues. From there the stories were picked up by the rest of the European press and took on a life of their own.

The point was sew chaos with the Allied Western bloc. While in their unique position, the East Germans had managed to raise active measures campaigns to an art-form, they acted at the direction and behest of Moscow. At the time, the KGB had a lonely little officer stationed in Dresden operating under cover of a government translator – although his German was never that good. While the man was never high enough up the food chain to direct an operation, Vladimir Putin was watching exactly how it was done.

Back in Tripoli, Gaddafi was delighted with the geo-political pile-on. He used the opportunity to ramp-up production of mustard gas and tried like the devil to get a nuclear weapon. Short of that, in December 1988, he almost certainly orchestrated the downing of Pan Am flight 103 over Lockerbie, Scotland.

International outrage pivoted back against the regime – turning him from victim to pariah over a news cycle. UN sanctions followed. What really scared Gaddafi, though, was the decline oil revenues. So to show what a swell guy he was, the colonel established the Al-Gaddafi Prize for Human Rights. The first recipient was Nelson Mandela, who returned the favor by awarding the colonel the Order of Good Hope and then publicly opposed the sanctions on Libya. Gaddafi, knowing a good thing when he saw it, declared himself against apartheid and apologized for the Arab slave trade.

Lost in his humanitarian love-in was what Gaddafi claimed was an old Libyan proverb: "If you treat them like dogs, they'll follow you like dogs." He was still keeping his foot on the neck of Cyrenaica, and they still hated him for it. In Benghazi, they took any position to counter old fizzy-head and they took to it with gusto. Qaddafi was secular and suddenly a hyper-traditional vision of Islam's place in the Middle East was very fashionable in the east.

Then 11 September 2001 happened.

Almost immediately, Gaddafi realized that the Islamists had over-egged the pudding. His rule over Libya had long been an expert balancing act of brutalizing the people to keep them down, but not enough to drive them to revolt. He could easily see – in a way that rich-kid turned unwashed holy warrior Osama bin Laden couldn't – that the casual kidnapping and murder Middle Eastern revolutionaries had been using to pester the West had now escalated to a point where nations were going to get erased. The fact that Libya was very close to developing a nuclear weapon was of little practical comfort for Gaddafi, who knew full well that his scientists were nowhere close to having a reliable delivery system for such a weapon. As one of the colonel's advisers reportedly told him "If we start the war we won't be able to hit Malta, if the US starts the war we will be wiped off the map." Or words to that effect.

Gaddafi started putting out feelers to try to, as British Prime Minister Tony Blair called it, "re-enter the community of nations." The effort was about as altruistic as his Al-Gaddafi Prize for Human Rights award. Gaddafi likely thought this was the only way to stay in power. To strengthen his position, Libyan scientists were racing to complete a nuclear weapon – not to vaporize anyone, but to have a sizable bargaining chip to "give up" in order to drive up the price of Libyan cooperation.

They were getting parts and technology from a man named A. Q. Khan from Pakistan. US forces, with the cooperation of the Italian navy, seized a shipment of equipment for refining fissionable material, as well as the directions on how to do it, as it sailed through the Suez Canal into the Mediterranean Sea. The ship, a German vessel named the *BBS China*, was guided into port at Tarantino, Italy, where it was discovered that A.Q. Khan was selling the same kit to both the Libyans and the Iranians.

With attacks being launched from Afghanistan and the Pakistanis selling nuclear bombs to Iranian and Libyans, the US felt compelled to do something.

So, we invaded Iraq.

IF THERE WAS A REAL, immediate positive to the US's ill-advised adventure in Iraq in 2003, it's that both Muammar Gaddafi and his hair could both see that his chemical weapons and subsidizing terrorist training camps out in the desert were going to be the end of him. Reportedly, when the colonel watched US forces flushed Saddam Hussein from a hole in the ground at a farm at Tikrit, Iraq, he went completely white with fear. The Americans really would simply erase a regime or even an entire country if it had half a mind. They didn't need proof or even a perfectly coherent reason – America just had to feel like doing it. Given the reality of the situation, Gaddafi thought it best to just come clean; dismantle his weapons program, turn out the terrorist training camps in his desert, and tell everyone who would listen that Nelson Mandela considered him a humanitarian leader.

Later, in 2008, an American diplomat wrote a report on Gaddafi stating that he was "a strong partner in the fight on terror" and noted – proving that a broken clock can be right twice a day – that Gaddafi had introduced full equality for women in the 1970's and had stepped on the Wahhabi extremism that Saudi Arabia had allowed to infect everyday life.

The upshot for Fizzyhead was that in order to ensure his existence and continue rule, he allowed Tripoli to more or less become a CIA black site. As Al-Qaeda had been trying to kill Qaddafi for years, this served the purposes of both the regime and the US-led War on Terror. The CIA agreed to the rendition of one of Libya's higher ranking al-Qaeda operatives, Abdullah al-Sadiq who had been fighting the US along-side the Taliban in Afghanistan of late. Correctly thinking that the Libyans were likely to get more out of the man, the CIA agreed to get him and turn al-Sadiq over to Tripoli.

Soon enough, al-Sadiq turned up in Malaysia seeking political asylum in Britain for himself and his wife. MI6 detained him long enough for the CIA to bundle him onto a ship and get him to Libya, where he was installed at the notorious Abu Salin prison for the next six unpleasant years. He was released in March of 2010 under a program of "deradicalization" with 33 other Islamists. He immediately went underground and emerged in May 2011 the fog of the civil war under his birth name, Abdelhakin Belhaj. As the leader of a rebel faction in Benghazi, he was working along the US Special Envoy to the Transitional National Government – the same diplomat who'd written that Gaddafi was "a strong partner against the fight on terror:, one J. Christopher Stevens.

My oh my, for the days of the revolution.

Dr. Latifa el-Jaouhar

CHAPTER EIGHTEEN:
A BEAUTIFUL PLACE TO BE

As my Turkish airlines flight began its descent into Benghazi, the attack on the US Special Mission compound was only about six weeks behind us. The old city that prides itself on being the "caretaker of the lost" was desperately trying to keep itself in check, but was coming apart. For his part, CIA Director John Brennan was – about the same time – was in Tripoli inspecting the US Embassy (which hadn't been attacked) and decided that while security measures in the capital seemed sound enough, the whole diplomatic operation was moving to Malta, and then to Tunisia. Officially at any rate, the medical mission I'd attached myself too was on its own. Earlier one of the field nurses had pointed out that surely doctors and nurses in were safe in the children's ward of a major hospital.

"Surely." I said – but we weren't necessarily. The Iranian had used children as human shields and mine sweepers during its entirely pointless Whirlwind War. Holy wars, however, tend toward the unholy pretty quickly. This was a fight for state control waged by groups who wanted to impose an order with themselves at the top of the pile. To justify themselves, they were using literally, not figuratively, the oldest trick in recorded civilization – specifically that "God wills it" bit Ur-Nammu codified back in Chapter Two. And because there was nothing holy about the proceedings, humanitarian aid volunteers *were* getting plucked off the street. Basically my "Surely..." was crap and I knew it. Still, a medical mission like this one couldn't operate without the medical supplies, and it wouldn't work without hope either.

As we taxied into the airport, Benghazi still had hope. The blast wall around the facility had been cheerfully spray painted with a giant hand, flashing new arrivals the peace sign along with a message that read in English: "Hello to You, and Welcome to Benghazi – The Cradle of the Revolution."

Relative to Western airports, the place is tiny, but busy. Soon we'd deplaned and I was standing in line with my bag and briefcase over my shoulder. Soon I was plopping my bags on the belt to take them under the x-ray. Then the entire process came to a sudden halt. The officer in charge took hold of by bag and unzipped it as a junior officer turned from the x-ray monitor peered in and shook his head slowly. Then he gave me the old Roman thumbs down.

In full disclosure, the last time that I'd been arrested for illegal possession of alcohol was when I was 17. I was in a heap to trouble then, but it was mostly with my parents; the courts just gave me a righteous finger-wagging. For all its flaws, Memphis is not a failed state, or even Detroit for that matter. After that teenage episode, I'd managed an entire undergraduate career of football games and spring breaks without much of a bother with the law.* And here I was in a rogue state – since failed and gearing up for a civil war – being led out of the customs shed (and away from any witnesses) over the bottle of Famous Grouse scotch, I'd bought that morning at the Atatürk airport. Mere possession I was told (at least I think that's what he was saying) was criminal.

I blame the big, heavyset blonde woman in the duty-free who didn't look Turkish at all. She told me that there was no issue with taking alcohol into Libya you just couldn't buy it there. This really had been the case in Nasiriya. The detention was vexing because, I'd already had one run in with the security that morning over donated medical supplies in Istanbul and I am not a man with inexhaustible supplies of luck.

Then I was outside the customs shed and being marched by two security men to another metal door away from the line of deplaning passengers. We went into a dingy white cinder-block room that, I noticed as soon and the door slammed shut, was empty. I was trying to get my head around any legal recourse available: These guys were in official looking uniform but the overriding reality was that Libya did not have a government. How official could these guys be? On the other end of the room was another door that seemed to reconnect with the airport building and some steps that went – down.

---

*That's not entirely true: I was charged with a DUI in Tuscaloosa while walking home. Too terrified to tell my parents, I acted in my own defense arguing that a) I'd been walking home and nowhere near a car, b) I'd been walking home *precisely* because I'd been too drunk to drive and c) while there was a public drunkenness ordinance, I hadn't been charged with violating it. The charges were dropped.

It's interesting where your mind goes at a time like this. I clearly remember wondering *What kind of comic novel is written in a North African prison?* By this point in my research, I'd seem a lot more than the original question I'd set out across Hell's half acre to ask. Starting out, I thought that I'd get a brutal dose of reality, put my questions to the people living it and see what I needed to see. Then I'd pack my bags, go home and write my book. Now the situation was developing into a different bucket of minnows altogether and entirely out of my control.

Since 9/11 – 2001, not 2011 – loved ones and you can others you dupe into picking you up at the airport can no longer wait for you at the gate. For the Memphis airport this meant meeting at the baggage claim on my return trips. Always there, coming into view from the feet up as I came down the short escalator from the main terminal to the baggage claim would be the Ladies Murff: Mrs M and our (then) middle-school daughter, Littlebit. As I came down the escalator they would begin appear until I could see Mrs. M's ethereal ginger hair and Littlebit's long black locks hanging past her shoulders. They never missed an arrival and I knew that once I saw those beautiful, smiling faces that I was home. I was safe. The Ladies Murff – and I hadn't realized this until I was going down grim concrete stairs in Benghazi – had been a sort of guide rope back to the "real" world, a physic anchor that allowed me to grope my way back out of this damned rabbit hole I'd gone down.

Now the two sets of feet were not at the foot of these steps waiting, but behind me, wearing boots. They were close on my heels and a hand gripped my upper arm. The best I could do was to tell myself that somewhere in a world gone hard and mean, the Ladies Murff were still out there, waiting for me at the bottom of another set of stairs. That made the whole thing , however it would end, a manageable equation: I just had to get up one set of stairs to the baggage claim at the Benghazi airport and down another to the baggage claim in Memphis. What could be simpler? It wasn't remotely that simple, and I knew it, but that's what that slippery hope is for.

In Memphis, the Ladies would ask about the trip and I'd tell them the funny bits and feel dashing and we'd have dinner at home and all would be well. Yes, I already knew that the nightmares would come soon enough, by this point they'd already started. The lifeless bodies of children and the faces of the hopeless parents: The tear streaked mask of grief on the mothers and the flat, faraway stare of the fathers who'd disconnected from their overloaded emotions. They'd all come in the night and ask me the same question: *Why?* Like most people foolish enough to become writers, I have a vivid imagination and for me the link between dream and waking isn't always clear. I'd go bolt upright in bed seized by some terror and Mrs. M would rise, almost float, up and pull me back down, those fingers in my hair and the nightmare would be gone.

My bed, however, is located in a world where most nightmares *are* driven away by the dawn. Some places – most places, really – sunlight doesn't so much erase a nightmare but just lets you see it coming down the street. Places like the one at the bottom of the steps in what appeared to be the tumble-down and closed off men's room in the Benghazi airport.

The cold sweat had already started in the customs. I had spent the morning talking my way out of smuggling charges in Istanbul for which I was innocent. Here I was actually guilty. Genuinely clueless, sure, but guilty nonetheless. Now the fear dropped from my chest, to the gut, down further in a big oily ball into my bowels. That mornings incident in Istanbul happened in Turkey, a NATO ally and (then) trying to get itself voted into the EU. Even if I had been hauled off, the matter would likely, eventually, sort itself out. Libya, on the other hand, didn't have a government in any real sense of the word. I knew full well that that bottle of Famous Grouse didn't really matter to them; it was an excuse, a symbol, a bargaining chip and that *did* matter. The smuggling charges were easily handled, it was the symbolism that would likely do me in. The only thing keeping a completely debilitating panic at bay was the thought of those two pretty smiling faces in Memphis. If I could just get to them – up one staircase and down another – I'd be home. I'd be safe.

Should you find yourself in such a position remember: Hollywood is full of shit. You can't out-tough the guy with the gun. You can't outsmart him either, because trigger fingers take IQs off the table. The best that you can do is make them not want to kill or detain you. Even that requires a plan of attack. To that end, remember that guy with the assault rifle is your *secondary* concern. The fella with the side arm is the one with whom you need to make friends. It doesn't entirely matter if kid with the assault rifle likes you or not, (which is a shame, because he'll be the easier mark) he's not the one calling the shots. The one with the side arm is. And that bald bastard kept trying to push the bottle of whisky into my hands. I threw them up in surrender and he pulled them down, forcing the bottle into my hands.

Not having a choice in the matter, I took the bottle, spun the top off and began to pour the whisky out with the bottle pressed to my crotch like my big, glass willy, writing my name on what was left of a stall divider. According to the late, great Robin

Williams, the number one rule of comedy is "When in doubt, go for the dick joke." I pointed the bottle up with a surprised look on my face, as a blob of brown water flew in the air. Then I drooped it back down with a sad, hangdog expression. Before I knew it, they were chuckling and I was reaching behind the bottle to scratch my cods as the last of the whisky dribbled out. Laughing with them and without waiting for a command, I tossed the fellow with the sidearm the bottle. It spun neck over butt through the air, and out of reflex he caught it. I was saying something lighthearted like, "Well, thanks for the heart attack, guys! Now, where is a good place to burn my boxers? I just shit my pants." and headed back the way I'd come. Oh, we all had a good laugh. At least that's the way I was playing it as I started walking away in a good-natured amble.

I don't like public speaking, and I understand that most Americans list it as their greatest fear, greater that actually dying. This was not like one of *those* fears – this was, for me at any rate, an unprecedented unknown. I never really thought that I'd get shot by the guards over a silly bottle of scotch, the fear was that I'd be detained by a completely off-the-books militia in a jail cell in what would be an exercise of Libyan sovereignty. If there was a starting gun for the post-revolution civil war, it had been six weeks earlier with the attack in Benghazi. You really want to avoid jail cells during civil wars, certainly, an Arab one when you are the only white man wearing a blue blazer in North Africa. This was an oily ball of fear that sank – kept sinking – as if the journey was a mile long.

Side-arm was calling after me, but I just kept walking, pressed through the door and kept moving. I was vaguely aware of being followed – but at a distance. In a conflict zone, security protocols do become criminally relaxed, but then again so does the chain of command. Gaddafi's Libya was similar to Saddam's Iraq in that any figure with a modicum of authority was used to executing orders delivered from on high. I was gambling that they weren't entirely sure *what* to do about me. I just had to head towards the ICHF team like a guided missile at a casual saunter. I was headed, specifically, for the nurses: Mostly women from the US, Canada, Australia and New Zealand. This was good for me because I'd already figured out that there is almost nothing in the world that Arab men fear more than Western women. If the authorities tried to waylay me there, it would trigger an international incident fueled by howling liberal white women. I knew it and so did Side-arm.

What I found when I joined the group was that yet another phalanx of confused airport security had confiscated most of the teams' baggage. This was something of a relief to me as this 20 bag drama superseded my whisky bottle. As it turned out, the airport's chief of security had not been alerted to our arrival. He didn't see a humanitarian medical mission, but a group of Westerners coming into the country and they needed to be shown who was boss. He'd plucked about half a dozen big black bags off the incoming baggage carousel and ordered an armed and uniformed lieutenant to drag them off to the side.

I was chatting with the nurses when I heard Dr. Gascon say, "Hey Murff, go get my case would ya?" The words hung badly for a moment. I considered myself as loyal to the cause as anyone, but I'd had about all the fun I could stand with the foreign airport authorities for one day. "It's over there." He pointed in a friendly, obvious way.

"Oh, I see it." I said.

"Well, go get it, would you?" He tapped his cane. Sure, the guy with the gun had wandered off, but it wasn't a very big building. As casually as I could, I ambled across baggage claim, it's possible I even whistled. To the guard, I pointed to the mural painted high on the wall and said, "Omar Muhktar…"

He smiled, "*N'am*" Yes.

"The Lion of the Desert" I said as I picked the doctor's gear out of the impounded pile. I doubt the guy knew any English, but seemed to know the phrase. We were still grinning at each other when I brought the bag over to Gascon with a winning smile plastered across my terrified face. On seeing this, the security chief started posing dramatically and shouting. Gascon sat on his case like a pasha, hands folded over his cane. The security chief ordered the rest of the bags locked into a tiny office and demanded Gascon get up. The doc roared back, daring any of them to touch it. The lieutenant returned and motioned for my help locking up our own bags. I demurred with a *Waddya gonna do?* shrug and drifted back into a pile of nurses.

The Arab World is still a "Big Man" culture, fiefdoms are savagely protected and slights to status are not taken lightly. Western culture is too, but we go to great lengths not to be quite so obvious about it, and plenty of our Big Men are women. Then comes some foreigner into *his* airport making him look like a fool by not being suitably impressed with his authority. The Benghazi Medical Center (BMC) had sent a representative to pick us up, and he now found himself caught between a Big Man and the Big Doctor. The language barrier didn't help. The rep's English wasn't very good, and it's doubtful that what little he had learned had been yelled at him in an irate Alabama accent while an international incident hung in the balance.

And this is why local fixers are so important for this sort of operation. Being Libyan, the hospital rep knew that the only solution to a Big Man horn lock-up is to find a Bigger Man with a larger set of horns. The rep raised the provincial Minister of Health on the line and the security chief disappeared into the bowels of the airport to take such an important call from so far up the latter. I never saw the man again. A few minutes later the frazzled lieutenant reappeared to wordlessly unlock the office where the bags were held.

THE MINISTRY OF HEALTH provided a bus that swung us by the hotel so we could drop off our bags before whisking us to the hospital where another ICHF component was coming out of surgery with a little girl named Assma. They'd come in without nearly the drama the night before from Australia and New Zealand via Dubai, as well as an American surgeon, Dr. Mary Wallis, had come in from Nicaragua. As a tagalong writer, I tending to feel about as useless as teats on a boar until one of the nurses said to the late arrivals, "Did you bring the supplies!"

I set the duffle down, finally, in the storeroom we'd requisitioned and watched the nurses from around the world fall on it like anal retentive kids at Christmas, unloading, sorting and shelving the contents with some system they knew with saying and I couldn't hope to follow.

Due to oil reserves, Libya has cash, the BMC is a beautiful, modern hospital. The lack of supplies has more to do with the war than poverty. What is scarce are qualified personnel. Under Gaddafi, every Libyan citizen was guaranteed a minimum income. This may sound like a grand, noble idea, but it is a double-edged sword. No one starves, but skilled professionals are hard to come by; most of the nurses in the country were on contract from India or the Philippines.

I'd met Dr. Wallis before in Guayaquil, Ecuador where'd she'd honestly impressed me as one of the sincerest people I'd ever met in my life. Tall, thin and ramrod straight, she looked to an alumnus of 12 years of Catholic schooling that she'd come right out of central casting for the part of Mother Superior. Wallis told me once that her Catholic high school had voted her most likely to become a nun. "That's silly because there are plenty of ways to serve the Lord outside of a religious order. My calling wasn't to be a nun. It was to be a doctor."

"Um humm." I mumbled. What I thought was *Well you talk like one too.* At her core, though, Wallis walked the walk as well: This was her calling and she was going to rise to the occasion and absolutely no one on this mortal coil had better get in her way.

"Have you met Latifa? You need to talk with her."

The BMC had given over a ward for the use of the medical mission team, and all went reasonably well it was big enough for the purpose. The patient list for the two-week mission was so long that a stay in the pediatric intensive care unit (PICU) of longer that 48 hours would cause a bed shortage. The trick was that the children had to keep moving: Come out of heart surgery, stay in the PICU for a day or two for observation and then cycle out to the general children's ward. There the mission nurses would check in on the kids from time to time, but wouldn't hover like a flock of foreign angles like in the PICU.

It was on that first afternoon that the program picked up the unexpected patient that threw the numbers off. The surgeons saw the math problem quicker than the nurses, who mooned over

Fellah – a tiny, underfed little girl who'd become something of a mascot for the team. At 15 months, she weighed in at 3.1 kilos (6.8 lbs), not much more than a loose sack of skin and bones. What little thin hair she had had been leached white and she'd managed to actually suck the skin off her right thumb.

Pam, a wonderful Canadian volunteer with a booming sense of humor, was predicting that the child wouldn't be alive when the mission packed up to go, but that prediction had been made before. At the first Benghazi mission, Fellah had been brought in for a VSD – a repair to a hole in the ventricle wall – but was too ill to undergo the procedure. Compounding that misfire was that the child's mother, thinking the situation hopeless, had stopped caring for or even feeding the child. The child's aunt had taken matters into her own hands and brought her in. When I asked where the mother was, I got only a single sad shake of the head. Even then she faced a near insurmountable issue with the useless local nurses. Not to put too fine a point on it, they sucked.

So, Pam concocted a plan to just smuggle the skinny kid back to Canada under her sweater. "You see," she explained, "when I go through the scanner, it'll just look like I'm pregnant."

"How's the little tapper going to stay put when you raise your arms over your head for the X-ray?"

"She'll cling." Pam laughed, "Like a little naked monkey."

Honestly, it wasn't the most far-fetched scheme I heard in country.

Finally I tracked down Dr. Latifa el-Jaouhari, the junior anesthesiologist, who Dr. Wallis said I needed to interview. She was coming into the PICU rolling her eyes. She'd just found a male nurse standing idly in the hallway fiddling with his smartphone. Under the old regime, the kid might have found a

job in the army and given a gun and all the thoughtless swagger
that comes with assault weapons. Instead, he'd found himself
more or less conscripted into being a nurse. Or the way he saw it,
women's work. Latifa had asked for some assistance. Or as she
saw it, his job. His eyes came away from the phone, but nothing
else. He didn't move but finally asked her, "Who died and made
you Muammar?"

If you're wondering, the "Fuck you" look is universal and
needs no translation.

Latifa couldn't really press the point and just sighed at me.
"This really is no way to run a country." She said in perfect
English. "We haven't quite got our head around this freedom
thing."

I was trying to be philosophical about it. "You know, the
government we set up* after our revolution only lasted about
seven years before we had to start over. Our first rebellion† only
about five years after that."

She smiled at this. "America wasn't always America." She
wagged a finger at me, "It wasn't always the land of the free. In
the beginning it was *exile*."

"You know your American history." Better, I thought, than
we know theirs.

She had learned her American history and perfected her
accent-free, even idiomatic, English living in Tampa until she was
eight years old. There she identified strongly with Martin Luther
King, Jr.: "I was from North Africa, I was an American. I
thought that that made me an African-American." It does, if

---

* Articles of Confederation.

† The Whiskey Rebellion

only by the definition of the words. The teacher didn't see it that way, but could never fully explain herself. Her three precocious career goals were 1) part-time super model, 2) archeologist (schoolgirl crush on Indiana Jones) and 3) UN delegate. While treasure hunting isn't particularly practical, she certainly has the face for the camera and the UN is as good a place as any to retire and not do much until violently forced.

She is not a militant, not particularly traditional and not terribly religious. Still, Latifa remembers the revolution as "the best time of my life." She showed me a blurry smartphone picture of a man, across the street from the military base before the walls were breached with bulldozers and tractors. He's a skinny guy, pulling his tee-shirt up, giving the soldier on the wall a clear target of his chest. "That's where he was." Latifa said, "Where *we* were. 'Just go ahead and shoot me, I don't care.' It's hard to fight people who don't care if they die." She stared at the photo for a long time before snapping her attention back to me.

"The solidarity, the sense of hope and purpose, the community!" her wide eyes alight with the excitement of the memory. "Benghazi during the revolution was a beautiful place to be!" Then her attention drifted past me, to some unfocused point and she said something that sounded very pretty in Arabic. She translated softly, "Benghazi arise, arise for the day you've awaited is here." Latifa got a shiver. So did I.

"When the bodies started coming in – and I had cousins who died in the war – people started bringing in spare mattresses for the wounded, bringing in bread and dates and other foods, pharmacists brought in medicine, anything to help. We didn't know where to put it. There was a hugging. Men don't shake hands with a woman who isn't a direct relative, and strangers were hugging me. *And it was okay!* Oh, it was a beautiful place to be."

    She sat back in her chair, "If I don't say it every day, I hear from someone. 'My oh my, for the days of the revolution.'"

.نحن قوم لا نستسلم، ننتصر أو نموت

We are a nation that knows no surrender, we win or we die.'

Omar Mukhtar

Chapter Nineteen:
The Man With the Golden Gun

On seeing what the American giant was capable of when it had half-a-mind, the colonel trimmed the disco haircut and the Sgt. Pepper military uniforms for an earthy, wholesome African dashiki. While the change of wardrobe might have convinced the world audience, the Libyans weren't so easily fooled.

In early 2011, the largely peaceful Arab Spring protests flashed across Tunisia and Egypt, and spilled over into Libya, where they stayed peaceful for about 48 hours. Sensing their opportunity, the Islamists in Benghazi and Derna called for a "Day of Rage" on 17 February. That was something of an understatement. What they did was tap into a long, only barely dormant frustration with a brutal and unhinged tyrant. Like that Tunisian fruit vendor, or the young man on Latifa's phone, the people just decided to set the place alight, and didn't care if they got killed in the process. When that happens, things tend to move fast: The courthouse on the coast road overlooking the Mediterranean was seized. But revolutions aren't generally won by filling paperwork out in triplicate, and unlike a coup d'état, they are very, very messy. Locals laid siege to the strategic and symbolic Kabita military center in the center of town. In a modern take on the final days of Byzantine Constantinople some 500 years earlier, they'd breeched the walls with bulldozers and later with captured tanks. After that there was no putting the *jinn* back in the bottle.

Himself a usurper, Gaddafi knew full well what the shape these things take: this wasn't mere protest but insurrection. The colonel reacted differently from his opposite numbers in Tunisia and Egypt. He fired on the protestors, killing 14. Then fired on the funerals of the deceased the next day, killing 24 more people. The regime didn't help itself when a pro-government mob in Tripoli sacked the British ambassador's residence while the army looked on. Gaddafi claimed that the rebels were linked to al-Qaeda, and to prove his point, let islamists out of prison. The intended purpose of the maneuver was almost certainly for the islamist to join the rebels in common cause and prove his point in a self-fulfilling prophecy triggering the West to come in and help him crush the rebels. In execution, it was a drastic miscalculation.

The largely peaceful protests in Egypt and Tunisia had established a promising opening gambit for the Arab Spring protests. So why did it all go so dramatically wrong in Libya?

Part of the explanation is dumb, simple timing – something people who write thrilling accounts of world events tend to downplay. Tunisia had taken the world by surprise. For that matter, so did the size and speed of the movement's spread in Egypt. In Cairo, there was a home grown (albeit underground) opposition in the form of the Muslim Brotherhood to step and guide things domestically. Gaddafi, for his part, had eradicated any element that might express dissent so that by the time that protest *did* spread to Libya, Tehran had gotten its game-plan together about how to co-opt the movement. Which worked especially well outside Gaddafi's central power base in the eastern towns like Derna and Benghazi, where. There was already a sympathy for political Islam.

At first Gaddafi stayed out of sight, and the rumors that he'd fled the country spurred the insurrection on. His son Saif al-Islam seemed willing to negotiate with the protestors until, on 20 February 2011, he announced that the street would be "rivers of blood" if the protestors didn't cut it out. The issue for the regime, as Latifa had pointed out to me with that desperate photo on her phone, was that threatening the protester with rivers of blood doesn't work on a population that doesn't care if it lives or dies.

One of the unsung early heroes of the revolution, however, wasn't in Benghazi at all, but New York. Ibrahim Dabbashi was the Libya's ambassador to the UN during the last years of the Gaddafi regime, when Father Fizzyhead was trying to rebrand himself as one of the world's great bulwarks against the same global terror he'd been funding for decades. Four days after the protests had tipped into revolt in Benghazi, Dabbashi led what might be called the diplomatic arm of the revolution. Knowing full well that the UN probably wouldn't take much notice unless he started working the room, he laid out a plan to end his boss's rule. It was Dabbashi, as much as anyone in the international community, who argued that the NATO airstrikes were crucial if

Benghazi wasn't going to be pummeled in one of Gaddafi's unhinged fits of revenge.* Within a matter of weeks, government tanks and armor were at the outskirts of the defenseless city, and Saif al-Islam was predicting the whole thing would be over in 24 hours. And it well may have been but for the better than two dozen air-strikes the British and French Air Forces flew over the next 48 that effectively smashed all of Gaddafi's armor.

In March, Chris Stevens was appointed Special Envoy to the Transitional National Government (TNG) and was dispatched to Valetta, Malta to meet with other diplomats run out of the Libya by the violence. The Libyan rebels expressly did *not* want foreign boots on the ground. They needed air-cover, yes, but it was their revolution and were justifiably terrified that any helpful invasion force would simply never leave. Gaddafi hadn't been the only Libyan who'd been watching the descent of Iraq for the last decade. And this was the tactical vacuum into which Iran's Qud's force brilliantly exploited. In the havoc loosed by a long dreamed of revolution, the average, fairly moderate Libyan was too paranoid, too frustrated and finally too exhausted to see the guiding hand.

As the US diplomats were meeting in Malta, Hezbollah, the Iranian-led state-within-a-state in Lebanon, began to trickle into the country from the east through Egypt with the help of the Egyptian Muslim Brotherhood. Unlike the Farsi speaking Iranians, the Lebanese spoke Arabic and were Arabs. Hezbollah came in to mingle with the worked-up locals and spread around

* The betrayal didn't go unnoticed. Gaddafi tried to replace Dabbashi with former Nicaraguan Foreign Minister and current Maryknoll priest, one Fr. Miguel d'EScoto Brockmann. The appointment was so strange that most at the UN just ignored the priest until he went away.

Iranian guns and money to the militias that were forming to oust Gaddafi. To be clear, Iran has no love lost for Sunni al Qaeda or the Muslim Brotherhood, but Tehran wanted Gaddafi and his secular socialism out. Hence the old proverb, "They enemy of my enemy is my friend." It was another one of those bad marriages that Tehran was willing to endure in order to recast the Arab spring from a "pro-democracy" to an "anti-Western" movement. In the spirit of Iran's Islamic Revolution, they'd get the job done and sort the nasty differences later.

Along with the Iranian money and guns, the Western assist to the revolution was a strange thing for many of the rapidly forming militias on the ground. After the fall of Saddam Hussein, Qaddafi was no longer sponsoring state terrorism, but places like Derna and Benghazi were churning out volunteers to go fight in the "crusaders" in Iraq. Derna, Libya was nearly tied with second place with Riyadh, Saudi Arabia for the number of foreign fighters in Iraq during the insurgency. This may have been a perverse piety to go fight the "Crusader War in Iraq," but in the long-suffering east of Libya it was a domestic way to thumb your nose at Qaddafi's *rapprochement* with the West. In addition, non-Libyan veterans of the Iraqi Sunni insurrection were flooding into the country. They had been fighting the crusaders for years only to find themselves free from crushing strikes of regime armor and air force as their bitter and sworn enemies in the Christian West paved the way for their victory. For the most part, the militants took a "Don't look a gift horse in the mouth" approach to things.

WHILE TEHRAN'S foreign adventures are no doubt duplicitous, conniving, dishonorable, Machiavellian and expressly intended to bring on the end of the world, they are well thought out. It's not certain that US policy on the Middle East is. Tehran would make a convenient pact with an enemy to some nasty end. Sometimes, it's doesn't look like we are entirely clear just who the hell is the enemy or the friend. Even our allies weren't entirely sure what we were doing.

France's performance in World War II was pretty damn shameful, but they aren't the "cheese-eating surrender monkeys" most Americans like to believe. Back in 1986, before Gaddafi had rebranded himself as a humanitarian and was still desperately trying to produce a nuclear weapon, Libyan forces had occupied the uranium-rich Aouzou strip along the border with Chad. It was not mystery about what why the Libyans were there, either

It was the French who instigated Operation *Épervier* (Sparrowhawk) to throw the Libyans out. Better than 20 years on, in 2008, the French were still in country when Chadian President Idriss Deby was fending off a challenge from Sudanese-backed rebels to seize control of the capital, N'Djamena.* If Dey wanted to remain in power, he'd need help and the French were already there. For its part, Paris absolutely did *not* want to get embroiled into a civil war in Chad, nor did it want the world to see the French forces retreating before a proxy war with the Sudanese. Paris propped up Dey with enough arms and support to keep the government intact. As part of the ongoing Operation *Épervier*, the force regularly sent armored patrols out along the border in the Sahara Desert.

On 4 April 2011, a French patrol picked up chatter in Arabic not too far ahead of their current position. The patrol's Arabic-

---

*By now, Dey had made up with the kinder rebranding of Gaddafi.

language specialist noted a couple of things: The convoy was stuck in the sand, and that the Arabic was the accent and style of the Persian Gulf – they weren't locals*. The patrol set off to ascertain just why a convoy was moving through Sudan towards what was looking like a rapidly forming the Libyan civil war.

The French patrol caught up to the convoy that turned out to be Qatari Special Forces – which was strange enough – carrying a large consignment of US and French made weapons. Qatar is a French ally as well as a large weapons client, so the patrol tried to keep things relaxed. Evidently, they did it pretty well as the Qatari C.O. – after explaining that he'd received his military education at the academy at St. Cyr† had a big white tent erected and rigged with a generator plus air conditioning. There they all had tea while the French awaited orders from HQ on what to do about the arms shipment. On discovery of the US component to the weapons, the *Chef d'Etat Major* (the French equivalent to the Chairman of the Joint Chiefs) would have contacted the CIA station chief at the US embassy in Paris to get on the same page. And in that air-conditioned tent in Chad, it seems inconceivable that the Qataris did not know what the answer would be: Stand down and keep you mouths shut about the whole thing.

This was all a bit chummy, but not that unexpected. Much has been made of the French president Sarkozy's decisiveness when it comes to leading the NATO intervention in Libya – it likely wasn't republican ideal or *egalitarie* but vindictiveness.

---

*While Arabic is spoken throughout the Middle East – it varies widely in accent and style – an Iraqi surgeon once told me that Egyptian Arabic "makes my ears hurt."

†France's version of the US's West Point or Great Britain's Sandhurst.

Qaddafi, once thinking he was getting in good with the US and no longer interested in what the tepid Europeans had to say, managed to piss of both Britain and France by refusing lucrative oil concession to both countries, and then not buying French made Rafale fighter jets. As it turned out, the French would send the jets on test runs to Libya anyway.

The weapons, while of US manufacture, did not come from the US – not officially at any rate. The Qataris got them from the Saudis, who'd bought them from the US as part of a $60 billion arms deal in 2010. To make the matter even more convoluted, you well may recall reading somewhere that the Saudis and the Qataris hate each other. They do. Given the passive-aggressive anti-American policy stance of the French, Paris reckoned that was as good a reason as any to spoon with the Qataris, who were early supporters of Osama bin Laden's propaganda against the Saudi government and royal family.

For their part, the Saudis have a strange relationship with the United States, and therefore, the world. And they do not like the fact that it is evolving in a way that isn't quite to the Saudi's advantage. Despite their huge arms purchases from the US, they don't have much of a military. Most of the armaments purchased from the United States are still in the packing grease, as it were. The thinking being that while plenty of countries might line up to invade the Arabian peninsula, only Iran could logistically pull it off. Even then it would be tricky as hell.

What Iran is calling a navy but looks a lot like second rate coast guard, which rules out a cross-gulf maritime attack. Any invasion of the Arabian Peninsula will require driving through Basra, a city of about 1.7 million. Yes, they are Shia, but they persistently refuse to rise up for the Iranians.

After that, there is Kuwait where the US still has plenty of troops stationed, even if the State Department isn't talking about them. And no one is asking them to leave, either. To be clear, without American intervention, neither Basra nor Kuwait will be much more than annoying roadblocks for Iran. After that, the invaders would face crossing some 350 miles of flat desert to hit the major oil producing centers of Abqaiq and Ras Tanura compound – and that is where they'd be heading. Between, there is simply nothing there and that cuts both ways, just ask T.E. Lawrence or Erwin Rommel. Assuming the invading army refuels and tops up provisions in Kuwait (in this scenario, miraculously abandoned by US troops), that's still a lot of clear, open desert where all food, water and fuel must be carried in train to support an invasion, and there is literally no cover from sorties by Saudi Arabia's vividly mediocre air force. It's got the latest equipment (they got it from us) whereas the Iranians are mostly flying Ford and Carter era F-14s. Their recent snuggling with the Russians has improved this situation, but not by much*. To get up to speed, the Saudi air force is currently on live, on-going training missions and doing a fair job of blowing the crap out of Yemen. So, progress, I guess.

In short, this is not going to be a fun drive for the Islamic Revolution. Still, if the Iranian army *can* make the run to the refining and launching compounds which happen to be in the countries grieved Shi'a zone without getting obliterated from above, Saudi Arabia just might be screwed. If Iran *did* manage it, the Saudi assumption is that the US would come in and settle the matter. And the smart money says that we would.

---

*For all its bluster, Russia is on its back feet.

315

Which explains why the Saudis are not concerned with their lack of a real special forces branch, and outsourced the operation of shipping arms to Libya to Qatar. For our part, the situation allows for the CIA to orchestrate implausible arms transfers from Saudis to Qatari's without American fingerprints being anywhere near the actual deal.

Soon it became clear, however, that the US *too clever by half* arms pipeline was plugged into to the same al-Qaeda veterans that US forces been fighting on Iraq. It really was the only plausible outcome for the adventure. President Obama tried to clean up the mess with a series of completely illegal weapons buy-backs in violation of the Security Act of 1947.*

The general reckoning, and good luck verifying it, is that about 400 stinger missiles (officially known as MANPADS) and 50 launchers went to *jihadis* that would eventually be turned against what we might call "the West." In September of 2011, the story was being picked up by the *Wall Street Journal* after related documents were found in Tripoli following Qaddafi's retreat from the city. According to that article, some two dozen Stingers went missing.

On 5 May, the day after the pow-wow between the French and the Qatari convoy, Chris Stevens took a boat from Malta into Benghazi, leading to breathless speculation in the press that Stevens was CIA. Normally, that is the sort of thing that the company handles, but if you are running a completely off-the-

---

* The same act, if you are wondering, with which Congress threatened to impeach Reagan over the Iran-Contra affair.

books operation, you wouldn't use one of your own diplomats because that, by definition, would make it very on-the-books.*

More likely, now that Qaddafi's regime was collapsing and the government defections were turning into a stampede, Secretary of State Hillary Clinton just wanted to put her stamp on what was already being called on the ground "Hillary's War." In eye-balling the White House, she'd crystalized her view of the Libyan revolution as "We came, we saw, he died."

Still, it was clear almost immediately that the arms shipments to the rebels were going to the wrong people – and the revolution was going pear-shaped. The small arms were one thing, what really caused a threat was the surface to air stinger missiles. You can take down a commercial airliner with one and now there were hundreds loose in eastern Libya in the hands of the same people we'd been fighting in Iraq. One of Steven's task was to collect the MANPADS from the various rebel groups now running amok all over the country.

The operation couldn't be run well from the embassy in Tripoli, so first home of the US Special Mission was the Tibesti Hotel, which also housed the international press. On 1 June a car bomb exploded in from the hotel. Steven's moved the mission within a CIA training site and listening post that was keeping tabs on the growing presence of Iranian intelligence officers and Quds force operatives.

WASHINGTON, D.C., 15 JUNE 2011: In a 32-page report to Congress the White House argued that the US military action

---

*There is no evidence that Stevens was CIA, but with decent tradecraft, there wouldn't be.

in Libya did NOT require congressional approval under the War Powers Act – even if US pilots were flying combat missions, and the US was providing 70% of the intel assets with the whole exercise costing the US taxpayer some $750 million.

The report went on to state that there were no jihadists involved in the fighting in Libya. It's a curious claim as the report was written *after* Obama had been forced to ask the Emir of Qatar to quit arming every al Qaeda affiliate in the top half of Africa. More to the point, the report went on to claim that no Islamists were fighting alongside the Transitional National Government. Even more curious, Chris Stevens' mission in country was more or less to court various Islamist groups and see if we could use them to our ends.

Back in Benghazi, there was the very off-the-books matter of the clandestine CIA Annex currently in a mad rush to recollect all the MANPADS and other weapons from all the Islamist groups that the White House was claiming a) weren't there and b) weren't armed with the weapons the CIA was desperately trying to get back from them.

To coordinate all the operations that weren't being conducted against enemies that weren't there, the CIA needed a base of operations. By June, Stevens had managed to secure a walled, 13-acre compound with 3 villas and a swimming pool northwest of the Annex at an ultimate cost to the taxpayer of about $70,000 per month. Lots of security improvements were ordered, but whether or not they were actually installed is another matter. Reportedly, there were parts of the decrepit wall that one could simply climb over.

BY JULY, the rebels had broken out of their stronghold and began to move towards Tripoli. The NATO no-fly zone gave them cover, but on the ground it was a close-run fight with steady rebel advances followed by confused retreats. Like waves of a rising tide, the advances pushed ever closer to the capital. By late August, the rebels were crawling through Tripoli's western suburbs − towards the sprawling Bab al-Aziziya compound − it's walled gardens and buildings forbidden to all but Gaddafi's inner circle.

The tail end of any war, when both sides know who is going to win out, can be oddly calm. During the heavy earlier fighting, when victory could still go either way, war crimes had been committed on both sides. Even Latifa, despite her romantic memories of the stand that crippled the tyrant, admitted that this must be true.

As the rebel flag went up over the old Ottoman Palace near Tripoli's Green Square, the city did not succumb to some medieval berserker's bloodbath. Despite loyalist neighborhoods still clinging on throughout the city, it remained eerily calm. In a rebel held building, the provisional government was staking its hopes of a post-revolution future on an unearthed investment report by Ernst & Young, detailing Libya's swell reintegration with the Western commercial world. Across town Saif al-Islam informed a semi-captive international press that he'd laid an ingenious trap for the unsuspecting rebels, who'd walked right into his cunning snare by taking over most of the capital.

After 42 years in power any prince, however awful, must have a power base, and Gaddafi's was the city of Sirte. He'd been born in a fishing village on its outskirts called Qasm Abu Hadi. As he rose to power, he turned the little coastal village into a regional capital and the people there knew it. It was here that he'd written his *Green Book* and in Sirte they knew that if their Sun King ever went away so would the large villas, the neatly maintained streets, their establishment prestige, their national leverage and privilege. So, it was in Sirte that Gaddafi and his ever shrinking gang of loyalists holed themselves up in an upscale and loyal neighborhood called District Two while the rest of the city was being blasted to pieces by the approaching rebel army.

Never one for subtle maneuvers, at about 8 am on the morning of 20 October, the Colonel's 75 car convoy made a break for it, heading west. Inside they were well-armed and wearing body armor, outside the convoy was a desperate blaze of gunfire that mowed down rebel checkpoints and civilians alike. Circling above was a French Air Force Raphale jet there to enforce the NATO no-fly zone along with a drone sending real-time images to NATO HQ. Neither the pilot nor anyone else knew who was in the convoy, only that it was huge and killing civilians in a blaze left and right. It was shortly before 8:30 that the pilot was given the go-ahead to strike. He did. The blast destroyed a couple of vehicles ahead of Gaddafi's, bringing the convoy to a halt as the concussion from the blast dazing everyone in the colonel's car.

In the confusion, the convoy was abandoned. Gaddafi was still wearing his body armor and armed with a golden revolver and a silver back-up pistol proving that, for all his other sins, he remained a top-notch Bond villain until the very end. In an attempt to clear a storm drainage ditch in which to hide, someone threw a grenade that evidently bounced back and exploded, killed a few aides, seriously wounding Gaddafi's arm and shoulder. So it was that Muammar Gaddafi, the man who'd become the Libyan State, and single-handedly controlling the largest oil and gas reserves in Africa, was pulled from a storm drain in his hometown. He was, predictably, recognized by his hair.

In true millennial fashion, what happened next was caught on video from a dozen different angles. As rebels gathered around Gaddafi, seems confused in the video, "What's this, my sons? What are you doing?" He is then frog marched to a group of trucks where, pressed against the hood, he is sodomized with a bayonet. He screamed *"harem alaikum"* as it was happening – which means, roughly, "It is a sin what you are doing!"

Perhaps the colonel had a point, but as far as the wages of sin go, he was absolutely a top-earner.

When the mob gains the day, it ceases to be any longer the mob. It is then called the nation. If it does not, why, then some are executed, and they are called the canaille, rebels, thieves and so forth.

Napoleon Bonaparte
to Dr. Barry O'Meara of St. Helena

CHAPTER TWENTY:
FETAHA

The Hotel Juliana in Benghazi is a modern, clean place with enough hot water if you don't linger and "Western" toilets as opposed to clean, tiled hole in the floor with a hose. Strictly speaking, they are more hygienic that the way we do it, but it the notion freaks you out, you'll need to check this before traveling in the Middle East. Like most anything else, it's just a matter of getting used to it - where there is no choice, there is not problem.

The hotel wi-fi is good, drawing a nightly crowd in the lobby to smoke, drink fruit juice, check smart phones and speak at each other in the time-honored manner of all at once. Get a room in the back of the hotel, away from the crowd, where you can open your window at night and listen to the sea lapping against the beach. My room was so close to the water that if I pitched an empty orange soda bottle, an odd shoe, or spare ammo clip out the window, I could almost hit the surf. To look at the shoreline, plenty of guests had already tried it.

As for the food, it was good if you stuck to the local cuisine. Most of the guests were international NGO sorts, German arms dealers and a few American contractors, so the management made a clumsy homage to the Western palette with fried mozzarella sticks for breakfast and cafeteria-style mystery meat. My advice is this: when in Libya, eat as the Libyans do: salads of fine tomatoes and cucumbers, hummus, yogurt and goat cheese. The caveat here is that one night they served lamb, or at least that's the way they sold it. I'm pretty sure it was goat.

Downstairs there was a nice, if slightly off-brand gift shop made up to look like an old-fashioned Mississippi Delta juke joint. Charming but crude paintings of Robert Johnson and his guitar sat alongside small figures of Louis Armstrong blowing away on his trumpet. When I'd into Basra earlier than year, I'd though that it was like landing on the moon. And it was, but I swear that this might have been the weirdest thing I'd saw - a bunch of Muslim Berbers trying to make like they'd been plucked off a farm outside Clarksdale. I don't know why this was so jarring: the blues was born in the Mississippi Delta, a flat, sparsely populated place where a large majority of the population had the ruling class engineer an entire social system that kept both hope and escape out of reach. That the blues came out of Clarksdale, Mississippi shouldn't be any stranger that that it landed in a place like Benghazi. Still, I visited the shop twice to make sure that, being a Memphian, I hadn't dreamed this bit up.

The pretend juke joint and the homage to its music, however random it seemed to me, offered more that a passing ray of hope in a place desperately in need of it. It was a shift beyond the mere survival mode to something that was aspirational: An exercise is what could be, rather than being entirely focused on surviving the moment, that a society needs in order to move forward. The signs, while fragile, were everywhere. In that grim twilight between the revolution and full-blown civil war, someone had built a hotel. I found myself standing by the half-completed swimming pool with the manager, Omar. He smiled triumphantly and assured me that the pool would be finished by spring. "We have a good future. In Libya, we have two great natural resources."

"Oil and…?"

"Tourism, of course." Omar said this as if I really should have known better. "Look at this…" We beheld the pool.

This was either an exercise in ambition, delusion, or very low standards of vacation travel. I took the cultural tack, "Well, Omar, help me understand something as an American; what would the women wear poolside? Not the *jilbāb*?"

"Ahh, yes. Women would be… ahhhh… discouraged…from the pool."

That sounded like the single most effective way to discourage men from the pool as well, but I kept that thought to myself. "What about Gadaffi's ban on alcohol? Will the new regime lift it?"

"No." he said with no small degree of approval, "There is no talk of this." Devout man, that Omar.

"Oh." I said deeply. Far be it from me to crush a man's one glimmer of hope in the foothills of war, but I just couldn't see how a bunch of stone sober men standing around a pool was going to turn an essentially homophobic country into an international tourism destination. Not with the Greek Isles, full of ouzo swilling, mostly nude Greeks, a scant 350 miles away.

Behind the hotel was the dodgy side of the Mediterranean Sea, oily and slick from the tankers coming in and out of port. "What about the ocean?" I asked and turned to face a cold surf beyond 50 feet of garbage strewn beach.

Omar sighed, "The beaches were mined when Gaddafi thought the US would invade." The trash had attracted, as it does, packs of feral dogs and – this was new – and foursome of feral horses. Some boys were trying to ride the horses, which seems like a good way to break your neck, but boys will be boys. In my experience, the wild animals and explosives tend to put bathers off.

In truth, the whole city is covered in garbage. The Arabs are, for all their passion, incredibly polite people. Unfortunately, very polite people tend to be easily offended. Language barriers never help these things, but I was curious to know if all this garbage was from the revolution or had Benghazi always been a trash heap.

I asked a surgical resident from Tripoli, a rival city about the waste disposal. "Oh yes," he said, "it's been like this for many years. Gaddafi ordered the garbage not picked up so Benghazi would be a dirty city."

"Why?"

"So, Tripoli would be clean." All things *are* relative.

No wonder Father Fizzyhead managed to turn the eastern half of the country against him. This may be the reason that most Libyans didn't seem to realize that their revolution had tipped into a civil war. By the summer of 2012 most Libyans would have said that the war was over and, like Latifa, said it with nostalgia. The revolutionary graffiti on the tumble-down walls are a lot of US, French and Qatari flags – about half the slogans were in English. I asked a young pilot trainee why the slogans were in a language most Libyans couldn't understand. "We want to tell our message to the world, not just Arabia."

"I thought that Gaddafi removed English from school curriculum."

He smiled proudly, it was boyish and wide, and he thumbed his chest. "We learned."

While I was in-country, Libyans were glued to their televisions to watch the aftershocks of the Arab Spring continue to unfold in neighboring Egypt, where the largely peaceful protests against Hosni Mubarak, the "Old Pharaoh*" had surgically removed the head of the government, leaving the rest of the body politic intact. They avoided a power vacuum, but also failed to muck out the stalls, as it were. In March of 2011, Secretary of State Hillary Clinton visited Cairo visiting with the leaders of the protests in Tahir Square that ousted Mubarak. The protesters were still on a euphoric victory lap, but Clinton was busy very coldly sorting out the existing chess pieces before her. She wanted to know what the movement leaders were planning to do ahead of Egypt's upcoming parliamentary elections. Reportedly, one of them dismissed Madame Secretary with "We don't *do* politics." They were winning and their righteous momentum would carry the day at the voting booth. That was the wrong answer.

---

*This is not a term of endearment in the Arab world - but a reference to pre-Muslim and decadent rulers. Emir, for instance, is much more respectable, and caliph until ISIS came around. Of course, the swastika was a symbol of spring until Hitler got his paws on it.

With the giant apparatus of state still intact, the next guy, Mohammad Morsi, stepped up along with a highly effective Muslim Brotherhood and in a transformation that completely validated George Orwell's *Animal Farm*, morphed into something nearly indistinguishable from the last fellow.

The Libyans, on the other hand, had taken things a bit further: cleaving off the head, cutting out the lungs, heart and, given the fate of Gaddafi's sons*, the balls of the old power structure. Unlike the Iraqis, they hadn't waited for a suspiciously interested superpower to invent a reason do it for them. The Libyans had reached their tipping point on their own.

The cheering solidarity in facing down a tyrant however, was inevitably replaced with the much more splintered and tedious task of rebuilding a society that had been long reduced to one overbearing, unhinged personality. Politics is such a nasty concept that many activists didn't want to touch it. They were rebuilding building a nation from scratch in a way post-revolutionary America never had to face. Like the Egyptians, they hadn't quite thought through what a post-Gaddafi Libya would look like. It had all happened too fast.

NO ONE WAS in charge but the sense of sticking together, of community, was strong. Yet, by the mid-summer of 2012, however, the vibrations in the city known as the "caregiver to the lost" were turning ugly. Building a new Libya that welcomed both the West and the Arab world was not a priority of Amar al-Sharia. The name means "Partisans of the Faith" and it – like al Qaeda – is more of a brand name than a single, coherent

---

*Dead, in prison or exile.

organization. One of its leaders, Mohammad Ali al Zahawi, told more than one reporter that his militia is "at war" with the liberals. In April, a bomb targeted a UN convoy. In May the Red Cross offices were attacked with rocket propelled grenades (RPG).

To get control of the situation, Chris Stevens returned to Tripoli as the new Ambassador to Libya for what was supposed to be a victory lap for the Obama/Clinton doctrine over the Bush Doctrine. Although, looking at the track record of what was actually done, rather than promised, it's hard to tell them apart. Consider: George W. Bush opened Gitmo to hold terrorists by executive order. The liberals cried foul and elected Barack Obama, who promised to close the thing in his first week and disengage from the War on Terror. He did neither, although he could have with the stroke of a pen, and liberals cheered as he increased drone attacks. Conservatives then fumed over what amounted to Obama continuing the policies of Bush. Enter Trump, running on roughly the same platform of disengagement of US forces as Obama. Suddenly the right was cheering over policies that enraged it four years earlier and the left was calling Trump a lunatic for doing what Obama promised to do and didn't. I digress.

No matter which doctrine you blamed or promoted, there was no victory to promote in Libya. The country collapsing into a violent power vacuum and vehicle for Iranian mayhem while the Clinton demanded that security in both Tripoli and Benghazi look like business as usual. Which, I suppose it was, just not the way Clinton was selling it.

As June ground on, the situation deteriorated after Washington announced the death of Yabya al-Libi, a Libyan born Al Qaeda operative in Pakistan. A bomb was thrown through the front gate at the US diplomatic mission where the Libyan militia acting as security acquitted themselves admirably, according to US security forces.

There were, however, lots of militia groups running amok, and not all of them swimming in revolutionary ideals. Most were for sale to the highest bidder. There was also the unsettling question of just who was going to run post-revolution Libya. In short, no one wanted to be the first to put their gun down, despite the CIA's attempts to get them all back. Then, on 7 June, there was that parade of militias staged and coordinated by Ansar al-Sharia on the corniche on Benghazi's seafront. It may have been promoted on Facebook, but the parade was just a side-door attempt to occupy the city by the jihadists. As it was, the mostly moderate locals were having none of it and started to push back. The militias moved out into the desert and fell back to Derna. It wouldn't be the last time people that called Benghazi home were forced to run the militants out of the city. Four days later, RGGs were used in a rocket attack on the British Ambassador, Dominic Asquith. Followed by the desecration of the British war cemetery in Tobruk.

All this time CIA was briefing the embassy in Tripoli about Iranian training of these militia, including Ansar al-Sharia. The State Department *did* change the status of the embassy in Tripoli and the Special Mission outpost in Benghazi to bring in additional security staff. It also decided to provide covert support to the Syrian rebels fighting against Bashar al-Assad. The knock-on effect of this was that every wanna-be arms dealer in the region began to clear out of Benghazi for southern Turkey, which would become the staging ground for all the powers coming in to meddle in the Syrian civil war. The CIA, for the most part, moved on to Syria as well.

For his part, Stevens on 25 June, Stevens sent a cable entitled "Libya's Fragile Security Deteriorates as Tribal Rivalries, Power Plays & Extremism Intensifies." And that's just the title. The report goes on to state "... al Qaeda flag has been spotted several times flying over government buildings and training facilities in Derna."

Later – in January of 2013 – Hillary Clinton testified that she had never bothered to read the cables from Stevens, nor had she ever consulted with Defense Secretary Leon Panetta over the continued loan of US Special Forces security teams for the mission. In short, she didn't do her job. Her defense, such as it is, is the same as Bush 43's. President Bush didn't actually lie to the public to get us into a war with Iraq – he was given bad information because he'd made it very hard to paint an honest assessment because telling the center of power what it wants to hear is good for the career. In Clinton's case, she was going to use the "Hillary's War" story to fling her into the White House. No one who took their career seriously was about to tell her that Benghazi had deteriorated into a shit-show.

There was still yet another factor alongside the ignored requests for added security. The larger discussion in the diplomatic corps was that US diplomats cannot do their jobs from fortresses. Across the world, local officials were refusing to go to the US embassies, as they find the security measures wildly insulting. Nor do they want to see an armored caravan disrupting local traffic like an invading army. Diplomats are neither politicians nor soldiers: their jobs are conducted through low-key meetings and back room deals, something that simply can't be done with an overt show of force. The global discussion at the State Department in the summer of 2012 was not increasing security, but decreasing it - making diplomats *more* accessible.

For their part, the Libyans, having decided that the war was over, forbid American boots on the ground. By the fall, the CIA had a twelve-man team in Benghazi training local intelligence officers. The CIA annex in the city was tolerated because practically, the Libyans knew that they couldn't put off the *jihadi* parades indefinitely without the help from the West. Yet, unlike the army, State Department and presidential hopefuls, the CIA operates well in the shadows. In addition, Ambassador Stevens was also very popular. While he had a security detail, he was very sensitive to the local optics, so he ducked security constantly. Or at least he tried. According to post-mortem interviews after the attack, the ambassador wasn't nearly as good at evading his security detail as he thought, they just kept enough distance so that he appeared alone.

The reality hardly mattered because the Libyans appreciated the effort. I was sitting with Dr. Laila Bugaighis, the then deputy director of the BMC – a nice lady in a Western pantsuit and long black hair gloriously uncovered – who told me, "Chris walked around without body guards all the time. He was our guest."

According to Kenneth Timmerman's account in his book *Dark Forces*, on 30 July the NSA listening post at the annex picked up some chatter – in Persian – about a Quds operation to send Iranian operatives into the area under the cover of humanitarian aid workers: In this case, a Red Cresent medical team. Beyond that, the details of plan was vague. The CIA chief sent word to the militia controlling the Benghazi airport to be on the lookout for a Red Crescent team coming in from Iran. The team arrived as scheduled and a tail was attached. The tail was still in contact with the Red Cresent van when it was ambushed in a hail of machine gun fire and the operatives kidnapped. A local CIA asset on the ground reported that it was a "Sunni-Shi'a" thing. Then, the CIA was informed that the Iranians had been driven to Tripoli and loaded on a plane for Tehran.

Which is not at all what happened. What wasn't known was that the Quds force planners knew that the operation – to kidnap Stevens to show the US that Iran could strike anywhere – had been blown. While it pains me to admit it, having an aligned with a Sunni militia "kidnap" the Iranian operatives, hold them for a while, then report them as having been deported to Tehran was a brilliant ploy. And on that had the fingerprints of Quds chief Qassem Sulimani all over it.* As it happened, the team began working with Ansar al-Sharia along with other sympathetic militias on a plan B.

Despite the maximum alert level, Ambassador Stevens came to Benghazi to met with tribal leaders at a restaurant on the night of 10 September 2012. It was supposed to be secret, but it didn't work out that way. Big Men love to put on a big show, and the local press showed up and suddenly the everyone knew that the American Ambassador was in town.

At 6:45 am the morning of 11 September, the local unarmed security detail at the mission compound noticed a Libyan policeman had parked his car at the front gate and climbed to the roof of a building across the street. The policeman was taking pictures of the mission's 13-acre compound. Complaints

---

*Honestly, it pains me to say much nice about Donald Trump as well, but he did order the airstrike that roasted Sulimani, and if this chaos is ever going to stop, the man really needed killing.

to local authorities were drafted by the local State Department security officer. Stevens pressed on with the day's business, which included a scheduled meeting with the head of a Turkish shipping company in Benghazi and Turkish Consul General Ali Sait Akin, who left the compound at 7:40 pm.

What looked like a garden variety anti-American protest began to gather in the street. At 9:42 pm, the protests broke into the first wave of the attack. According to Kimmerman's account: Ex- Navy SEAL Tyronne (Ty) Woods was told three separate times to stand down during the initial 22 minutes of the mission compound attack, and by then the compound was engulfed in flames. On a normal day, it is only a five minute drive to get from the CIA annex to the Special Mission compound. This wasn't a normal day, but the unrest had not taken over the whole area, so it is curious that it wasn't until 10:28 pm that reinforcements arrived. Then it took another quarter of an hour to fight their way through the crowd into the compound.

Woods, along with fellow ex-SEAL Glen Doherty would die seven hours later defending the Annex which was hit by a well-targeted mortar attack. Understand that a mortar looks simple, but it is not a particularly easy weapon to master, requiring specialized training from *someone's* military. This was not a protest or riot gotten out of hand, this was a coordinated attack. And the coordinated parts were too well timed to be mere opportunism.

The events of 11 September had the flavor of a sweeping geo-political statement rather than a targeted hit. It would have been much easier to kill the ambassador out and somewhat unguarded than attempt to get him within a walled compound.

The State Department blamed it on some nut-job movie trailer with a junior high AV club production value, then a terrorist attack by al Qaeda. Almost to a man, eyewitnesses pinned the attack on Ansar al-Sharia. With its snazzy logo of crossed AK-47s, a fist and a Koran, it is a recognizable brand.

Latifa told me that she was on duty at the BMC when the body of an "Anglo-Saxon" was brought in. That alone was confusing enough, then rumors started spreading he was the US Ambassador. The hospital staff finally identified him by calling the numbers on his cell phone. "We did what we could," Latifa said, "but it was CO_2 poisoning, from the smoke."

A US helicopter took up his remains. "We thought it was an Apache." Latifa told me, peering off into some unfocused distance the we people do when recalling something both indelible and unreal. "We thought the US air strikes would begin." But they didn't.

In the aftermath of his death, Benghazi was left with was a profound sense of *fateha*. I heard that word several times when Steven's name came up. It means scandal or shame to a degree that English translations don't touch and the average modern blameless American probably couldn't grasp even if they could articulate it. "He was a guest in our country, after America helped us oust Gaddafi. And we did *this*!" Latifa told me. Then, then she turned back to me with those dark Arab eyes, but sounding like a Florida girl said, "C'mon people. We're better than this!"

She was ashamed.

The West is in the grips of a fashionably indignant age, and we have a tedious habit of getting indignant about things about which we don't really care. We are indignant about human rights violations in China, but have a home filled with products of Chinese sweatshops. Indignant, yes, but not terribly embarrassed by our hypocrisy. This is because people don't get ashamed about things that don't matter to them.

Chris Stevens, to the vast majority of Benghazians, mattered.

"The past isn't dead. It isn't even the past."
William Faulkner

CHAPTER TWENTY-ONE:
CLANS, HASHISH AND FEAR OF YOUR MOTHER

Granted, the above quote was made by a man who likely didn't know what fiscal quarter it was, but the point stands. The Iraqi's fascination with William Faulkner is a less random that it first appeared to me on that night in Nasiriya, or that pretend Mississippi juke joint on the beach in Benghazi. That far side of the moon foreignness was fading and if not understanding, some patterns were emerging. Not necessarily along the lines of what Machiavelli called "the Frank and the Turk" or even East and West. Just how any human society acts. And being a dim-witted human, sometimes you have to go to the far side of the moon to see what is right before you.

What had happened in Libya wasn't like Darius' palace coup, or even the civil wars of the late Roman empire that involved dueling legions more than they did the terrified citizenry. Latifa had pointed out the parallel between the Libyan and American revolutions, but it was a flawed comparison. In Libya, there was no ready cadre of homegrown leaders with the administrative experience to keep the wheels on the road to form the next government. Gaddafi's bending the entire state to the over-bearing personality had ensured that the Libyans wouldn't be so lucky. This wasn't even an Egyptian style Arab Spring uprising that led to what we might call a popular coup.

What happened in Libya was a scorched earth revolution that didn't only take out a leader, but the entire government. With its socialist *jamahiriya* removing the government meant striping all of society back to survival mode. And even Ur-Nammu standing atop his Ziggurat in Ur could see that a society in survival mode was not where you wanted to be.

What was so tragic in Libya was to see the ideals and solidarity of the revolution get crushed in the resulting vacuum. They were trying to build a society from scratch, and weren't doing a half bad job of it. Latifa had been right when she said that America was exile. Once across the Atlantic, the settlers were largely left alone to get on with it. Libya wouldn't be so lucky. No matter how well intended, competing external pressures and actors would make it nearly impossible to build something stable – like laying the foundation of a house in the middle of a hurricane. Less metaphorically, the simple idea of Libya – as a nation – didn't have nearly the historical weight to it to withstand the vacuum.

For example, the idea of France as a nation is five hundred years old. The revolutionaries in Paris could scream *vive la France* while lopping off the king's head and not see the conflict. The only revolutionary talk I heard here was "Benghazi arise, arise for the day you've awaited is here." The country that Gaddafi took over in 1969 had no great sense of a Libyan nation, it was just some lines drawn in the sand by the Italians. There wasn't even a nostalgia for the old Ottoman days. There was a sense of *Ummah*, the Muslim community, and after that, things got decidedly clannish.

No one was in charge. The sense of sticking together after the trauma of the revolution was strong, but the politico's couldn't stay away forever. You could almost see the looming problem in the very architecture. Middle class homes are largish buildings filled with extended families occupying private apartments inside. Inside these walled compounds are delightful and immaculate gardens. The roads and beaches and public places are a wreck of filth and garbage; yet behind the walls of every home, restaurant, hospital or mosque, there is a tidy garden. If you believe that a culture's architecture reflects the people who live there, then the message is clear: "Once inside the walls you are one of us and will be taken care of. Outside the walls, you are on your own."

Still, the *souks* were full of people milling through miles of cheap American and European goods. The power was on and people where going about their business. As far as I could see, The city's fragile peace was being held together by a sub-structure of fear of your mother, the threat of well-armed clan retribution, and the mellowing effects of hashish.

But an arrangement like that can't last forever.

ONE PARTICULARLY fearsome red flag, in a place carpeted with them, was that after the attack on the Special Mission complex efforts at collecting stinger missiles and

MANPADS dropped off the cliff. Something that I'd failed to point out to Mrs. M.

I was with some nurses in a taxi – the three ladies in the back seat with myself riding up next to the driver, because even in a civil war, manner count. We roaring the past the wrecked mission compound, still fire damaged from the attacks. The driver pointed to the building and made some gun noises as we merged into that wild din of Arab traffic. "You know this building?"

"Yes, I got it!" I said a little testily. What can I say, I was still touchy about it.

The driver didn't speak much English, so he busied himself texting his girlfriend and the rest of North Africa between the occasional glance at the road. He laid on the horn in a constant blast that made me think he was guiding the car by sonar. Then we'd pass some other site of awful revolutionary derring-do and he'd make more war noises. He had an outstanding howitzer.

Finally, he poked me in the ribs and said, "You this building!" as we plowed into gridlock at 50 mph. Before me was a five-story building which had had its front blown clean off.

"Good Lord!" I said.

He was actually pointing to the boarded up Catholic Church left over from when the Italians ran the place. "You Christian, yes?" Under the circumstances, it sounded like a trick question. "We have oil and we have tourism." There it was again, this talk of tourism. On the other hand, the Bahamas were once considered a death wish, so why not admire the Libyan ambition? Still, I was still fixated on the blown out structure. It looked like a dull, modernist dollhouse for a very dirty, 85-foot little girl. Which, in a nutshell, is the current state of Libyan tourism.

That's when the cracks and reports started. The nurses in the back seat of the taxi looked over at me to see if the distant pops were fireworks or assault rifles. Maybe it was because I was American, or a Southerner, or a guy, but they assumed I could tell the difference. I can. It's a game Memphians play on hot summer nights. At any rate, after a couple of days in Benghazi I just said: "Look up" meaning fireworks, and "Don't go that way" meaning *don't go that way*.

The crack of gunfire can be deceiving. The long-off reports rolling along the shoreline weren't the sounds of battle but joyriding: Short bursts coming from the same location but not returned. They call it "happy fire." It sounds harmless enough, but the surly rules of gravity can't be denied. A bullet fired into the air must come down...somewhere.

The common accounting is that there are more guns than people in Libya. Another taxi driver – whose English was better than the fellow jabbing me in the ribs on a revolution high – assured me that there is an assault rifle or RPG (or both) in the trunk of every car. After the ouster, though, it was considered bad form to be too obvious about it. Yet, on the front steps of the Benghazi Medical Center I watched two men – one in a *kurta*, the traditional long white shirt, and the other in a fatigues jacket and jeans – open their trunks and compare an arsenal that would make the NRA proud. They did this, with wives and kids waiting in the car, with the same nonchalance as Americans comparing smartphones or fly-fishing rods. In no way did the scene attract the attention of the security guard who was using the forward site of his rifle to scratch the back of his head.

Inside the hospital, things were more normal. The surgical residents were eager to learn. Despite the carping of Islamist politicos and all that Great Satan business, to have trained "under the Americans" is a great feather in the professional cap. The growing chaos outside, if anything, seemed to give the surgical residents a focus that could not be found in the lower ranks of hospital personnel. The orderlies and nurses were coming in late, not following simple protocol and seemed to think that getting a text was a perfectly reasonable excuse to leave in the middle of feeding an infant patient. What plans they couldn't bear to miss in a country without alcohol, or any place to meet girls without a fearsome phalanx of aunts around, is baffling to me. They surfed the Internet with such enthusiasm that the hospital had to create a separate, password-protected network for the medical team. When I asked the resident from Tripoli who'd set it up for the password, he threw out his chest and smiled, "'American dream', one word. So you won't forget."

In Libya, nursing isn't a high-status job, nor does it pay well. With the universal basic income under the Gaddafi regime, there had been a chronic shortage of nurses. There simply wasn't a lot of incentive for anyone to take what they perceived to be low-status work for roughly the same amount of money you made staying at home smoking hash. Gaddafi's solution was to import an order of Polish nuns, trained as nurses, to hold the place together. Most of the nurses when I was there were contract workers from the Philippines and India.*

The mission settled into a routine of patients arriving from the OR and personnel changes. "Hand offs" were made twice a

*Six weeks later, even most of these fled as well.

day, 8am and 8pm, when both shifts went from bed to bed discussing patient status, what had gone haywire in the last twelve hours, and what was done about it. Dr. Gascon would call out questions and demand answers, interrupting wrong responses with a loud, barking "No!" that would be devoid of any explanation as to why it was wrong. Then he kept hammering them with questions. Learning to think under pressure, while an entire room is watching, is part of the process.

He wasn't much easier on the volunteers than the resident trainees. "Pam!" He called to the sunny Canadian, "Has that kid got downs syndrome?"

"The chart doesn't say."

"And the chart is always right?" Gascon's sarcasm could get over-the-top. "Did. You. Check. For. Red. Flags?"

"I'm looking at the ears and I can't tell… oh wait a minute," Pam looked the little boy over again, "He's got 12 fingers….and 12 toes."

"OH!" I could almost hear his eyes rolling from across the PICU. "Think that's a red flag?"

Amused at the rise she'd gotten out of him, Pam looked over to me with a grin. "He's just being Ed."

This was the same wrinkle we'd hit in that pasha court with the Minister of Health in Nasiriya. Heart defects and downs syndrome are connected, although the how of it isn't well understood. In the Arab world, conditions like downs syndrome and extra digits are common due to cousins marrying. The government claims that it doesn't happen, but in a place like this, there is no good way around it.

Then there was the case of Fellah, the tiny, underfed patient that Pam had been plotting to smuggle back to Canada via a hysterical pregnancy. Sitting on the bed with her, Gascon seemed like a giant – a weirdly gentle one. The sarcasm reserved for trainees, local politicians and tagalong writers disappeared. "Without the operation she'll never get well enough. Where is the mother?" She'd been brought in by her aunt, a doctor, who only shook her head: Mom had given up and was no longer feeding her, and was waiting for the child to die. Her thumb, the one off which she'd sucked the skin, had been taped, but the odds just kept getting longer.

Gascon looked at the child and stared off out the window, but only for a moment. There was very little chance of her surviving until the next mission trip without surgery. And in her state, however, the surgery would likely kill her. Snapping back, he ordered the child quarantined at the far end of the PICU and to be given a feeding tube consisting of olive oil and milk. It sounded barbaric to me because I think the feeding tubes should be filled with some high-tech medicine that I can't pronounce. "Protein and fat. It's what she needs and it's what we've got."

Meanwhile, Pam was making a vain attempt at training two distracted male nurses, one of who walked away in mid-sentence to answer a text. She called after him in that nasal boom of the Great White North, "In Canada you'd get fired for that!"

"I had a text!"

The other nurse pulled out his ear-buds long enough to join the debate that in no way involved him – an honored pastime in the Arab world. "We are living in a democratic society now!" he said with a smirk.

And so they were. Even if, at times, it was hard to tell. When the children moved out of the PICU, they went to the children's wing of the hospital. There at the end of the hall of the pediatric wards was another one of those scenes that makes you wonder why we're fighting essentially culture wars with people who are fundamentally the same as us. The moms gathered in the common room. Yes, these were wearing black *abaya* and were beautifully tattooed with henna, but in the end they were just moms in a children's hospital. The nursing volunteers would drift over to their wing to check up on the little tappers, the moms, mostly through hand gestures, would snare them in the common area and give them glorious henna tattoos up their arms. It gave the moms something to think about other than the weapons grade anxiety of your child having heart surgery.

The nurses loved it. Some were even invited to something of an Arab gals night out. Given the circumstances, it was actually a night in, and during the day. Either way, I wasn't invited. Still, as conservative as the country is, traditional dress is not compulsory in Libya, just custom. In Benghazi there was more shopping than you'd think. The Muslim world's naughty little secret is that under all those billowing sheets and robes, Arab women are closet fashionistas. Storefronts displaying risqué cocktail dresses line the street. If you duck into the street *souks*, you can find a whole rainbow of intriguing *I Dream of Jeanie* inspired lingerie.

To get to the bottom of the mystery of the Arab woman's wardrobe, I asked Latifa, who'd only taken to the headscarf in the last five years, about it. "Western women think it's a sign of oppression. But look at the unmarried women." She was pointing to a pretty, curvy gal on her cellphone – her pout and diva whine needed no translation. Now that I was looking at her, there wasn't anything remarkable about her clothes other that the headscarf. I understand from the Ladies Murff that my sense of fashion is so out of date that I wouldn't have even if the headscarf was the new thing. "They're dressed modestly by American standards," she said, "but those are cute, formfitting clothes. Arab men like curves."

Latifa went on to describe what was, I assume, some local meme or cartoon: On one side you have a Western woman in a skimpy bikini and dark sunglasses covering her eyes. She's looking at an Arab woman in a black *abaya* and veil with only her eyes exposed. The Western woman thinks, "How terrible, that woman is so oppressed she is only allowed expose her eyes." But the Arab woman is thinking, "How terrible, that woman is so oppressed she's only allowed to cover her eyes."

I have to admit, I'd never thought about it like that before.

As Latifa explained, "It's only after we get married, generally, that we dress traditionally. We say to our husbands, I want *this* only for you." She looked at me to make sure I understood. "It's important that he thinks it's his idea."

"Why?"

"Oh, you know how men are."

"No, not 'why are you manipulating your husband'…I'm familiar with that tactic. Southern ladies do the same thing all the time."

She gave me a slightly confused smile, "You *know* that they're doing it?"

"Of course."

"It looks like your Southern women could use some advice from Arab women. We'll show them how it's done so that you never know."

I laughed. "I don't think that they need any more advantages. So, why do you dress like that?"

"It's comfortable. I mean, look at it."

Which, if the doctor is to be believed, means that the international symbol of female oppression in the Arab world is, in fact, just a long, comfy mu-mu.

I HAD INTENDED to trek out into the desert. Any Libyan will tell you is a priceless, unspoiled beauty. Evidently you need to go out there in groups. Head out alone like Fizzyhead to sit among the *jinn* and they'll tell you things you don't need to hear. Our fixers informed us that some bedouins were "arguing over a patch of sand" and the trip was canceled. The surgical resident too low on the ladder to get the official memo told me a different story. "Oh, we chased the bad militias out into the desert." He laughed and then looked at me almost sheepishly, "You don't want to go there right now." I asked if there were any plans to go after the *jihadis*. He laughed again. They might as well try to extradite from Mars.

When the Libyans refer to "the desert" they mean a place better than twice the size of Texas, with a population of less than two million. It was into this wilderness that many of the Ansar al-Sharia militants were run after a pro-American mob torched the organization's Benghazi HQ. The Iranian operatives went back to Tehran, but Hezbollah lingered on in Derna. The desert is breathtaking beauty and terrifying harshness. For a people who depend on a tight knit community for their very survival, spending too much time alone and isolated in the haunts of the *jinn*, is dangerous pastime. Personally, I found a well-armed, half-baked militia more unsettling, but to each their own.

Instead, the mission took a bus along the littoral road to the biblical city of Cyrene, where the biblical Simon was born. There was a lot of trash there as well, so maybe it's not just

Benghazi. The scenery is like southern California with citrus groves, not very grand mountains and, I swear, the sent of hashish billowing everywhere. Marijuana is technically illegal, and the authorities take a dim view of smuggling, but tend to turn the blind eye to homegrown botanicals and an entire nation of illicit moonshiners. The Libyan version is called *sahillia*, usually taken neat and chased with fruit juice.

In Cyrene, there are some Roman ruins built on Greek ruins, over built with a Byzantine spa. It was magnificent, stretching back unbroken through modern times through antiquity, the link between Europe, Africa and the Middle East. It was a thousand years of frolicking in tepid waters without one good cleaning.

All of which was about to give me some multi-cultural hope for this famously sectarian region. Until I met a man for Egypt, and looking back I should have known he had a chip on his shoulder: He asked where I'm from. Now, I'm as proud to be an American as any red-blooded honcho, but admitting it in parts abroad invites lectures from helpful locals eager to point out just how awful you are. On cue, this guy started in on politics: he *something'd* President Obama. I didn't understand him and nothing in his manner indicated approval or disapproval, just avid , finger-jabbing certainty. My guess is that he disapproved, because he felt the same way about Carter, Reagan, Bushes one and two, and Clinton. I just can't see how anyone could approve of *all* of those guys.

Yet, the man insisted, tan suit flapping around his thin frame, that he was a lover of all mankind. Maybe he did approve of all those ex-presidents. It's not that English was all that bad, he just never stopped to breath. He open his palms to the air as he told

me, "I love all the people of the world. Are you Christian?"
There was that trick question again. "Catholic?"

"Yes." Explaining my actual status seemed daunting.

"Orthodox or Roman?"

Some people can really split hairs. "Roman."

"I love all men...Catholic, Protestant, Muslim, Hindu." He thought for a moment, "All but Israel."

"That's not really *all* mankind is it?*"

"Tell me," he eyed me slyly, "if you are not a Jew, and do not live in Palestine, why do you care where they live?"

"Well," I asked back, "If *you* are not a Jew, and do not live in Palestine, why do *you* care where they live?"

That really seemed to stump the old guy.

THE NEXT DAY, Sunday, I found myself walking down a dim, dirty corridor along-side Mary Wallis – the pediatric cardiac surgeon who'd disappointed her classmates by not becoming a nun. We were headed to the only Christian church in Benghazi – not the old, boarded up Italian cathedral, but a small a pretty Catholic chapel that was part of the deal Gaddafi had struck with the government of Poland and the Catholic church for the safe keeping of the Polish nuns he'd imported as nurses. The church was a standalone building housed, for its own protection, in the back of the walled compound of a much larger mosque. For better than a generation, Libya had operated on along secular lines, and with no Shi'a population to speak of, so there wasn't any inter-religious chapping, either. I never really picked up a consistent anti-Catholic vibe, despite the questions. I suspect

---

*Mrs. M thinks I have a death-wish. I like to think I'm naturally curious.

any vandalism, under the old regime had more to do with hating the Italians rather than Catholics.

Outside the compound, however, the church was very hard to find. Even Dr. Wallis wasn't exactly sure, and she'd been going to church every day. And that's what worried me. Not her devotion to the faith, if anything I was jealous because I'd love to have that much faith in anything. I was going to mass more out of curiosity than piety. What bothered me was the pattern: The same dawn mass everyday by the same Western woman. Wallis was too tall for these parts, and her life, her faith, a solid expertise in her profession gave her the air of certainty you don't much see in a wrecked society. In short, she looked like an important white person. Granted, this was Sunday, so it wasn't dawn, but the service schedule wouldn't be too hard to figure out.

Western NGO sorts had been snatched off the street and the Iranians had already embedded operatives in with a Red Crescent team. During my adventures with Benghazi airport security, what was passing for the authorities had stopped looking through my bag when they'd found the bottle of scotch. They never found the Beretta locking blade that had been in the lining next to an internal brace. A knife at a gun fight might not seem like much, but it may well be all you need. Any travel that requires a commercial flight makes bringing a pistol tricky. True, finding one in a conflict zone is both easy and cheap, but the black-market is no place to be without introductions – they'd as soon kidnap you themselves as deliver the hardware. As for a knife, check you bag and you are 90% there.

It was the threat of a kidnapping that bothered me. Chances are that, if they come, they aren't going to just descend on you guns blazing and make a spectacle of themselves. They do that to an ambassador to make a geo-political point. You, gentle reader, aren't that important. Neither am I. More likely, you'll start to notice you've been boxed in with car and someone will get out – Thing 1 – and *show* you the gun, rather than stick it in your ribs. The point is that you freeze with fear so that he can lay hands on you and bundle you off into the get-away car that will take you to a ransom or likely death. You aren't going to want to get in the car, so take note of where the gun is. There will be at least one other person – Thing 2 – with a gun. Now, Thing 2 may be pointing a gun at you, but if so, he's pointing it at Thing 1 as well. Take advantage of this because even in the world of terrorism, these people have to work together.

In the movies, this is the point where the hero shows us how cool he is under pressure. This is wrong. This is, in fact, the time to show – theatrically – just how scared you are. Go down like your knees have buckled (but don't like them touch the ground, go into a squat like you've just messed your pants). Before you go down, slip your hand into your right pocket, where you'll have your knife. As Thing 1 grabs your shoulder to bring you back to your feet, stab him in the groin – or if you aren't that quick, in the belly. Getting stabbed in the groin, I understand, is an unsettling experience, so like you're swooning around like a panicking idiot, pull the startled Thing 1 with your left hand to put him in between you and Thing 2. *Keep your right hand on the knife handle* and pull up towards. If you've gone too deep, just tilt the handle up at an angle and slice through until your hand in near his pistol grip. That's when you let go of the knife and take his gun.

At this point you're probably just going to have to go ahead and shoot Thing 2. Even if you miss, he'll be looking to beat a hasty retreat. For one thing, he'll assume that you're on a rampage while using his *jihad* buddy as a human shield. Don't worry about the driver, he'll already long gone.

Groin wounds of this magnitude bleed out pretty quickly, which will save you from actually having to shoot Thing 1, but you will have to wash your pants. Not sure what to tell you about dry cleaning.

Admittedly, these are strange thoughts to be having as while looking for a church. Then again, I'm of somewhat Norman descent, so maybe it's congenital. I was scanning the alleyway, but Dr. Wallis was looking for the inconspicuous green door set in the wall. The she found it with the calm certainty of faith. Above the arch, in the concrete was simply carved HAEC EST DOMUS DEI. It was probably the only Latin in the city. Inside the compound, the grounds were well kept. Here, again, was the language of their architectural style. Once inside, you were protected – even a Catholic church. They are, after all, People of the Book.

IN THAT STRANGE TWILIGHT between revolution and civil war, even the Libyans didn't think that that revolutionary solidarity and a sense of community couldn't hold the place together indefinitely. Gascon, for his part, is possessed of a vision of the way the world could be with some standard protocols and training methods. But what about the volunteers who fly off halfway across the globe – burning vacation days to do their day job for nothing, under these appalling conditions? The average American has two kids. Picture having eight. All of them ill or otherwise traumatized at the same time, speaking a foreign language, with massive chest wounds and almost no access to painkillers. Picture this in a country that hasn't seen a happy hour in 45 years.

I'd asked the mission anesthesiologist how he dealt with the added chaos of his job done under such conditions. He had an air of almost zen about him. "You just...do." It seemed to me that everyone was trying to make it work, because you just do. But the *jihadis* wouldn't stay in the desert forever, they had US weapons and Iranian money and planning. And I knew it as well they did. I recall writing in a report at the time "Libya's future is theirs for the taking." And it was. It still is. But, like the tiny Fellah on the far end of the PICU, the odds were appallingly long.

The simple truth is that most jobs that are worth doing are hard. The passions that drive us to be better than we are, and sometimes better than we can even imagine ourselves, are *always* taxing. The tasks that produce that satisfied exhaustion and deep sleep of the happy make us what we are.

In a savage world full of terrible tragedy, the minor victories matter. With her mother AWOL, Fellah became something of a mascot to the team. At one of the final hand-offs of the mission, as the full team of medical volunteers from the US, Australia, Malaysia, India, Belarus, Canada, Iran, Columbia, Pakistan, Holland and Libya had gathered, the departing nurse announced, saving the best for last, that overnight Fellah had a bowel movement. That was it – the big news. Shit happened.

The room exploded in applause.

...I kept on looking for a sign
In the middle of the night
But I couldn't see the light
No, I couldn't see the light
I kept on looking for a way
To take me through the night
I couldn't get it right
I couldn't get it right...
Climax Blues Band
"Couldn't Get It Right"

CHAPTER TWENTY-TWO:
POTHOLE OF THE GODS

And just what am I, or anyone else for that matter, supposed to make of all this?

Under the circumstances, the desperate little thing filling her diaper seemed, if not a miracle, certainly a victory. I'd like to extended the metaphor to what was happening in the rest of the country, or the Middle East, or the rest of the world. – and as graphic metaphors go it would have been fair enough. It was hardly a victory for anyone.

The mad scramble to get out of Libya had not started by the time I was leaving for the Benghazi airport. It would, soon enough, in a few weeks. The heartbreaking thing wasn't the physical destruction so much as the destruction of potential – like watching peace negotiations reach that crucial junction just before the hand-shake, and some jackass throws a sucker punch and the whole thing implodes. The Libyans well may have sorted the mess out on their own if they'd been allowed to, but that was asking too much. Without all the outside "help", its possible (but only just) that the bewildering network of tribal militias might have, out of mere survival, drifted under the largest banner of the UN-backed Government of National Accord (GNA) – corrupt, inefficient, and petty, but within the system. The largest oil reserves on the continent, however, ensured every self-declared general had some foreign backer willing to bankroll his army.

The red flags of proxy war were unfurling along the coast, and if I'm going to be honest, I wanted to stay. I don't have a death wish, I just bore easily. With the medical mission wrapped up, however, by brief was complete. My job involved flying back to Istanbul without any hard to explain luggage. There I had a much needed in one of my favorite cities. The next morning I hopscotched to Amsterdam then Milwaukee and, without breathing a draft of fresh air, flew down to Memphis.

When I touched down I found, as I knew that I would, the Ladies Murff at the bottom of the escalator at the baggage claim. They were smiling, happy to see me, the only two creatures on Earth capable pulling me out of the rabbit hole which I'd gone down. I reached them, hugged them close and kissed their hair. And like that, I was safe. That terrifying glob of fear that had turned my insides cold and clammy would, with distance, be recast as the sort of funny story you tell at a cocktail party. Yes, the nightmares were waiting, I knew that much. But these nightmares were the sort that could be driven away with a touch or the sun. The nightmares I'd left behind were of a more stubborn variety.

US troops had drawn down in Iraq, and surged back against the both the rise of ISIS in the northern provinces and stampeding trough Syria to take advantage of the chaos there like some religion-soaked mafia of the desert carrying on about the End of Days. While in the south, Iran came in with its proxy militias and money and carrying on about the End of Days - Shi'a style. Stuck in the middle, Iraq's geopolitical position swung wildly from "America save us from Iranian domination" to "Iran save us from American domination."

Like Iraq, Libya had money and oil reserves – but that was a double-edged sword: there was simply too much money on the table for patchwork of revolutionary militias not to make a late in the game power-grab. Or for the surrounding powers to jockey for influence. It was never about religion though - wholesome of crack-pot. This was primarily a fight about identity, fueled by commodity prices. But you need more than that to fight a war, Ur-Nammu knew it when he first pulled the "God will's it" wheeze.

Just a few weeks after I'd left Benghazi, Libya came apart again. The center was unable to hold in the vacuum filled with foreign arms and money. Turkey stepped in, with help from Qatar, to support the UN backed Government of National Accord (GNA) in Tripoli with drones, material and – because modern proxy wars require some degree of plausible deniability – mercenaries from Syria. To the east in Benghazi, the city called the "Cradle of the Revolution", rebel backed militias would begin to coalesce under the banner of "General" Khalifa Haftar's Libyan National Army (LNA). Haftar had gotten

support of Russia, the United Arab Emirates, Egypt and…
France. Paris's reasoning for bucking its allies is that Haftar had
managed to sell himself as a bulwark against radical Islamism.
Considering that the entire eastern rebellion was seeded with
Iranian money and arms, this is a little hard to swallow. More
likely, neither Russia nor France really wanted the new fledgling
government in control of that much oil beholden to a place like
Turkey.

Whatever its reasons, the political maneuver put France on
the opposing side of the UN (in which France has a permanent
seat on the Security Council) and its NATO ally, Turkey. It also
put them on the same side as the Russians, against whom they
are preparing for a degraded European invasion back home.
Confusing? Well, orgies generally are.

All of this foreign support has been about as helpful as you
can imagine. Humanitarian missions were scrapped, but the
foreign nurses had mostly fled anyway. Not long afterwards, I
learned that the little Catholic church I'd been to with Dr. Wallis
had been burned, vandalized and used as both outhouse and
weapons depot. Then I heard that the Benghazi Medical Center
had been shelled. My thoughts ran to little Fellah, but she hadn't
made it that far. And that's what gets me – not just her but all the
ones that wouldn't make it a pediatric heart program was now on
hold. And I'd learned first hand in Iraq that societies don't really
get put on hold: they move forward or they regress.

The press is pretty good at covering the broad strokes of
political saber-rattling and cities falling to this army or that
faction, as well as the individual human stories – the lives ruined
and lost. It's much harder and more abstract to report on
unrealized future: Things that could have happened but won't.

The potential had been there in Libya. After two ICHF training missions in Benghazi, the program was doing better that after five years of mission in Iraq. Perhaps it was because Libyans had ousted their nightmare on their own and had more skin in the game, or were more willing to put their necks on the line. That quote from Winston Churchill nagged me, "Nations that went down fighting rose again. But who surrender tamely were finished." The truth is that I have no idea why, only that real progress was being made before the foreign actors came in. Those vomit inducing disappointments are just part of the exercise. Which is what make those little victories like Fellah's more poignant, more meaningful.

TWENTY YEARS is a very long war. Long enough, possibly, to forget how to live in peace. On 14 February 2021, President Joe Biden vowed to pull the US troops out of that Graveyard of Empires, Afghanistan, on the twentieth anniversary of the 9/11 attack that put us there in the first place. At one point, his former boss, Barack Obama, planned to clear out as well – but then surged. And in between the two, during the administration of all things polar opposite Obama/Biden, so did Trump. And he did, sort of. But not really, or Biden wouldn't be dealing with it.

The fear that kept the US in Afghanistan, as well as in Iraq, is that pesky transition hiccup that has been a problem for so many regimes since Cyrus the Great pared his family tree into a straight line by marrying his daughters to his brothers. The Roman republic had a workable system of power transfer on which everyone agreed, but it was a fragile precedent. After Caesar wrecked it, the emperors never quite got the hang of passing the keys to the next fellow. Eventually, it cost them the whole show.

Let's face it, the only real advantage to a monarchy, after the generation or two required to spoil the kids rotten, is that all agree on the power transfers are on some sort of, in not divine, at least biological auto-pilot. The British – God bless them – have maintained theirs by ensuring it is all symbolism and very little substance.

For US foreign policy, for all our talk about making the world safe for democracy, as well as our nation-building adventures, we've never been entire sure why our transferred have gone so smoothly – for the most part.* And so we can't seem to make it work for anyone else unless we are holding a gun to their head. Any power, individual or national, can enforce a *superficial* peace with the barrel of a gun, but you can't instill buy-in into a system. If the nation-building goal also includes freedom, then people with the same baseline cultural assumptions will have to come to some workable arrangement within their own existing cultural framework. It might get ugly. Scratch that, there is no way it won't get ugly. In the end, some common ground must be found. People don't have to trust each other, only the system.

No war lasts forever, although to look at Europe's Hundred Years War, some have certainly tried. As I was putting on the last polish to the galley of this strange book, Libya announced an interim national government and the main rebel force under General Khalifa Hafter, if not put down its arms, agreed to terms. Again, I find myself typing the words "Libya's future is theirs for the taking." Still, stranger things have happened.

---

* I'm looking at you, Donald Trump.

THE UNITED STATES is a super power whether we like it or not. At the end of World War II, we found ourselves as the last power standing in the free world – a superpower by default. For whatever reason, the rules-based liberal system the United States conceived and defended after World War II was trusted, even by those who didn't particularly like America. The Soviet bloc trusted the liberal system so well that they devoted more time and energy to their "active measures" – pioneered by Russia, perfected by the East Germans – sowing chaos among the West than to actually improving the East.*

Our global adventures should be focused on maintaining and defending that order, not nation-building. No nation, no matter how powerful can build another people's nation for them any more than you can work on your neighbor's wonky marriage. We shouldn't try.

The Persians, the Romans and the early Caliphates of Islam, despite their kaleidoscope of human flaws, had cracked the nut of making foreign people stand in line to sign up for membership in the club. They did this by offering a stable system with clearly defined and enforced rules. While it's unfashionable to remember it, most of global system under the British wasn't the formal Empire, but what they called the "informal" one: Countries that agreed to follow the rules to gain access to the market. When the United States found itself in a position to mold the global system

---

*The curious thing about the anti-nuclear movement shows that it a) started in Germany spreading west and b) focused on protesting the American nukes pointed at Soviet Union rather than the Soviet nukes pointed at Europe.

to our vision our first instinct was the same – just keep the shop open for anyone willing to abide by the rules of the club.

In 1945, the United States could afford to be aspirational – to see the world *as it could be* – with free market access and no empires, with liberal but clear rules. By creating that space it created the conditions from which a new order grew that did more over the course of 70 years, to raise more people out of poverty than any other system in the history of mankind.

We won the Cold War not through regime change, although it wasn't for a lack of trying. Mostly, those ill-advised attempts in places like Vietnam, Iran and the rest of the floor length list, either failed or, succeeded wildly in making the problem much worse by supporting brutal dictators simply because they checked the "I'm No Pinko" box. No, we won with our long game: Denying authoritarian actors access to a better system. The system may be unfashionable with the academic and barista sets these days, but those people have always been more fashionable than practical. In short, our ideology didn't win out, it was our stuff, and the freedom to monkey around our the stuff the way we wanted that won. For lack of a finer term, we won through gross materialism. Once the people behind the iron curtain realized that the world included blue jeans and rock & roll, they wanted them. And the government designed to deny them collapsed.

SO, WE ARE A SUPER POWER, whether we like it or not. The Cold War is over, and the unipolar period afterward has closed as well. We are living in a multi-polar world that is splitting into violent fractals of nationalism in retreat from the global system. Even Ur-Nammu, contemplating his Great

Ziggurat, that footstool to the gods, knew that you couldn't accomplish much with anarchy as your baseline. So did later and greater rulers. In the meeting of "Communication" that hotel conference room in Nasiriya, they knew to mention the law code of Hammurabi before bragging about the Cradle of Civilization and the Epic of Gilgamesh. Society can't flourish without stability and order. No one ever built an impressively useless monument or wrote an epic tale while in the grip of flight or fight.

The power of the United States has a lot to do with harnessing individual ambition to its own end, but also that we won the geographical and historical jackpot. So, it isn't entirely in our power to step away from the role of superpower, even if the majority of voters want to. Nor can we escape the fact that we are a target, the power to beat if another power wants to make a name for itself. And if we choose to stand alone, like Napoleon, we will face a global coalition that we cannot beat. We ignore the truth at your own peril.

What is up to us is to decide what sort of superpower we want to be. As we've learned in the last two decades, forcing another people into our Nation-in-a-Box concepts is a fight that will never end. History tells us that the trick is much simpler than that: Get them to sign up on their own.

Before the ideology bloodbaths of the Cold War, the United States was largely seen as what we might call a humanitarian power. We still are, even if a ham-handed one that has gotten pissed off enough to do something rash. We've spent a lot more blood and treasure trying to create conditions for a stable democracy than we did knocking over hateful Big Men. Granted,

practically speaking, intentions don't matter – and the road to
hell is paved with the good and noble sort.

Nadwa Qaragholi, of Living Light International, related a
metaphor to me while I was in Iraq: Don't change the change the
color of a piece of paper by soaking it in ink, you'll destroy the
paper. Better, then, to just apply drops of ink, and let the color
spread on its own. Granted, anyone showing that much patience
and common sense isn't likely to get a parade thrown for them.
And she would know.

Airstrikes, for the record, absolutely incinerate the paper.

And that, if anything else, is our blind spot. Not that were
aren't exactly sure why our system works and therefore can't
really export it, but that our system made us so rich we can't
conceive of a problem without a price tag. And we are the world
leader in solving problems with a price tag – just look at the
Berlin Air Lift, using the single most expensive and unwieldy
method of transport (by a factor several times) we delivered some
2.3 million tons of material to keep West Berlin well-fed and
warm for better than a year. Long enough to outpace the
Russians who had the place surrounded on their domestic
doorstep!

If we could buy a solution in the land of oil and religion,
we'd have already cut the check, be out the door and hailing a
taxi. But we can't. I'd suggest that we all go to our corners and
pray about it, but that only seems to be exasperate the problem.

MY PERSONAL OPINION on holy places is, admittedly, a
bit out of joint from the experts – but the Catholics put me to the
curb, so I don't have any skin in with the organized religions.
Still, if I'm going to hell it isn't going to because a priest raised

being pedantic to a sacrament. Or, for that matter, because the following opinion: I don't care what the back story is, places like Jerusalem and Mecca just don't seem like very holy to me. The clerics at each others throats over their shrines sure as hell don't. Perhaps God did put a divine foot down there in the sand 2,000 years ago. It is lovely to think so. All that appears to be left of that *Dei, vestigium pedi* is a deep imprint that has since filled with enough earth and water and human stain to become brackish and foul.

And it is a stubborn stain – the what we call the Gulf War, the locals call the Crusader War. Saladin saw the wisdom in patching up the Sunni/Shi'a split in his fief, but the Iranians are still trying to use the crack to take the place over. Canossa settled less that the Pope Gregory and the Holy Roman Emperor supposed. It was the Thirty Years war led to an exhausted, "Let's agree to disagree."

What strikes the historian is that for all its *meaning*, Jerusalem has no strategic importance and never has. Baghdad spent centuries as the center of the world, the Persia empire was once the global colossus, both Rome and Constantinople were both the seats of empires, and after being rebranded as Istanbul, it was the seat of a second one. None of which you can say about a place like Jerusalem. Mecca lacks the divisiveness, but it's kept under lock and key by one of the groups tearing up the Holy Land.

In my experience, such as it is, holiness doesn't need to be locked down, and with the right kind of eye, it's all over the place. The dictum *"Give a man a fish and he eats for a day, teach him to fish and he eats for a lifetime."* is good. Folding it into a humanitarian model to litter the world with functioning pediatric heart centers is something else all together. Or volunteers flying around the globe to do their job on their vacation days around the developing world. Or a short Iraqi woman gracefully browbeating some bureaucratic blowhard into doing the right thing with no hope of kickback. If these things aren't holy, then I really don't know what is or what possibly could be.

As for the formal religious shrines, I think of places like the Blue Mosque in Istanbul; not because it has two extra minarets for added flare, but it had the power to awe the self-righteous. No mean feat. Or St. Paul's Cathedral in London, where I saw a priest – maybe 130 pounds in full habit – hush a milling crowd of tourists into complete silence by asking, without raising his pleasant quiet voice, "Excuse me, I'm delighted that you are all here. The Church of England is very proud of St. Paul's. It is time for services, so please remember that this is, first and foremost, a church."

Perhaps, for me, the holiest of them all was that small Catholic church in Benghazi, because it was in a place that in tribal, fundamentally human logic, it shouldn't have been there, but was. It was kept safe, not by the projected power of Rome, but by being on the grounds of a mosque that could see the value of the shrine to a brigade of Polish nuns who needed a place to connect with God in their own manner. That otherwise unremarkable collaboration just might have been one of the holiest things that I've ever seen.

Soon after I'd gotten on a plane that would take me back to the Ladies Murff, the *jihadis* had come in into Benghazi in force. They burned the walls of the pleasant little church, urinated and defecated on its altar, and then used big room as a weapons depot. What they didn't realize was that they hadn't desecrated the church at all. What they'd done was profanely desecrate the mosque that had once given it shelter.

Ever since Hammurabi shot his mouth off as being called by the gods, and Darius raised the claim to an art form, humans been trying to build a Kingdom of Heaven on Earth. The communists, socialists, fascists and NAZI might have thought that they were side stepping the issue by taking religion out of the equation but a fanatic is a fanatic. They seem pretty good at finding gods and devils without any religion. If anything, their approach seems to make the unhinged fanaticism even worse.

The great religions and human traditions teach us, and deep down most of us already know it, that peace is found in the journey, not the destination. Down here were we are all too fundamentally human to ever really get it right. So, Heaven, however we imagine it, is fundamentally above our pay grade.

Down here we just keep making a pothole of the gods.

Richard Murff

Three dedicated Iraqi ladies who, despite speaking English, went through an interpreter to get their photo in this book.

ACKNOWLEDGMENTS

A book that presents the weird scope as this one owes its existence to a great deal of people, many of whom I can't mention by name, but you know who you are and I thank you. Chances are I've already bought you a drink, and for those I haven't, well, the next round is on me.

The International Children's Heart Foundation allowed me to tag along on some of their medical missions, and for that, I'm grateful. Nadwa Qaragholi, of Living Light International, was a wonderful contact who has become a wonderful friend.

This book is littered with historical and public figures – but more importantly – a lot of private citizens who've worked hard to make this world a better place. While society tends to punish good deeds with alarming speed, my personal opinion is that these people deserve what little privacy the modern world permits, so in nearly every case I've changed the names of the private citizens herein.

About the Author

Richard Murff has covered humanitarian issues across Latin America, Iraq, Ukraine, Libya and Clarksdale, MS, to name a few places. He has ghostwritten memoirs, business books and regional histories, with less impressive jobs such as writing sermons for a preacher who was very likely certifiably insane.

Murff spent his early career in advertising and marketing for a handful of global corporations. After several years in the financial sector specializing in capital markets for government debt and collateralized securities, the economy blew-up.

His books include the upcoming *Drunk as Lords, Haint Punch, Yellowcake, One Last Hour* and as editor and contributor, *Memphians*. His work has appeared in *The Bitter Southerner, Delta, The American Spectator, Sail, The Daily News, Oxford Town,* and others.

He lives in Memphis, Tennessee with his wife and daughter. The Mint Julep cookie was created in his honor.

SELECT BIBLIOGRAPHY

Anderson, Scott, *Lawrence in Arabia.* Anchor: New York, 2013
Barr, James, *A Line in the Sand: The Anglo-French Struggle for the Middle East, 1914-1948.* W.W. Norton & Co.: New York, 2012
Chulov, Martin and Luke Harding, *Libya: Murder in Benghazi and the Fall of Gaddafi.* Guardian Shorts, London, 2012.
Coughlin, Con, *Khomeini's Ghost: The Iranian Revolution and the Rise of Militant Islam.* Ecco: New York, 2009
Haidt, John, *The Righteous Mind: Why Good People are Divided by Politics and Religion.* Vintage, New York, 2013
Herodotus, *Histories.* Quality Paperback Club, New York, 1997
Hoffer, Eric *True Believer.* HarperPerennial, New York, 2002
Holland, Tom, *The Forge of Christendom: The End of Days and the Epic Rise of the West.* Anchor, New York, 2009
Holland, Tom, *Persian Fire.* Anchor, New York, 2007
Kahneman, Daniel and Amos Tversky. "On the Psychology of Prediction." Psychological Review 80, no. 4 (1973): 237-51.
Kinzer, Stephen, *All The Shah's Men: An American Coup and the Roots of Middle East Terror.* John Wiley & Sons: New Jersey, 2008
Lawrence, T.E. *Seven Pillars of Wisdom: A Triumph.* Anchor, New York, 1991
Nolan, Cathal, J., *The Allure of Battle: A History of How Wars Have Been Won and Lost.* Oxford University Press: New York 2017
Machiavelli, Niccolo, *The Prince.* Burnaby: Memphis, TN, 2020
Rogan, Eugene, *The Arabs: A History*, Basic Books, New York, 2009
Nagel, John A. *Learning to Eat Soup with a Knife: Counterinsurgency Lessons from Malaya and Vietnam.* University of Chicago Press: Chicago, 2005
Timmerman, Kenneth R., *Dark Forces: The Truth About What Happened in Benghazi*, Broadside Books, New York, 2014

Wright, Lawrence, *The Terror Years: From Al-Qaeda to the Islamic State*. Alfred A. Knoff, New York, 2016

Catherwood, Christopher, *Churchill's Folly: How Winston Churchill Created Modern Iraq*, Carrol & Graff, New York, 2005

"American Peace Commissioners to John Jay," March 28, 1786, "Thomas Jefferson Papers," Series 1. General Correspondence. 1651–1827, Library of Congress.

Philip Gengembre Hubert (1872). "Making of America Project." *The Atlantic Monthly, p. 413*

Zeihan, Peter, *The Accidental Superpower*, Twelve, New York, 2014

9 780979 698842